TRICKS

Over 79 Experts

OF

Reveal the Secrets

THE

Behind What They Do

TRADE

Best

Edited by Jerry Dunn

Houghton Mifflin Company

Boston

For information about permission to reproduce selections from this book, write to Permissions, Houghton Mifflin Company, 2 Park Street, Boston, Massachusetts 02108.

Excerpts from "One Starry Night" and "Jerry Lee's Boogie" by Jeffrey Gutcheon copyright © 1978 J. Gutcheon/Uncle Mike Music ASCAP. "How to Punctuate" by Russell Baker reprinted by permission of International Paper. "How to Tie a Bow Tie" by Gene Shalit copyright © 1991 by Gene Shalit. "Telephone Fundraising Strategies" by David Levy copyright © 1988 by the Grantsmanship Center; reprinted by permission. "How to Be a Couch Potato" material from *The Official Couch Potato Handbook* by Jack Mingo and Bob Armstrong, used by permission of Last Gasp of San Francisco. "How to Be Funny" by Steve Allen copyright © 1987 by Steve Allen; reprinted by permission of McGraw-Hill Publishing Company. All illustrations, except the musical scores and where otherwise noted, are by Victor Paredes.

Library of Congress Cataloging-in-Publication Data
Tricks of the trade : over 79 experts reveal the secrets behind what they do best / edited by Jerry Dunn.
    p.   cm.
  Includes index.
  ISBN 0-395-58083-8
  1. Curiosities and wonders. 2. Life skills. 3. Social skills. 4. Tricks.
I. Dunn, Jerry Camarillo.
AG243.T68 1991 91-17505
031.02—dc20   CIP

Printed in the United States of America

Book design by Jennie Bush, Designworks, Inc.

VB 10 9 8 7 6 5 4 3 2

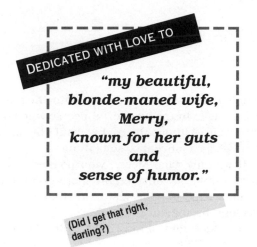

DEDICATED WITH LOVE TO

"my beautiful,
blonde-maned wife,
Merry,
known for her guts
and
sense of humor."

(Did I get that right, darling?)

THANKS

Helping a stranger who burst into their lives asking for advice came easily to the wonderful people who contributed to *Tricks of the Trade*. Without them, this would be one of those blank books you use as a journal or something.

It was my wife, Merry, who pointed out that advice from experts would be considerably more exciting if some of them were famous experts. She also contributed her invaluable editorial wisdom throughout the book.

Art Buchwald, Julia Child, Wilbur Garrett, and the late and lamented William French Smith all agreed to early interviews, whose inclusion in the book proposal helped greatly to sell the project.

My agent, Alice Martell, has been a touchstone of intelligence, humor, and unflagging faith. She fully lives up to both elements of her lighthearted nickname, "Attila the Honey." Henry Ferris, my editor, Luise M. Erdmann, my manuscript editor, and Becky Saikia-Wilson, manuscript editing supervisor, all lent their substantial talents to the book. The designer, Jennie Bush, did a great job, and Victor Paredes provided fine illustrations.

Joan Tapper made valuable suggestions. Cyd Smith of the Sterling Publishing Company helped me locate entrants in the *Guinness Book of World Records*. Bill Bowers, Gene Jones of the Jugglers Network, and the fine staff of the library in Ojai, California, all offered help and good-natured interest in the project. Jürgen Hilmer provided photographs.

And finally, Peter Workman, Frances Atkeson, Maria Mudd, Joe Donohue, John Nuñez, Susan Petty, Tom and Judy Munzig, and Jean Smith all put on their thinking caps to come up with ideas for the book. Now let's put them on again, friends, and do a sequel! What do you say?

Thanks

vii

Contents

FOR MEN AND WOMEN ONLY

NEW TRICKS FOR OLD DOGS

INDEXES

INTRODUCTION

There is no human problem which could not be solved if people would simply do as I advise.

—*Gore Vidal*

I believe in taking good advice. And I need it. Just check *Who's Who* or *The Guinness Book of World Records*, and you won't find me in there. Business savvy? I'm the kind of guy who would open a tall man's shop in Tokyo. As for athletic prowess, the last time I had a headache my wife said, "I've told you a thousand times: When you get out of bed, it's *feet* first."

Oh, I'm not a totally maladroit lunk-knob. I've learned to do a few things reasonably well: write magazine stories for a living, perform sleight-of-hand magic for entertainment. I can also make a passable omelette. But the things I don't know how to do are as numberless as the stars. When I try to bluff at poker, I always get caught red-handed and red-faced. When I light a fire in our fireplace, I vanish, coughing, into billows of smoke. Trying to ice-skate backwards, I do a banana peel onto my backside. My vacation snapshots look like illustrations in a photography instruction manual—all the "don'ts."

So I thought I'd seek advice on how to do these and many other things well. As a journalist who's spent years interviewing accomplished people, I've observed that many of them have distilled a few basic rules for success in their field. I guessed that their rules could help a foozler like me avoid a lot of mistakes. It was my wife, Merry, who suggested seeking out experts that have achieved fame. They are more knowledgeable—and perhaps more inspiring.

I sent out scores of letters, and the people who responded are, by definition, the nice ones. There's no thrill quite like picking up the telephone and hearing a familiar voice say, "Hi! This is the Greatest Who Ever Lived! Muhammad Ali! You wrote me a letter?" We spent nearly an hour talking about his patented ploys for avoiding punches.

Of course, not every expert is able to explain the talent he or she has developed to perfection. Jazzman Miles Davis once commented, "I'll play it first and tell you what it is later." Doing a thing with magnificent skill often involves deep mystery; it seems to come out of nowhere. When I wrote to Isaac Asimov, for example, asking for tips on how to improve one's writing, this author of more than four hundred books sent back a courteous and revealing note: "I don't know how to improve writing. I started writing at 11, and I already knew how just by instinct. I have never learned anything since. Please try someone who *consciously* knows how to write."

I took his advice, setting out to find experts who could not only "play it" but could also tell us "what it is." For instance, although no one had ever asked Chevy Chase how to do a pratfall—his comedy trademark—he laid it out (so to speak) in a way that is both hilarious and easy to follow. His chapter is a lesson from a master. Another example: Art Buchwald gives hundreds of entertaining speeches a year, and if you follow his do's and don'ts, as set forth here, you'll definitely be on your way to public speaking success. Want to cook a perfect egg? Ask Julia Child. Carry a tune? Go to Michael Jackson's vocal coach. They're all here, along with dozens more experts who offer you their special knowledge.

Learning new tricks can be profoundly important, especially as we grow to be old dogs. Tom (*In Search of Excellence*) Peters tells a story about Michael McCaskey, the president of the Chicago Bears and a former teacher at the Harvard Business School. Like clockwork, every few years McCaskey takes up something new, such as water skiing, just to experience afresh the perspective

of the novice. This exercise serves to remind him to assume nothing and to keep his ideas simple.

I figure there's always room for self-improvement (especially in
my own case, having made ineptitude a way of life). It helps to
remember that Henry David Thoreau once was a pencil maker,
Albert Einstein a patent office clerk, and former President Gerald
Ford a male model. Just look at what they achieved! Using this
book, you, too, will be able to accomplish all sorts of things—
from dribbling a basketball between your legs (taught by one of
the Harlem Globetrotters) to communicating with teenagers (Erma
Bombeck) to winning a debate (William F. Buckley, Jr.).

I'll be seeing you in *Who's Who.*

WHAT "TRICKS OF THE TRADE" DO *YOU* WANT TO LEARN?

If there's a skill you'd like to master—anything, you name it!—or an expert you'd like to hear from, let us know. (If we use your idea, you'll get actual credit, right there in print, for all your friends to see.)

Please mail your ideas to:
Jerry Dunn
Tricks of the Trade
P. O. Box 336
Ojai, CA 93024

1

SOCIAL SKILLS

HOW TO DO A PRATFALL

Chevy Chase

Like Charlie Chaplin and Buster Keaton, Chevy Chase has made the pratfall his comedy trademark.

Although it may look cloddish, an actor on-stage needs finely tuned skills to fall flat on his face in a way that looks real, looks funny, and doesn't cause bodily injury. Offstage, too, there's no social occasion that can't be improved by a thunderous crash over the coffee table followed by an understated "whoops." My rules:

Stay in motion.

I learned how to fall when I played college soccer; we were taught to roll whenever we fell on the field. And that's the basic principle behind any pratfall—you never land. You're always in motion, so no one portion of your body (particularly pointed portions!) hits without the force being absorbed by other points along the anatomy. It helps to be tall, because you can put your arms and legs out and roll over them in a series of moves to absorb the shock.

> **A comedian does funny things; a good comedian does things funny.**
> —*Buster Keaton*

On the other hand, John Belushi felt that because of the way he was built, he could just go fall on anything. I would watch him try to do pratfalls, and it was like a brick hitting the ground. There was a thud like a huge registered mail sack. He didn't really have the fine details down, but it looked funny. For that type of build, it's good to have a lot of mass and fat (and a lot of hair on your back). These are shock absorbers that a tall, skinny guy like me doesn't have.

The only time I really got hurt on *Saturday Night Live* was when I played Gerald Ford in a debate against Danny Aykroyd as Jimmy Carter. I thought it might be funny to end the debate by simply falling forward while holding on to the podium. The podium was made of hardwood, however, and I went to the hospital with internal injuries. The stunt violated the rule of always rolling, staying in motion; instead, I took a direct shock.

Fall through obstacles.

I used to go to dinner with Paul Simon and *Saturday Night* producer Lorne Michaels. We'd be walking across the street in the Village to a Chinese restaurant, and I'd hit the curb with my foot, which gave me enough momentum so I'd stumble forward. But I was always careful to fall *through* something, like trash cans. And whenever I did a pratfall on *Saturday Night*, I made sure to arrange some tables and chairs to crash through. These things help break your fall. The idea is that you never quite hit the floor without hitting a number of little floors first.

THE CHRISTMAS PARTY
PRATFALL

Here's a festive pratfall for the holiday season.

Let's say you're going to a Christmas party and you have packages in your hands. The first thing to happen, once the door opens, is to sort of muff the packages. Somehow drop one.

From now on, it's important that you always look as if you're trying to retrieve the beginning of the error. One Christmas package drops, you reach out to grab it before it hits the ground—and you drop two or three others. As you're leaning forward and moving to pick up these packages, you trip over one of them—they are now at your feet—thereby making a lot of paper noise and crushing a few boxes. You don't fall all the way to the floor, though, because your hands are down reaching for the packages. You're just starting to stumble.

You go through the first two or three greeters at about hip level—and into the coffee table. Always hit the leg of the table (or couch, or whatever) with the toe of your shoe only. Hitting with your toe not only prevents injury to your shin but also checks your motion, giving you some momentum that prompts the rest of your upper body to whip over the table. It also creates mayhem.

Noise improves a pratfall.

I always find it advantageous to grab on to as many things as possible that will break away throughout the fall. This way you make noise, and the more noise, the worse the fall seems to be. Glass is good, metal objects—anything that clatters. I think a pratfall is better in direct proportion to the noise level.

One thing I don't find funny in movies, though, is the guy who falls out a window and screams the whole time; I'm against anything but normal conversation during a fall. Any noise should come from the objects you fall through.

Make the fall look real.

To be funny, a pratfall has to look real. It's a strange thing, but if the fall looks at all fake, you generally hurt yourself.

Fall when it is least expected.

When a pratfall guy gets on some stairs, you can be almost sure he's going to take a fall. But I think the best kind of pratfall is totally unexpected: You're just walking along, then you trip over or through something.

> **You might as well fall flat on your face as lean over too far backward.**
> —*James Thurber*

Have no fear.

The first really funny pratfall I did was in college at the dorm, mindlessly falling down some stairs and then out a door, through a series of rocks and bramble bushes—with no fear whatsoever that I would get hurt. And the "no fear" concept works because you *don't* get hurt. Football coaches teach you this when you're blocking and tackling: Go all out, and don't hold back.

Be aware of your environs.

You must be totally on your toes. It's like understanding the size of your car if you're driving between a couple of buses at top speed: You just *feel* the width of your car and know you'll make it, although there may be only an inch on each side. Well, you have to feel that same thing with your body. It's kind of instinctual, but it's also something you can learn.

One of the better pratfalls I enjoyed taking was off the top of the Christmas tree as Gerald Ford on *Saturday Night*. We had Ford decorating the tree and singing "Easter Parade." I was at least fifteen feet off the ground; I simply held on to the top branches, leaned forward, and let myself go. I knew that as the tree hit the floor, it would break my fall.

Know where you're going to finish.

You must think *before* you make the moves. You can't just say, "I'm gonna go for it!" without knowing where you'll end up—and that means within an inch.

HOW TO BANG YOUR NOSE AGAINST A DOOR

Here's a great move anybody can learn.
You're going into a restaurant. The person in front of you opens the door, they hear a bang and an "OOoooph!" and then you're pretending to hold your nose and spit out teeth.

It's simple: The door hits your *toe*. That causes the noise and stops the door, which never touches your face; it barely grazes it, like the wind.

Some fine points: Be close enough to the door so that from any angle it looks as if it hit you; you almost have to *feel* it hit your face. (If you stay too far from the door, people will see the air.) To pull off this stunt, you have to know that your foot is going to stop the door at the perfect place. You can't be scared; you have to feel it out and just do it. Also, if you want to spit out "teeth," try using Chiclets. All in all, it's a delicate maneuver—but a great one.

Land in the "classic position."

It's almost invariably funnier to end a pratfall on your back, with your legs up and spread in the air. A good facial expression to use is "pain." (Or, if you're playing Gerald Ford, maybe have *no* expression.) If you say anything at the end, I think understatement is funniest, like, "No problem!"

It's something only the great minds can handle.

COMMUNICATING WITH A TEENAGER

Erma Bombeck

Erma Bombeck started her career by writing obituaries for the Dayton, Ohio, *Journal-Herald* ("I had a great rapport with all the funeral homes"), then wrote a housekeeping column that she characterized as "sort of a sick 'Heloise.'" Today her humor column, "At Wit's End," is syndicated in more than nine hundred newspapers, and she has produced a string of best-selling books.

It's important where and when you talk to teenagers. You make a big mistake trying to be heard above MTV, because you can't get their attention. So don't allow any competition—Michael Jackson will win every time.

Don't let dinnertime turn into the Trials at Nuremberg.

You show me parents who continually confront their teenagers at the dinner table, and I'll show you parents eating alone. When you're lecturing teenagers and they begin to hum and leave the room, you can sense there is hostility.

Don't ever say you understand teenagers. It breaks down the hostile relationship between you that it takes to understand one another.

Accept that most conversation in the teenage years is a confrontation. It's sad but true. A lot of problems are surfacing, and you don't have a chance to just sit down and bond. I mean, that's something you do to your teeth. Forget bonding. It's cute when the baby is lying on your stomach, but other than that, it just doesn't happen.

Use guilt.

The idea is to make teenagers feel they are so rotten that they do not deserve to continue breathing. Tell them they've ruined your entire life. Even add some graphics: Maybe you can bring a tape recorder into the labor room and play it back to them when they get older; it may help them realize what you've gone through to bring them into the world. I don't see anything wrong with guilt—I call it "the gift that keeps on giving." You pass it on to your kids; then they grow up and pass it on to theirs. So we have generations of it, and it seems to work very well.

Don't give them unrealistic ultimatums.

I used to tell my children, "If you don't shape up, I am walking out of this house and you will never—see me—again." But you shouldn't threaten things you can't deliver on . . . because kids will hold you to it.

> The best way to give advice to your children is to find out what they want and advise them to do it.
> —*Harry S. Truman*

Don't send contradictory messages.

Parents do this all the time without even being aware of it. In one sentence you'll say, "Go to your room this instant; don't turn your back on me." In the larger sense, it's a serious problem for them. On the one hand we're saying, "Grow up and be independent," and on the other, "Wait, we've got some more stuff to teach you." We constantly send them mixed messages.

Get some new clichés.

The old ones are *really* tired: "While you're under this roof," and "If you want to be treated as an adult, act like one," and "When I was a kid . . ." Your teenagers have heard it all before, so they tune you out immediately.

These are not "the best years of their lives."

These are the toughest, most miserable years of their lives. Teenagers are so insecure about themselves. They don't know how to act, and they're scared to death about everything—how they fit into the world, their looks, their careers, what their peers think. They don't know who to trust or even whether to trust themselves. They just do what they think they're *supposed* to do at that particular time in their life. So they need all the love they can get.

Forgiveness is a major religion during teenage years.

Forgiveness is what child-raising is all about, because teenagers are going to screw up and fall on their faces. There will be times when they slam the door and say, "I hate you! I don't ever want to see you again." Get ready for it—and just forgive, forgive, forgive.

Always temper punishment with an equal amount of love.

My mother taught me this, and it's very important, because we sometimes get lopsided. We bark at our kids all the time, but we forget to balance it with love at the other end.

Shut up and listen once in a while.

The sin of all parents is that they talk too much. They lay out the crime, then they go back and say it again. After reiterating it a bit more, they choreograph it and dance around. The child stands there but doesn't get to respond. Finally, you remark, "Well, if you have nothing to say . . ." You didn't give him a *chance* to say anything. We parents are so used to being the authoritative figures that we just don't know when to shut up.

Accept that kids are going to lie.

Innocent parents are always saying, "Why would *my* child have a reason to lie?" Well, start making a list. They lie constantly to save their skins. This is a situation where you have to do a

> ## A Couple of Truisms
>
> • Never compare your teenagers' lives to how you were raised. If Grandma ever tells the truth, you could lose your credibility.
>
> • Let them know you've made a mistake in your lifetime. Don't overdo it, of course. You just say, "I can remember making a mistake once." That sort of covers you.

George Bush: You lower your expectations. Lower them almost to a level that you can't believe, and then you're not going to be disappointed.

Kids need love the most when they deserve it the least.

When your teenager has behaved so badly you want to set him adrift on an iceberg, this is the time he really needs you. When the kid doesn't want to talk about it, can't talk about it, really screwed up royally—that's when he needs your love. It's a time when you think, "God, I wish I had become a nun," but it's precisely when you two should get together.

If you can cry together, you can laugh together.

The teenage years are not *all* serious times, and it helps if everyone can laugh about things. I believe that if you don't have a sense of humor in this world, you're not going to make it. How can you survive an illness, survive disappointments, survive your *life*, without humor? Because you need to put things in perspective.

I don't think a sense of humor is something you're just born with, though. The parents must have it first, and then the children have to develop and hone it for themselves. My kids did that, probably just to survive, because this is a very fast-moving family. We don't wait for you to get the jokes; we keep zipping along. Humor has worked well with my kids; it really pays off.

> Having children is like having a bowling alley installed in your brain.
> —*Martin Mull*

Don't stop being a parent.

I don't think kids like it if their parents stop being parents. But sometimes adults fall into the "old pal" syndrome: They think the age gap is narrowing, and all of a sudden they have a right to join their teenagers and talk about their music and find some common ground. I contend that teenagers don't need a pal. They've got pals. They need a parent. It doesn't mean you have to be at odds with everything they do, but you still have to be that parental figure.

Furthermore, you have to be a parent for a long time. My kids are grown, and now I'm in a position where I keep my mouth shut about how they spend their money and take care of their cars. But even though they are in their thirties, they still come to me and ask, "What do you think?"—of the girl, of the job, and so forth. Let's face it, you're the only one who loves them enough, who knows them well enough, to tell them the truth. They're going to take it, because they know the spirit in which you're giving it out. You simply have this niche in their lives, this little place, that you really have to guard and that lasts all your lives.

HOW TO GIVE ADVICE TO TEENAGERS— WITHOUT HAVING THEM HATE YOU

Giving advice to teenagers is simple: You don't. You're more like a psychiatrist—you sit there, you listen, and you let them arrive at the answer themselves. That's the skillful way to do it.

As an example, try to keep quiet when they bring home boyfriends or girlfriends you can't stand. My kids have had some real winners, I can tell you. When my daughter was in high school, I handled this situation badly by pointing out all the flaws of the boy in question. The more flaws I pointed out, the more my daughter was absolutely sure he was going to be the best friend she ever had. If you put yourself in this position—"Choose me or the other"— you'll lose. (It's hard to accept, because you want to say, "Did your boyfriend make you six thousand meals a year and do your crummy laundry? No!" But that has nothing to do with it.) What you're doing is criticizing their judgment—saying they can't do anything right; they can't even pick a friend. What happens, eventually, is that they discover the boyfriend's flaws all by themselves. They don't need you. With teenagers, most of the things you worry about never happen if you just sort of lay back. Of course, I say that in hindsight— which has 20–20 vision—now that I'm older and wiser.

Having said that, there are certain situations where teenagers say, "Can I go? Give me a yes or no." If they put it that way, say "no." They'll get very angry and respond, "I *knew* you'd say that! Why not?" Then you give them the reason. If they don't like the reason, tough-o. Parents find this hard to do because they think, "My kids are going to hate me." They think their daughter is going to run away from home and live on a commune with a guy with a burlap shirt and a hoe. Their son is going to end up on a curb in Denver. Not necessarily. Kids know that some of these decisions are tough. And sometimes they're just testing you. They may act like they're complaining: "Oh, my mother, you wouldn't *believe* her; this woman drives me nuts! She wants to know who I'm out with, how long I'm staying, what time I get home." Actually, they're bragging. What they're really saying is: "My mother loves me."

How to Fend Off a Mugger

Curtis Sliwa

Curtis Sliwa and his wife, Lisa, founded the Guardian Angels safety patrols, an interracial group of unarmed young men and women who patrol areas where crime has changed the quality of life. Having started in 1979 with thirteen people, the group now numbers five thousand members in sixty-seven cities.

If you have little skill and no confidence, your best approach may be just to accede, give up your valuables, and pose no resistance to a mugging. But if you feel you're capable and that it's important to make a stand, you should prepare in advance—practice some techniques, run through simulations with a friend, create situations in your mind—the same way you work out to a Jane Fonda videotape. Because the time to start figuring things out is not when you're in the middle of being mugged or sexually assaulted.

The basic idea is to "hit and run"—to debilitate your attacker long enough for you to get away from danger. The following techniques are good for the person who doesn't think of himself as being physically tough or capable:

1. Use the palm of your hand.

Most people have never thrown a punch in their lives, so never ball up your hand and try to punch someone as if you were Mike Tyson. Boxers bandage their hands before throwing blows, so they have a cushion. Standing in the middle of a parking lot with no gloves or tape on your hands is not the time to throw your first punch and then realize: "Oh, I just broke my knuckles and dislocated my finger. My arm feels paralyzed." That wasn't your intention when you hit the guy.

Instead, use your palm. It's hard and often calloused; you can even smash it into the ground and still have your hand in one piece. You're going to take that palm and jam it up into the attacker's nose (underneath is best). The nose is a very delicate item, all cartilage, and when a guy gets hit in the nose, his eyes start to tear up and he sometimes suffers a temporary loss of his mental and physical faculties. (If he's hit hard enough, the cartilage will go right up through the bridge of his nose and could rearrange the furniture upstairs. That would save the taxpayers $32,500 a year, but it obviously takes a lot of experience to do.) This move doesn't require great strength, and even a petite or elderly person can deliver a debilitating blow that may cause the attacker to let go temporarily and allow the victim to get out of the situation.

2. Go for the genitals.

About 98 percent of attackers are men. If you have a little maneuverability and feel you can get in another strike, the obvious next target is the genital area. Your knee is your best weapon. It requires the least amount of movement; you're just lifting your knee as you would to walk up steps. You don't need a lot of flexibility. A thrust with the knee is going to cause pain—a language that the attacker probably understands well—and may give you time to flee.

3. Try to wear the right shoes.

Flat shoes or sneakers put you in a better situation than women's high (or even low) heels or men's dress shoes with leather soles. These shoes slip and slide, which can cause problems since you don't have any traction. Typically, an attacker grapples with you, grabs you in a headlock, pushes you. If you're slipping and sliding because your shoes don't grip the pavement, your self-defense techniques may not do much good: You're already on the floor. All the attacker has to do is grab your clothing and shake you out—as he would a tablecloth, trying to get rid of breadcrumbs. One thing men can do: Have rubber treads put on the heels and toes of your shoes; they won't take away from the dress look, but will give your shoes more traction.

4. Stomp the attacker's foot.

Whether you're grabbed from behind or in front, a quick jab downward with your shoe on someone's instep is going to cause a good deal of pain; it will probably cause the attacker to release you. You may miss the first time, so be ready to do it again.

THREE THINGS MUGGERS LOOK FOR IN A POTENTIAL VICTIM

Wearing headphones. Headphones cut off your senses. Whether you're on the jogging path, doing the laundry in the basement of your apartment building, strolling in the park, getting your car in a parking lot, or dittybopping down the street, as long as you have those tunes blasting in your ear, you can't hear someone running up behind you. A crowd of people on the sidewalk could be yelling, "Hey, look out—that guy's got a knife!" but you've cut off your preemptive radar. The potential mugger or rapist knows that a person wearing earphones is oblivious of what's going on around him and will make an easy victim.

Being under the influence of alcohol. People who are looking to strike often try to sense if you've been drinking alcohol. They know from personal experience how much it impairs your senses and reactions. And they can tell from your attitude that you're not alert, not poised; you've got that dumb smile on your face. You look like a good target.

Going to the cash machine without being alert. There's no armed guard as you make a withdrawal at a cash machine. Although it seems almost comedic, most people stand there and count their money. (You can't do anything to the machine anyway, even if it did gyp you out of $20!) People are oblivious about what a setup they put themselves in. A mugger can loiter across the street or crouch in a car, watch you count your money, and know almost exactly what kind of a score he'll make. To avoid being a victim: Be alert to anyone else in the area. Don't use the machine if your instincts tell you to get out of there. Wait to count your money until you're in a secure place.

Don't always assume that your strike is going to land squarely where you intended it to. Once your shot has the desired effect, run.

5. Kick the attacker in the shins.

A kick to the shins is very effective, no matter how big or strong the attacker is. Use the side of your foot or your heel, whatever is nearest the guy's shin. If you've ever nicked your shinbone on a coffee table, you know that you can feel the pain for the next half hour.

6. Grab his ears.

Everyone's got ears, and everyone hates it when people grab them. Ears are better to pull than hair, because with the gels and grease people use on their hair now, you may not be able to get a good grip.

7. Do a headbutt.

Especially if you're short and petite and the attacker is towering over you, you can just thrust your head upward and butt the person. If you hit him underneath the chin, it drives his jawbone up and causes real pain. It can discombobulate the attacker without causing you any damage.

Some other tips:

Don't try to hit an attacker's torso or arms. They're the strongest parts of the body, even on the computer wimp who's never worked out a day in his life. Concentrate on the most vulnerable areas.

Be aware that in defending yourself you will probably get hit and suffer some damage yourself. You don't come out of a fight the way it happens in the movies. The attacker has the advantage of surprise, and even guys who are used to roughhousing can be paralyzed with fear when they get hit the first time.

What you do once you realize, "Hey, I'm being attacked!" is

what really counts. Your main objective is to get out of there. Don't stop to see if you're bleeding or try to figure out where the attack came from. You have to trust your animal instinct at this point; if you try to intellectualize, you're dead meat—it's the wrong time. The moment you stop moving away, an attacker can renew his assault. Keep heading toward wherever there is light, traffic, and activity.

If you haven't thought about being the victim of a crime in this day and age, no matter where you live, you're a fool. You may worry about health problems—your caloric intake and proper exercise—but you're more likely to suffer from an attack. So you have to think about what you're going to do—in advance.

HOW TO BE FUNNY

Steve Allen

The creator of *The Tonight Show*, Steve Allen has been called "television's Renaissance man"—the composer of four thousand songs (such as "This Could Be the Start of Something Big") and the author of dozens of books (including *How to Be Funny).*

Rub elbows with funny people.

We tend to take on the social coloration of those with whom we spend a lot of time. Although few of us will have the chance to dine with Robin Williams, Jay Leno, or Garrison Keillor, we can nevertheless brainwash ourselves with their creative output by watching and listening to their recorded humor via television and radio, films, and comedy albums. Not only can you enjoy it the first time, but the experience can be easily repeated, which is especially helpful if your intentions are analytical. Also, read the work of our great humorists: James Thurber, Robert Benchley, S. J. Perelman, Woody Allen, and others all the way back to Mark Twain. This immersion in the business of being funny will have at least one immediate effect: You will laugh and enjoy life more. This will make you more relaxed and probably more humorous yourself—a person whose company other people will look forward to sharing.

Remember that comedy is about tragedy.

The raw material of most comedy is painful. After all, what are jokes about? They're about how dumb people are, how drunk they were last night, how broke they are, how poor, how bowlegged, sexually frustrated, greedy, or lazy. To refer to the Christian moral tradition, jokes are about the seven deadly sins: pride, covetousness, lust, anger, gluttony, envy, and sloth.

Study the construction of jokes.

In general, the straight line of a joke sets up a premise, an expectation. Then the funny ending—the punch line—in some sense contradicts the original assumption by refusing to follow what had seemed a reasonable train of thought. Here is an example from one of Spike Jones's comedy records:

> *(A telephone rings.)*
> WOMAN: Hello? *(She listens.)* You don't say. *(Pause; she receives another message.)* No, you don't say! You *don't* say. *(Pause.)* You don't say. Okay, good-bye.
> MAN: Who was that?
> WOMAN: He didn't say.

> **The test of a real comedian is whether you laugh at him before he opens his mouth.**
> —*George Jean Nathan*

Try these formulas for constructing gags.

Wordplay This type of joke often rests upon a deliberate misunderstanding of an idiomatic combination of words. A classic example is Henny Youngman's famous "Take my wife—please." Critics sometimes cite that joke as a *bad* example, but it's terrific. To be amused by that line, you have to understand that Henny has just said, "Women are crazy today." Then he adds, "Take my wife—please." It's a wonderful play on two separate meanings of the verb "to take": "to consider" and "to physically carry or move from place to place."

An example of wordplay from my own career is an ad-libbed answer to a question from the audience:

QUESTION: Your wife, Jayne Meadows, was born in Wuchang, China. Does she have any Chinese blood?

ANSWER: Yes, she keeps a small jar of it in the garage.

The Reverse Saying the exact opposite of what is expected is another elementary form of humor. The shock of mental surprise evokes laughter. Example: "This woman I know is so ugly that when she sees a mouse—the *mouse* jumps up on a chair."

Exaggeration Not every exaggeration is automatically a joke, so this formula calls for ingenuity. It's not funny to say, "My health is so bad I'm the sickest man in the world." But it is funny to say, "My health is so bad my doctor just advised me not to start reading any to-be-continued stories."

Implication Many jokes involve making a more or less obvious point but managing not to state it directly. A good illustration is the following exchange that took place between Art Linkletter and a seven-year-old boy he interviewed on one of his shows years ago.

"Were you born in California?" Art asked the child.

"No," he replied. "We moved here from Kansas City four months ago."

"Why did you move to Los Angeles?"

"My daddy wanted to see if he liked it."

"How do you like it?"

"We're moving back next week."

Naturally, the child's line got a tremendous reaction. But if he had said, "We *don't* like Los Angeles," that would have been simply stating the bald fact and would have produced little or no laughter.

Switching Take an old joke and revamp it to fit a new situation. For instance, one night during a television show I received a question from someone in the audience:

"Is that your own hair?"

I paused for a moment, patted my hair, and said, "In another two payments it will be, yes."

This is an example of "switching" a line that I had heard on the radio back in the late 1930s. The original line had nothing whatever to do with hairpieces; it may have related to an automobile or any other expensive item. Somebody asked something like, "Is that your car?" and the comic said, "In another two payments, it will be."

Your own formula A joke formula I made up myself involves splitting a compound word, changing its meaning, and adding the phrase "and you know how painful that can be." The word "hornswoggle" was the first term to be subjected to it. Exactly why "hornswoggle" was mentioned in the first place, I have absolutely no recollection, but it did prompt me to say, "And if you've ever had your horn swoggled, you know how painful that can be." A line like that can become a sort of trademark for you, which is a good thing, because you can make people laugh over and over. In your daily life, be sure to notice if something you say strikes people as funny and would bear repeating on different occasions.

Learn to tell humorous stories.

Don't memorize a lot of jokes. I'd recommend—at least at first—against memorizing a stock of jokes, like, "Say, have you heard the one about the two Armenians who . . ." Far more effective is the comic anecdote in which you tell something that actually happened to you or to someone you know. Obviously, there should be an inherently comic element in the event itself. Almost everyone has the ability to tell a funny story of this type.

Don't pump air into your story. As you proceed, it's best not to say, "This part will really kill you," or "Wait till you hear this." If the events detailed are really funny, leave the laughter to your listener. It's not necessary to advertise the components of your narrative.

Be selective in choosing figures of speech. Few things let the air out of a story quicker than using passé expres-

---

Funny and Unfunny Foods

Someone—I believe it was the late humorist Irvin S. Cobb—developed a list of meats rated according to our perception of them as funny or unfunny. According to Cobb's analysis, beef—just by itself—is not funny at all, whereas pork is at least slightly amusing. Beef can become amusing, though, when it is in the form of meatballs or hamburger. As hash, it is more amusing still. Liver, Cobb thought, was slightly funny, but wieners and sausages far more humorous.

—*How to Be Funny*,
by Steve Allen, with Jane Wollman

sions. For example, until around late 1984 it was cute to use Joan Rivers's expression, "Can we talk?" But you wouldn't want to use the line now, because it was a fad phrase and therefore inevitably of passing interest, so using it would suggest you aren't keeping up with what's "in."

Check audience response. Be sure to note if anyone (or no one) is laughing at your jokes. Even young children have a good sense of this. If they do something cute or funny—whether accidentally or on purpose—they will keep it in the act, so to speak, or abandon the approach, on the basis of how much laughter and smiling their antics elicit.

Develop your skill at ad-libbing. In everyday conversation, there's no time to mull over which joke formula to use at a particular moment. You have to make instantaneous, almost automatic, decisions. An exercise for people who want to learn to speak more articulately, whether for creating humor or not, is to simply pretend you're on radio or TV and do a play-by-play description of whatever you're experiencing or observing. For example, you can talk about everything you're passing in your car. "Good morning, ladies and gentlemen, this is Steve Allen broadcasting from my Model A. It's a sunny morning here in downtown Phoenix, and I'm at the corner of Fourth and Jefferson. There's an old woman walking her dog." It's all innocuous chatter, but it *does* keep your mouth moving and helps train you to speak in grammatical sentences. The next step is trying to ad-lib some funny lines along with the narrative. "There's an old woman walking her German shepherd. It's not a dog, folks. It's a young blond guy from Stuttgart."

Almost anything can produce a funny thought. For example, I bought one of those cars with a computerized voice track that says, "Your keys are in the ignition." Let's think up a funny response:

> **About half.**
> —Pope John XXIII, when asked how many people worked in the Vatican (in A Dictionary of Contemporary Quotations, ed. Jonathon Green)

STRAIGHT MAN: Your keys are in the ignition.

COMEDIAN: Well, I certainly hope so. If they were in the glove compartment, we'd *never* get out of here.

Another possibility:

STRAIGHT MAN: Your keys are in the ignition.

COMEDIAN: Thank God. If my *nose* were in the ignition, I'd be in big trouble.

Needless to say, if we replaced "nose" with a part of the human body associated with the sexual or eliminatory functions, the laughter would be even louder because of the shock factor.

To help you with ad-libbing, you may want to try some of these homework assignments:

1. Ad-lib a joke on your current weight-loss diet, being locked out, and a bad snowstorm.

2. Recall an awkward or embarrassing situation. How could you have used humor to get yourself off the hook?

The goal is to develop an attitude of mind that keeps you on the lookout for the actual or potential comedy that's part of daily life.

HOW TO SEE THE HUMAN AURA

Rosalyn Bruyere

Rosalyn Bruyere, the founder and director of the Healing Light Center Church in Glendale, California, is a researcher, healer, and teacher of laying-on-of-hands healing. She is the author of *Wheels of Light: A Study of the Chakras* and is involved with the traditional medicine teachings of Native Americans.

How I learned to see

Although my grandmother and great-grandmother were both psychic, I'd never focused on anything esoteric. I was one of the typical women who dropped out of college (where I studied electrical engineering), got married, and had babies. Then my two sons started seeing what they called "colored fuzz" around people. They saw auras.

For the first time, I recalled that as a child I'd had the same ability. In order to raise my boys responsibly, I had to make some sense of our experiences. I read all the old spiritualist books, the Taoist masters, Sufis—a little of everything—and found that no two of them agreed on what the aura was, never mind what it looked like. If you read three books, one of them would say that if you had a blue aura you were spiritual; another said you were depressed; and another one said you were enlightened. Give me a break! So, after plowing through nearly seventy books, I quit trying to read my way to a solution.

A good friend took me to a spiritualist medium who became my teacher, and I spent eighteen months really developing the skill of seeing an aura. Once I began to see it, there was so much more than anybody had written about. It's not one color, but multiple colors. And what you can see is *interactions* between people—more important, really, than what we usually think of the aura as being all about. People who stay in the mystical mode want to interpret it too simplistically—if the aura is orange, the person is angry; if it's blue, he's spaced out. They want to label things. When they see the slightest glimmer of color around the edge of someone's head, they think they're seeing the aura— and they are, about six inches of it. But the aura extends all over your whole body. Looking at a small part would be like trying to diagnose breast cancer from a toe injury.

So, for me all the mythology about auras isn't very useful. The useful part came when I was involved in lengthy research at UCLA which had to do with the auric field as an indicator of health. Whatever it is that psychics see, some of the disturbances visible to them in the aura indicate not just physical health, but also mental, emotional, and even spiritual health. (In most traditional religions, such as the Native American, high shamans had the ability to see these disturbances, so they could tell in advance when someone was growing ill and what kind of intervention was needed to keep the tribe healthy.) So I began using my sight primarily for healing and diagnosis.

For the last ten years, I've also tried to convey the idea that seeing auras is an interpersonal skill with real value on a global level. I first understood this in 1974 during a trip to the Middle East. I had observed that Americans and Europeans tend to have auras that shift between yellow, green, and blue. (Yellow indicates left-brain activity, which is linear and logical; then, when people "take a commercial break" and kind of space out, the aura goes into blue.) In Greece I saw more orange than I'd ever observed in America. Orange is the color of emotion, so I said to myself, "Gee, you mean there really *is* something to the Mediterranean temperament?"

When I got to Egypt I found people with auras of orange, pink, puce, magenta, and peacock blue. It was like being in a world of psychics, because these were the same colors I'd seen in spiritual groups. It was Disneyland for consciousness junkies! Arabs, being right-brain, see the world emotionally and psychically, not in a linear fashion. What governs them isn't what they *think* about things, but how they *feel*. Then I arrived in Jerusalem and everyone had yellow auras; the Israelis were dominated by linear thinking. Suddenly I understood why these two groups don't get along. Arabs and Israelis are literally "on different wavelengths."

If people learn to see auras, it may help them to understand and accept others who are different.

The scientific approach

I like the scientific method, setting forth a premise and seeing what you can find out through disciplined procedures. From science we've learned that the aura is three to ten times faster than what we call visible light; it's a higher frequency. So people who see auras can "see faster."

Actually, I prefer not to use the term "visible light," because in viewing auras I'm not seeing "invisible light"; I'm seeing the rest of the visible light spectrum. Most people just tune this out, an ability we learn as children. A study done in Italy showed that 60 percent of the kids tested saw auras, but by the time they were socialized and in school at ages five to seven, they'd lost it. They were focused instead on linear, concrete things, such as reading what's on a page. Tuning out is a common process: When you needed to study in college and your roommate wouldn't turn off the radio, you developed a way of tuning out the music so that you could concentrate on physics. As children, we're slowed down in our learning curve in order to grasp the basics—but we may never speed back up. Part of our brain just sits there, dormant.

Developing your ability to see

The way to see auras is to look at living things. The aura is easier to see around a human being, because it's closer to your frequency. But you can also see it on a dog, a plant, or anything else that has an electrical current, even a telephone wire. (Without any practice, most people can glance at high-tension wires and see what looks like radiation off a hot road. They're seeing the wire's aura, without the colors.)

Focus on a person, setting your focal length on their forehead. As you look, your peripheral vision will give you kind of a shadow image. People usually say that this is either beige, white, or blue fuzz that extends anywhere from three to ten inches beyond the physical body. At first you may become aware that *something* is there, but you won't be able to see it. Don't get frustrated and stop looking, or tell yourself you're not doing it the right way. Just keep on. The way to improve is by relaxing and letting your peripheral vision come into play. You're soft-focusing rather than hard-focusing. Just proceed very casually and comfortably. You can practice by looking at people when you're stopped at a traffic signal, standing in a supermarket line, or almost anywhere.

Eventually, you'll know that you're distinctly seeing something. It's usually clear, beige, white, or blue—but very pale, like the thinnest watering of a watercolor. It's transparent; because you're looking past the edge of the body, you can see right through the aura. By the way, have patience with yourself, because you're going to see auras on some days, but not others. No one has deciphered this cycle.

At first people see a single color, the one that's closest to their own frequency. You could say that you're seeing through your own aura. I always remember the beautiful scriptural reference from St. Paul: "You see but through a glass darkly." Because you're blue, you see the blue in other people. This goes on for a period of months.

Then you begin to notice that skin tones are somehow translucent. When you look at someone who has a lot of skin exposed and no makeup on—a woman wearing a low-cut dress, for instance, or a bathing suit—you'll see a sheen over the body. At this point your sense of color starts to be different. As you look down the front of someone's body, you'll see three or four different tints. Everything starts to fall together.

But this is also a confusing stage. You've seen something, and you think you have data—but what does it mean? Actually, not a lot. Unless you see a localized patch of significant color in one area—which could be pathology or muscle strain—it doesn't have any specific meaning. The aura really has to do with the state of consciousness that the person happens to be in at the moment you glance at them.

Here's an example from our job-oriented culture. A woman who stays at home all day, with her children running around, has a kind of soft focus she uses for tracking them; this gives her a blue-purple aura. Then her stockbroker husband comes home and deals with things in a very linear and logical way; his aura is yellow. It takes them through dinnertime before they're in sync again. There's a period of adjustment when people with different jobs come together. And often what is so attractive about that other person is that they are different. The wife thinks, "Thank goodness, some adult conversation." And the husband feels, "What a relief to be home" in the emotional bosom of his family. When people start to see these interpersonal subtleties and take a real interest, they start to grow at a rapid clip.

The most fun about the aura is that the average person sitting in their living room can grasp it pretty easily. Then they can use it however they want to. In my case, I'm interested in how the auric field is related to biochemistry and the mind. But the guy sitting on the couch on Saturday afternoon might care only about the aura of the team he's betting on. (With a lot of practice, you can actually see auras on TV. It's easier to see them on film; for instance, I can tell you instantly whether an actor is into the part or not.) Most of my students, from ambulance drivers to psychotherapists, use their new ability in the healing arts.

Sensing the aura

Here's something you can do for fun when you have friends at home. Rub your hands together until they get very, very warm; then shake the heat off. Now slowly bring your hands together until you feel what seems like a fuzzy ball between your hands. When you feel this fuzzy ball, you're right at the edge of where the aura on one hand bounces against the aura on the other. It's subtle. If you move in closer, so that your hands are three inches apart, you'll feel them draw together magnetically. This happens when the aura on one hand touches the skin on the other; it's drawn in.

Using this method, you can scan a person's aura even if you can't see it. Start by feeling that fuzzy ball between your hands. Then direct your hand at someone else, and see if you can feel your aura bounce off his body. You'll sense a difference in texture (which, with my electrical engineering training, feels to me like capacitance); your hand knows it's being compelled in a different direction.

As you scan over a person's front or back, you may find an area of congested energy, which you sense through extra pressure on your hand. Or you may find an area where there's no energy at all. These represent places where there are physical difficulties, and the person will verify that something is wrong in that part of the body—an ulcer, or whatever it may be. After six months of practice, at least 70 percent of us can develop this ability.

Using your hands to scan helps you to learn that the aura is actually there. And continually touching the aura also helps your eye learn where to look, because you can feel the edge of the aura, even if you don't see a thing. Eventually, you develop "hand-eye coordination." This is exactly how I was trained.

After six months about forty percent of us can see the colors of the aura, and a new world opens.

How to Whistle Beethoven's Ninth Symphony

David Harp

Whistlers look happy—and why not? Whistling is a great way to express yourself; it's an instant, portable relaxation break. However, while there's nothing better than a good whistler, nothing is worse than someone whistling off-key. The way to better whistling is easy: Learn to whistle in tune by practicing a few scales; then dress up your whistling with simple vibrato and the advanced warble.

Scales

Scales are the musical alphabet, the do-re-mi's that go together to make a song. By whistling scales, you'll learn to hit notes accurately. Play the notes of the following four scales on a piano; after each note try to duplicate the pitch by whistling. Then try to whistle the whole scale, up and down.

Chromatic Scale

Begin on C and just play up thirteen black and white notes until you get to the next C. To make it easy, we give each note a

> **You know how to whistle, don't you? Just put your lips together and blow.**
> —*Lauren Bacall*

syllable name; the white notes are in capital letters, the black notes in lower case:

DO di RE ri ME FA fi SO si LA li TI DO

Major Scale

Without this basic scale of Western classical and folk music, you can't even whistle a tune as simple as "Twinkle, Twinkle, Little Star." It is made up of all the white notes on the piano from C to C; these are spelled out by the capitalized syllables of the chromatic scale:

DO RE MI FA SO LA TI DO

Minor Scale

Creating a more plaintive or wistful sound, the minor scale figures in folk and Gypsy music:

DO RE ri FA SO si li DO

Blues Scale

The seven notes of this Afro-American scale sound "bluesy" in any combination:

DO ri FA fi SO li DO

Tip: If you have trouble making accurate jumps—let's say from DO to ri—practice by softly whistling the notes that come in between; you move up the ladder by steps. First, whistle **DO** di RE **ri**. Once you're used to the sound of the gap between DO and ri, drop the intermediate tones and make a direct jump, taking you from the first to the second note of the blues scale.

Or find a song that begins with the same jump; the first two notes of "Greensleeves" ("A-las") are also a DO and a ri.

Vibrato

A pleasing quality can be added to your whistling through minute fluctuations of pitch, called vibrato. The technique is to move your tongue as if you were saying "you you you." Good

> **Hell is full of musical amateurs.**
> —*George Bernard Shaw*, Man and Superman

whistlers seem to prefer small, smooth variations of pitch, which means not moving the tongue very much. (Keeping the tip of your tongue braced against your lower front teeth will allow only the middle of the tongue to move.) As a matter of musical taste, don't use vibrato on every note; save it for when you want to be expressive or to emphasize a note.

The Warble

A beautiful liquid effect, the warble may take you six months to master. You warble by using an articulation that sounds like "oodle" or "loodle" as you whistle. There are four main ways to employ it: (1) a single "loo" or a group of "loo"s, to emphasize single notes; (2) "oodle" or "loodle," to break a tone into two parts; (3) "loodle-oo," to divide a tone into three parts; and (4) the continuous warble of "oodleloodleloodleloodle," which creates a delightful liquid trill.

Now let's put together everything we've learned and . . .

Whistle Beethoven's Ninth Symphony

Here are the first sixteen bars of Beethoven's Ninth Symphony ("Ode to Joy"), with notations suggesting where to use vibrato (v) or a warble ("oodle" or "loo").

How Politicians
Work a Room

Robert Orben

The author of forty-six
books of humor mate-
rial for show business
figures and speakers,
Robert Orben was
director of the White
House Speechwriting
Department for
President Gerald R.
Ford.

Politicians learn the art of "working a room"—
making a good impression, touching base
with as many people as possible (including
all the important figures), moving in and out
of different groups gracefully and with charm.
The masters follow these rules, whether by
instinct or calculation.

They never let a circle of people close in.

Once people realize it's possible to approach a public figure—
let's say at a charity benefit or political gathering—they will gather around and hem him in. But the politician's goal is to circu-
late through the entire crowd, so the whole trick for him is to
keep moving—never to stand with two feet solidly in place and
have a ring drawn around him. People generally understand that
a "big name" is a busy person and that others want to talk to
him, so they accept that he will move along after a few pleasant
words and questions.

They touch other people.

To be physically touched by a celebrity is flattering: You feel
that he has a warm, personal interest in you. So politicians often

give a handshake with two hands, one shaking your hand, the other gripping your forearm. To make a point, they touch your arm or shoulder. They establish contact and make you feel good about them.

They're careful of what they say.

A person who gets to talk with a nationally known politician is likely to remember the conversation forever. So politicians don't say things they wouldn't want to see repeated in print. The story of what a public figure indiscreetly said at a reception seven years ago will be retold a hundred times.

When it's time to leave, they are ushered out.

Ideally, the person in charge makes an announcement like: "The senator would love to spend the rest of the evening here, but unfortunately he has another engagement he's committed to

ON REMEMBERING PEOPLE

Richard M. Nixon

When I was in the House and even in the Senate, I could almost unerringly remember the names of hundreds of county chairmen, city chairmen, precinct chairmen, volunteer workers, newspaper reporters and publishers, and prominent business people.

As president I was not as efficient, not because I was older but because there were just so many more to remember. But whenever I knew I was going to meet people at a reception, a dinner, or other function, I thought that the least I could do was to remember guests' names, occupations, family backgrounds, and hometowns. I always made it a practice, when time permitted, to study the guest list for at least a half hour before each event. My secret, if it could be called that, was that after this brief moment of study, whenever I heard a name, a place, or a position, it immediately triggered my thinking processes and I would be able to put them together. When someone came through the line, the usher would give me the name and I would say, "I'm glad to see you again. I remember when we met at a rally in Cedar Rapids in 1952." Most people were naturally pleased and surprised and no doubt wondered how I did it. It was not because of any natural gift. I worked at it. People were my business.

Richard M. Nixon was the thirty-seventh president of the United States.

attend. He'd like very much to come back on another occasion to spend more time with what has to be the most interesting group that has ever graced this room." Applause, applause; the celebrity waves, and he's into the car.

HOW YOU CAN WORK A ROOM

A minister talking to his parishioners during the social hour after services may not call it "working the room," but that's what he's doing. And so are you when you attend a professional meeting or sales conference, a PTA social, a political fund-raiser, or a glamorous cocktail party.

The idea of walking into a room filled with strangers, however, makes most of us uncomfortable. If we don't avoid it altogether, we feel shy and nervous. But learning how to "work a room" helps you feel outgoing and confident. Whether you want to find new friends or business contacts, promote your political cause or charity, or meet an attractive person of the opposite sex, here's how to make your way around the room.

There is almost no wrong way to approach someone. Most people are eternally grateful for someone's taking the initiative and starting a conversation. Even a cliché like "Do you come here often?" is better than nothing because it breaks the ice. And usually there's a better conversational peg to hang your hat on. At a meeting of stamp collectors, a logical approach would be, "How long have you been collecting?" or "Do you specialize?" For practice in approaching strangers, attend meetings of community, religious, and fraternal organizations, which socialize regularly. You'll soon feel comfortable striking up conversations.

Listen and respond. One of the best ways of being considered a bright, charming conversationalist is to be a good listener. People *love* to talk about themselves; just get them started. This means asking questions, almost as if you were a writer interviewing someone you know nothing about. Express reactions to their answers—kind of like George Burns: "Oh, really? I didn't know that! That's interesting. Ah-hah!" You don't need to exercise great conversational skills to be charming, but only to show interest in the other person.

Learn how to move to a new group without offending the last. It's the nature of a social event for people to mingle—meeting and greeting and moving on. In making the rounds, the main thing is not to hurt feelings by giving people the impression they're being dropped after a few minutes. As long as you come up with an acceptable reason (or even a plausible subterfuge) for moving on, that's okay.

First, you can't be caught looking around the room as if searching for someone more important than the person you're talking to. (This kind of behavior is epidemic at Washington receptions.) Some people scan the crowd by taking off their glasses and peering through them as if something were on the lens, meanwhile looking around the room. You can, of course, glance around the room quite consciously and explain, "There's so-and-so, the person who's running this event, and I have to touch base with her." That's a perfectly acceptable reason for leaving a group.

A good, all-purpose device is never to have a full glass of whatever you're drinking, whether it's Coca-Cola or a martini, so you can excuse yourself, saying, "I'm going to get a refill, and I'll get back *if I can*." (People understand that it's easy to get waylaid at a crowded social gathering.) Go to the bar and ask for just a splash. On your way back join a different group.

Try to include people who are standing alone. If I'm talking with a few people and see somebody hovering nearby—almost part of the group but not really—I will always motion for them to come in, and in one sentence I explain what we're talking about. They're very grateful, as I would be in a similar situation.

Touch base with everyone before you leave. If you were at a party with six couples, you wouldn't just pick up and say thank you to the host and hostess; you'd make the rounds before leaving. Similarly, if the group is small enough, go around saying your goodbyes and expressing the hope that you can continue your conversation on another occasion. (If it's a group of two hundred, obviously, you just have to disappear.)

Choosing Gifts for Boys and Girls of All Ages

Stevanne Auerbach

What toys should you buy for children of different ages? Keeping in mind that children develop at different rates and have different interests, here are some good general guidelines:

Stevanne Auerbach, Ph.D., is the director of the San Francisco International Toy Museum, which displays new toys for children to play with as well as antique toys for them to look at. She is the author of *Toy Chest*, a book about child development as it relates to toys.

Babies (toys should be hypoallergenic, soft, and washable)

Teddy bears
Soft foam balls
Crib toys—activity centers
Mirrors
Mobiles—new babies can start with a black-and-white version (they can't see colors yet); then they enjoy a more colorful one. You can also make your own mobiles with pictures cut from magazines.
Bath toys—wash-mitt puppets, boats, squirters

Toddlers (to age 3)

Push-pull toys that make noise
Shovels and pails
Jack-in-the-boxes

Ride-on toys—low-slung, well-balanced three-wheeler bikes; fire engines or tractors to straddle; KiddyCoupe

Ring stacks—a stand with posts and colored rings

Pounding sets—whacking pegs into holes is fun and helps work out frustrations, though it's hard on adult ears

Bop bags—cartoon figures that are easy to blow up and knock down; another way to release pent-up frustrations

Puzzles with large pieces

Blocks—large, easy pieces

Bubble pipes

Books—large, washable

Preschooler (ages 3–5)

Picture and story books

Blocks

Beanbags—throw into baskets, make up games

ColorForms—plastic people, numbers, letters; they stick on a plastic sheet and can be peeled off to use again

Crayons, art supplies—fingerpaints, Play-Doh, etc.

Construction toys with large pieces, such as Duplo

Slinky—be sure to supervise play on the stairs

Toy piano or electronic keyboard—also xylophones and other musical toys

Dolls—some have clothes with zippers, snaps, and laces to teach a child the skills of dressing oneself

Doctor kits and other role-playing toys

Ages 5–8

Tape recorders—listen to story and music tapes; record the child's own voice; parents record stories for child to listen to

Microphones—for singing, telling jokes and stories

ViewMaster viewers—stories, animals, geography, and more

Playtime Classics

• **Ant Farm:** Teaches about the environment and is just plain fun to watch.

• **Barbie Dolls:** Barbie has been through many changes in her lifetime since 1959. Because she can be dressed so many different ways, she's versatile and represents both a working girl (jet pilot, TV anchor, etc.) and a glamour girl.

• **Etch-A-Sketch:** Creative; good toy to take on trips.

• **Hula Hoop:** Fun exercise for all ages, and you can't get hurt.

• **Slinky:** The original metal Slinky lasts longer; the newer plastic ones pull, twist, and come undone.

• **Tinkertoys:** Regular Tinkertoys are perfect for ages 4–9; Giant Tinkertoys are fun for younger kids . . . and adults.

• **Yo-Yo:** For the novice and enthusiast, there's even a magazine called *Yo-Yo Times*.

Hand puppets

Tools—kids want real tools, not toy plastic ones; supervision is needed

Checkers—get a magnetic version for traveling

Paper dolls

Transparent clocks and similar toys that show a machine's inner workings

More advanced construction toys—Tinkertoys, Playmobil play sets, Legos

Yo-yos—good for outdoor play or on a trip

Bicycles

Hula Hoops

Kites—some can be precisely steered

Transportation toys—cars and trucks

Ages 9–12

Collectibles—dolls, small cars, baseball cards, marbles, and so on

Dollhouses—children can learn to wallpaper and decorate them with miniature furnishings

Electric trains—fun to develop a layout of towns and countryside

Crafts kits—good for making presents that the child can give

Model kits

More complicated construction toys—Erector sets, Lego space ships

Beauty/glamour supplies—for girls to try grownup styles

Electronic games—portable or video systems. (A tip: Be sure your child plays with a balance of toys—physical, educational, creative, indoor, outdoor—and doesn't end up glued to video games or any other single activity for a prolonged time.)

Books

Videotapes

Board games—Junior Monopoly, Scrabble, checkers, etc.

Magic sets—performing tricks builds confidence in front of a group

Play is serious work for children. There is fantasy in it, of course, but also reality. Kids learn how to get along with other people, and they find out about the world they'll inhabit when they're older.

There are three basic types of toy: Active toys, like rocking horses and Hula Hoops, get kids physically involved. Educational toys, such as Lego sets, blocks, and books, teach new skills or knowledge. Creative toys, like fingerpaints and puppet theaters, let children use their imaginations.

In choosing toys, there are a few simple principles. First, a toy should be fun. It doesn't take much for a child to have a good time. As every parent knows, kids often spend more time playing with the box a toy comes in than with the toy itself. That's why it's a great idea to give children cardboard cartons they can pretend are boats; to fill a drawer in the kitchen with wooden spoons, plastic cups and bowls, and pots and pans they can play with; and to throw a cloth over a card table so they can have a tent or theater.

A toy should be appropriate to the child's age; otherwise, it will frustrate the too-young child or bore the older one. Gender doesn't matter so much. Boys and girls like to play with many of the same things, so don't limit their choices. Boys enjoy stuffed animals and puppets, and girls need to play with trucks and construction toys.

A toy should also be safe. Each year there are 100,000 injuries involving toys. Especially with children under five, watch for loose pieces, sharp edges, and paint without a "nontoxic" label. As for toy weapons, I'm against them. About 25,000 kids each year are injured by toy guns. And more than 200 children are killed by picking up guns they *thought* were toys. It seems foolish to put a gun in a kid's hands, particularly with 150,000 other toys on the market. Children will play aggressively when they need to, and they can make their own little guns with their fingers or Legos. But when a parent provides a toy gun, it gives the child the wrong message.

Kids must learn to respect their toys and not leave them scattered all over the place, so be sure to provide plenty of easy storage—boxes, shelves, cupboards, cartons. (One idea is to sling a hammock to hold stuffed animals and dolls; it's great fun for the child, too.) If a toy needs batteries, be sure to put in the right size before giving the toy to the child; this prevents frustration.

Don't give children too many toys, or they'll be overwhelmed. Instead, buy a few really good toys that will last for a long time. Toys with more than one use are said to have "high play value." A teddy bear, for instance, promotes a child's affections, and he or she can also make up stories about it, which stimulates language development.

To find out what toys your children want, just take them on a trip to the toy store; let them wander and develop a "wish list." (Obviously, you don't have to buy everything on the list!) Choose good basic toys. But do get at least one "hot" item that the child has seen advertised and really wants.

Don't let toys substitute for your attention and time to play together. Remember, the parent is the child's first "big toy."

Puppet theater and puppets—kids enjoy making their own

Real adventure toys—tents, sleeping bags, walkie-talkies; for children in transition from toys to "real world" activities

Sports gear—soccer ball, tennis racket, horseshoes, roller skates

Ages 12–15

Camera

Video camera—although expensive, a good value for older children who can learn to use it properly and create their own movies

Walkman

Tape recorder and tapes

Complicated construction toys—Fisher Techniks, etc.

Backgammon, chess—because of the strategy involved, more interesting and challenging than video games

Crafts and crafts books—to develop new skills, such as embroidery

Small sewing machine

Stationery—with rubber stamps, children can create their own printed pieces

Model kits—boats, planes, cars

Planetarium—projects the stars on a bedroom ceiling

Terrarium—kids can plant from seedlings

Gardening supplies for growing vegetables, flowers

Sports gear

Maps, geography items—a child going on a trip can learn about the destination and how to get there

THE <u>REAL</u> SECRETS OF THREE-CARD MONTE

Harry Anderson

Harry Anderson, the star of television's long-running *Night Court*, is also a comedian and magician whose stage act includes a version of three-card monte. In his scuffling days, he once made a living on the streets operating a three-shell game.

When you bring out your wallet to play three-card monte, consider your money spent. You can't win. In this game the monte tosser throws a queen and two other cards face down on the table, mixes them around a bit—and you're sure you know where the queen lies. But when you put your money down, your card never turns out to be the queen. The tosser is always one step ahead of you. There are two main reasons:

1. The monte tosser is not manipulating cards; he is manipulating human greed.

2. The monte tosser wins not by sleight-of-hand, but by a convincing bit of theater.

When a monte tosser works his game, it is really a little drama in which he plays the leading role, with his shills and "muscle" as supporting players. You can see this act played out every day on the streets of New York and other cities.

Years ago, slick operators used to toss monte at racetracks, county fairs, train stations—even on moving trains. Another passenger might strike up a conversation with you about how "back in Kansas" he saw "this fella throwin' these cards." He starts to

> **If a pickpocket meets a holy man, he will see only his pockets.**
> —*Hari Dass Baba*

explain the game, using three of his own cards—say, a queen of hearts and two black deuces—just to show you what the guy was doing. You watch the demonstration and notice that he's very clumsy because he's not a "broad tosser," or monte dealer. He's just a fellow reenacting the scene for you. Each time he throws the cards, you can see where the queen, or "money card," goes. But as he talks and tosses, this fellow seems to get an inflated idea of his own skill: "Hey, this is pretty easy; I could make money with this game!"

Actually, your fellow passenger is a clever con man acting out a part. This bit of theater is what will beat you, not his skill at

THE MONTE CAST OF CHARACTERS

The **tosser** is the man throwing the cards—the only member of the cast you're aware of unless trouble develops. The modern monte gang usually uses a young tosser, so he doesn't look like an experienced card mechanic—although, of course, he is. (Somewhere in our minds we think we can get the better of children.)

The older and better actors in the gang work as **shills.** As you watch the game from the sidelines, you see some people losing and some winning; *all* of them may be shills. You notice that the losers don't seem to be following the dealer's toss very well. But the clever fellow is winning because he *is* following the toss. Not only that, he's picking the same card you'd pick! So you begin to follow the toss; then you make your move and enter the game—and you lose.

The tosser separates his **customers** into "mooches" and "wise guys." The mooch, who doesn't know anything and blindly trusts the toss, might think the money card is in, say, position A. The wise guy, who thinks he knows everything and is onto the game, will believe the money card has gone to position B. But the money card is, in fact, at position C. Tossers say that in three-card monte there's one card for the mooch, there's one card for the wise guy—and then there's the winner, the money card.

The **muscle** are tough members of the monte gang who stay on the sidelines unnoticed, watching for the police and also making a show of force if need be. If a player gets abusive, tries to grab his money back, or says he's going to call the cops, one of the muscle boys threatens him and suggests there's going to be a fight. (Actual violence is uncommon, since it would bring the police and end the game for the day, which isn't good business.) Eventually, the situation cools down; but by the time the player turns around again, the tosser and his shills have gone; the cards are gone; the money is gone; the game has vanished.

sleight-of-hand. It's like Edgar Bergen with Charlie McCarthy: If the character the ventriloquist creates is believable enough, it doesn't matter whether the lips are moving. It's not really a trick of the lips; it's a trick of characterization. And monte isn't a game of handling cards; it's a game of handling human nature.

You believe this character on the train to be a fool who doesn't know what he's doing—although he's ready to bet that he *does*. And here is where your human greed comes into the equation. Are you willing to take advantage of him? He's counting on the fact that you are very willing. If he's correct, you become his "fish," and he'll win your last dollar.

So greed draws you into the game. It also trips you up along the way. As an example, take the old "bent corner" ploy *(for details, see "How to Throw Three-Card Monte")*. The question is, if you notice a bent corner on the money card—a bend that the tosser is apparently unaware of—are you willing to cash in on it? It's an ethical question. (If you were playing in a poker game with friends at home and noticed that the ace of spades was nicked, the right thing would be to point it out to the other players and get a new deck. Whether you actually do this may depend in part on how honest you are and in part on how much money you've lost in the game so far.)

Very few among us are as pure as the Dalai Lama. And so you might bet on the card with the bent corner. If you do, you'll be shocked when it turns out to be the deuce, not the queen. You've been had. And you can't complain, because that would show you were trying to take unfair advantage.

The game of three-card monte assumes there's a little larceny in all of us. It simply exploits our willingness to take advantage of another person.

> **Whatever deceives seems to produce a magical enchantment.**
> —*Plato*

A little game from Hanki-Poo,
Two cards for me, and one for you.
Keep your eye on the Queen—
$5 will get you $10,
$10 will get you $20 . . .

A three-card monte dealer sometimes chants this ditty to attract you to his game, which is a swindle presented as a simple sporting proposition. He shows three cards and tosses them face down on the table. Your job is to find the queen. If you're right, you win; otherwise, you lose. The truth is, you don't stand a chance. Even if you know the sleight-of-hand moves and secret dodges revealed below, you won't be able to follow the queen in the hands of a master operator. You can, however, learn how to toss three-card monte to entertain your friends:

The Cards You'll need a queen (let's say hearts) and two cards of the opposite color (like black twos). If the black cards are identical, extracted from two different decks, you can work a diabolical deceit (described below under "The 'Bent Corner Ploy'").

Monte tossers prefer Bee brand cards, whose backs are entirely covered with a pattern of diamonds that camouflages the secret "move." But you can also use Bicycle and other cards with a white border.

To prepare the cards, stack them and bend them lengthwise down the center until the long sides meet; then release the pressure. They will now have a bridge or "crimp," which makes it easy to lift them from the table.

Hold the crimped cards stacked and carefully squared up; bend up the outer right cor-

ners; then bend them down again. This prepares the cards for the "Bent Corner Ploy" used at the end of the game.

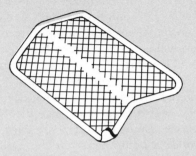

All three cards should look the same from the back. Be sure there are no smudges or other marks that could give your audience a clue which card is the queen.

The Toss Your left hand will hold one card. Your right hand will hold two cards, one

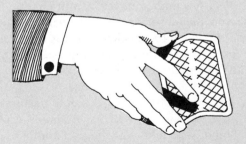

above the other; to make an "honest toss" you'll throw the bottom card but for a "fake toss" the top card. Both tosses look the same. Here's how:

Lay the cards face down in a row, with the queen in the middle. With your right hand, pick up a two by the ends, holding it at the crimp; it is gripped between the balls of your thumb and second finger, which extend below the card. Move your hand over the queen, letting the left sides of the two cards touch, and pick it up, also between the balls of your thumb and second finger. A gap of half an inch separates the right edges of the two cards.

Raise the cards off the table and rotate the hand to show the face of the queen. At this point the third fingertip presses lightly against the index corner of the queen.

To make an honest throw: As you swing the hand face down, release the bottom card by loosening the grip of the third finger; the card drops face down and a bit to the left. Your hand finishes the swing in its original position over the table.

To make a fake throw: The movement is identical, except that as you turn your right hand face down, you release the *top* card.

Do this by letting go with the second finger. This finger quickly grips the lower card, and the third finger straightens out. Thus, by the time the right hand comes to a stop, it appears that the second finger is still holding the upper card, while the third finger is now unoccupied, having dropped the lower card.

Whether it's an honest or a fake throw, the card should drop flat to the table, without bouncing or turning.

A Simple Routine *First Toss* Lay out the cards with the queen in the middle. Pick up a two with the left hand, and rotate your hand to show the face of the card. "A black two," you say. The right hand picks up the other two and displays it the same way. "Another black two." Move the right hand over the queen and pick it up, as described in "The Toss." Rotate the hand to display the card, saying, "And the queen—the money card! Keep your eye on the queen."

Toss the queen fairly to the center; then pick it up in tossing position in the left hand, show it, and make another honest toss of the queen. Repeat these tosses, each time showing the face of the queen. The fifth time, toss the queen fairly to the middle; then cross your right hand over your left and drop both twos, one on each side of the queen. "Even if I crisscross my hands, you can probably guess that the queen is in the middle."

(From this point on, you treat the proceedings as a demonstration instead of a guessing game that challenges the spectators. This way they'll be fooled but not embarrassed when you reveal where the queen is—or is not—located.)

Second Toss Pick up the cards and repeat the first four throws of the sequence. On the fifth throw, make a fake toss, throwing the top card to the left-hand position. Drop the card in the left hand next to it, in the middle position, and then drop the card in the right hand on the right end. The queen appears to be on your left side but is actually on the right. Show the card at the left end, saying, "Most people would swear that the queen went here, but they'd be wrong." Reveal the queen at the right end.

The "Bent Corner Ploy" Tell your audience: "When the monte tosser really wants to clean you out, he resorts to a special trick that depends entirely on your willingness to take advantage of him. He pretends to drop something, and while he's bending down one of the players—actually, his shill—reaches over and slyly bends up the corner of the queen, making sure you notice it."

As you say this, show the queen, then turn it face down and bend up the outer right corner a bit.

"This player starts winning every time. Since the monte tosser hasn't noticed the bent corner, you decide to take advantage of the situation and bet all the money you've got. He throws the cards . . ."

Lay out the cards with the queen in the middle. Pick up a two with the right hand and show its face ("one black card"), then turn it face down again. While the left hand picks up the other two and shows it ("another black card") and while the spectators' attention is focused on the left hand, the right hand's third finger (or little finger if you find it easier) secretly bends up the corner of its card. It's easy because you already bent the corner. The bent corner is concealed by the right third and little fingers.

The right hand now picks up the queen under the two, displays it, and makes an honest toss. Then the left hand picks up the queen and makes an honest toss. The right hand picks up the queen and makes a fake toss, throwing the two with the bent corner to the middle position. The spectators think it's the queen.

Cross the left hand over the right, preparing to drop the left-hand card at the right end. During this motion your left arm hides your right hand long enough for the right third (or little) finger to secretly straighten out the corner on the queen. Drop the two from the left hand. Then the right hand drops the queen at the left end.

Now comes a "convincer" that will totally fool the spectators. You say, "The monte tosser pretends to be on your side. He says, 'Don't bet on this card . . . or this one.'" As you talk, pick up the queen from the left end, without showing it, and beneath it pick up the two from the right end. Rotate the hand to show the two ("Don't bet on this card!"). Make a fake toss, throwing the queen to the left end. Rotate the right hand to display the "other" two, which is actually the same card you just showed, saying "or this one!" (This is the reason you use two identical black cards.) Drop the two face down at the right end. Apparently, you've shown both twos very fairly.

"Now, who wouldn't be willing to bet the ranch that the queen is in the middle? Well, just be glad you didn't . . ." Reveal that the middle card with a bent corner isn't the queen but a two.

The Moral "And that, ladies and gentlemen, is why you should *never* play another man's game."

—*J. D.*

HOW TO SERVE TEA AS IT'S DONE AT THE RITZ OF LONDON

Michael Twomey

Michael Twomey is the master of ceremonies at the Palm Court of the Ritz in London, one of the world's most celebrated places to take tea. He joined the staff of the hotel forty-five years ago, when he was fifteen years old.

Tea is a lovely thing, a bit of English tradition in which our visitors can take part. At the Ritz I preside over tea each afternoon at the Palm Court, an absolutely delightful room that was originally called the Winter Garden for its glass roof that opens to the sky. We do tea in two seatings by reservation, and we insist on jackets and ties. The sense of occasion is paramount with us. It's coming to *take* tea, rather than to drink tea. Occasionally, the Queen Mother will come by, or someone else our clients may recognize. We serve many Americans; perhaps this is our way of getting back after the Boston Tea Party!

In my forty-five years at the Ritz, I've gained a reasonable idea about how to serve tea:

First, the water: My idea is that it should be drawn freshly. In the morning in the average domestic home, the tap should be allowed to run a little while, so that the water in the pipes is cleared and you get fresh, oxygenated water. The water must now be heated to boiling. But it should boil for a short time only; if the water boils too long, it loses a little oxygen, which makes the tea taste rather bland. When everything is done freshly, the water sort of sparkles, and it highlights the tea.

> **If this is coffee, please bring me some tea; but if this is tea, please bring me some coffee.**
> —*Abraham Lincoln*

After the kettle boils, put some of the water into the teapot and swirl it around for a few seconds to heat the pot. Now add tea—a heaping teaspoon of leaves for each person, plus "one for the pot." It should be loose tea. (Tea bags don't seem to produce the same result.) Then pour in the boiling water. This infuses the tea to perfection. In the old days they used to say that you should let the tea stand for four to five minutes, but I don't think it's essential to leave it as long as that. Three minutes is fine.

Now the tea can be poured, which is done through a strainer. On the table you should also have a second teapot, full of boiling hot water. If the tea is too strong for someone's taste, you can add a little boiling water to the cup. Once the teapot is empty, pour in the supplemental hot water for your second cup of tea.

I'd say that 99 percent of English people take milk with their tea. I'm an advocate of putting fresh, cold milk in the cup first. As the tea is poured, the milk sort of warms up with the tea. I find that if milk is added afterwards to a boiling cup of tea, it tends slightly to scald it and change the flavor of the tea a little bit, which is noticeable to a connoisseur. (Other people say the milk should go in afterwards, however, so that you can judge how much you need.)

I'm amazed at the amount of tea people drink—in the Palm Court, it's an average four to six cups per person. Perhaps it's no wonder. Drinking tea is a lovely way to revive yourself. When I get home at the end of the day, what's the first thing I always do myself? Have a nice cup of tea.

Tea Etiquette

• **What should I do if I slosh tea into my saucer?** This can happen when your cup is overfilled. The acceptable thing is to pick up both your cup and saucer and, in a dignified manner, bring the saucer to your lap or chest, as it were. As you drink, the saucer remains below the cup, which should prevent any indiscreet drips from going on your dress. Eventually, your hostess will probably notice and change the saucer for you.

• **Why do those little sandwiches have the crusts cut off?** Basically, to achieve daintiness. We cut the bread very thin and sliver the cucumber in order to make a morsel, rather than something you have to attack. At the Ritz we give five little sandwiches—cucumber, of course, and smoked salmon, smoked chicken, low-fat cheese, and ham. It's daintier not having to cope with crusts. (Personally, however, I like crusts.)

A CARNIVAL AGE-AND-WEIGHT GUESSER REVEALS HIS SECRETS

Bill "Willy the Jester" Stewart

In the costume of "Willy the Jester," Bill Stewart runs his guessing game at the medieval village inside the Excalibur Hotel in Las Vegas. Years ago, on the road with a carnival where he operated "one of those shows where a girl changes into a gorilla," he learned the age and weight game from an old-timer named Charlie.

I've spent twenty years, mostly on the carnival circuit, guessing how old people are and how much they weigh. It's a real encounter with human nature. Sometimes I make guesses for three thousand customers a day, and the way the game is constructed gives me two advantages right off the bat.

The first is illustrated by a funny line that David Letterman uses on his TV show when a guest comes on with a ridiculous-looking necktie: "Hey, I like that tie. What happened—the guy couldn't guess your weight?" Even though the line is a dig at what I do, I get a big laugh out of it, and it contains a basic truth: The worth of the prize is much less than what customers pay to play the game. I charge $2 for a guess, but my prizes wholesale for only 50¢. I can't lose running this game. Of course, customers can see that the prizes aren't worth what it costs to play, but prizes aren't what they're after. Usually it's an ego trip—for instance, they think they look younger than their age and want to fool me—or they just like being the center of attention for a few moments.

A second advantage for me lies in the rules of the game. I have to guess ages within two years, weights within three pounds, and birthday months within two months. If you think about this, the percentages in my favor are much higher than they appear. On age guessing, the phrase "within two years" really gives me a spread of five years. If I peg someone at 28, and he's anywhere from 26 to 30, I win. For weights I have a spread of seven pounds. Only on birthday months are the odds slightly against me: I have a spread of five months, which leaves seven months for the player.

Most adults don't ask me to guess their birthday months, though. The category was really created for kids, since it's too easy to guess an 8-year-old's age within a five-year range. If an adult picks the birthday month category, it's usually for one of two reasons: They've seen a prize they want and are going for it, or else they're having a birthday that day. So I take a chance and pick the current month, and it works for me quite a bit.

Here are my secrets for guessing ages and weights.

> **During a carnival, men put masks over their masks.**
> —Xavier Forneret

Age

Age is the toughest category to guess. Especially with cosmetic surgery nowadays, women may appear to be in their 30s but really be in their upper 40s.

Gray hair is a fooler and will get you in trouble. I've had customers in their 20s who have as many gray hairs as I have at 46. I study the face, and if I don't see crow's feet and wrinkles, I figure that the gray is premature; it doesn't mean a thing. I've picked off guys with gray hair and receding hairlines at 26 years old because their faces looked young. Another clue is when they have gray hair in the dome but not in the mustache; it tells me the hair is prematurely gray, so I take a few years off.

When someone is trying very hard to make sure I notice the gray—a guy might come up and deliberately take off his hat so that I can see his hair—you can bet your life I'm going to put his age ten years under what the average person would guess.

Wrinkles and crow's feet aren't entirely reliable indicators of age; maybe the person has worked outside a lot and has premature wrinkles. But generally wrinkles do peg someone as older. I try to get a person's face into the light so that I can see small wrinkles. (Also, I'm trying to make a show out of the whole thing by putting them in the spotlight, and they enjoy being the central figure for the moment.) Another trick is to get them to laugh or smile, because that's when age wrinkles show up in people's faces. I might say, "Don't you giggle at me, or I'll make you 12 years old!" which always gets a smile out of them.

I don't look at people's teeth—although if I ever had a horse come up and play the game I would. But I do notice braces. Some girls will make a big point of flashing their braces, like they're trying to say, "I'm a teenager"—but teenagers with braces keep their mouths shut. So if a girl shows me her braces deliberately, I might put her in her upper 20s; she's probably a working girl who decided to fix her teeth now that she can afford it.

Surprisingly, some of the most important clues come from looking at people's hands. There are two things I watch for. First, if it's a girl who could be a teenager but looks older, I immediately look for a wedding band or engagement ring, which would bump her up from 16 years old. Second, as we get older, age spots appear on our hands, and these give away women with young-looking faces or cosmetic surgery. I had a customer recently who looked 45, but her hands said she was at least 50; she turned out to be 56.

Some of the most useful clues about age don't even come from the customers themselves. The people they're with sometimes give it away. If I get a teenage girl who's made up to look 25, but she's there with five giggling 14-year-olds, she's got no chance; I'm going to put her at 14. Or a woman might point to her husband in the crowd and tell me, "*He* wants you to guess my age." By looking at her spouse, I can get a clue how old she is.

If I *really* overguess a woman's age, she might get steamed and react like she's about to start World War III. But I have a good alibi line: "See, I wasn't really guessing *you*. I was guessing that real old guy you're with!" The wife gets a kick out of that.

A clue to kids' ages is in the way they present themselves. I had a boy who stood about 4'6", a kid the average person would have guessed at 10 years old. But the way he came up and spoke directly and maturely—"I want you to guess my age, sir"—made me put him at 14, which was a direct hit. If kids handle themselves well, they're usually a little older than they look.

A person's physical condition offers fewer hints than you'd expect. Nowadays, some people are in peak condition well into their 50s. And if you do get someone with middle-age spread, it's not necessarily an added clue, because by that time the double chin and sagging posture and other signs of age are already there.

But clothing can be a big giveaway. A teenager who looks older than she is but comes up wearing a New Kids on the Block T-shirt is dead in the water. On the other hand, I had a girl who looked very young but was wearing a sweatshirt from the Bolshoi Ballet. Since today's teenagers don't even know where Russia is, let alone what the Bolshoi is, I pegged her in the 30s and got her.

In the end, a lot of age guessing is instinct. After you look at everything I've mentioned, sometimes the best thing to do is just forget all of it and go with your gut feeling. Here's a little story that happened not long ago: I guessed a nice little old lady right on the button at 101. (I remembered Willard Scott on TV with his pictures of people turning 100 years old, and she looked like one of them.) But when I held up the pad of paper with my guess on it—the crowd sees it before the lady announces her age or knows what I guessed—her family's faces just fell. You could sense it was the lady's birthday, since the whole family was there and she was dressed up with a little flower on, so I thought I'd better fix the situation. I asked, "How old are you, dear?" She answered, "I'm 101 today!" I said, "God bless you; you look great for your age. I wrote 72, so go get your prize." She never saw my guess. It made everyone feel great, and I felt great, too.

Weight

The first thing I do is gauge a person's height, using myself as a measuring stick. I'm 6'4", and if someone comes up to my elbow, or my shoulder, or my chin, I know how tall they are.

There are some standard ratios of height and weight, but I've found that doctors' and air force charts are absurdly low on weight. (For instance, I weigh 290 pounds; at 230 I'd be almost slim, but for years the air force chart said a man 6'4" should weigh 172 pounds. At 172 pounds I'd be a handrail!)

Generally, I'd put men of 5'6" in the 140-to-160-pound category; moving toward 6' I'd go into the 170-to-200-pound range. Where they fall within the range depends on their bulk.

The woman who has her weight guessed in public is often the petite type who wants to show everyone what a perfect figure she has; she's usually somewhere between 110 and 120. Another common customer is the tall woman who appears slender; I peg this type at 130 to 150. (Some tall women with perfect figures can weigh 155 pounds, and they're amazed when I hit it.) Surprisingly enough, women can weigh as much as men of the same height; just because she's a girl, you can't figure she weighs less.

A great technique is to mentally compare the customers to friends whose weights you know. For example, I used to have three buddies who were boxers—a lightweight, a welterweight, and a middleweight. I remem-

---

Here's One Carnival Game That's Not Crooked

• In the weight-guessing game, people often suspect there's some sort of hidden pressure plate in the floor that tells the operator how much a customer weighs. I've never even heard of that being tried.

• In the past, some dishonest carnies did cheat at the game (although I can't imagine anyone doing it now) by writing down *two* ages on their pad of paper. The operator wouldn't show his guess until the customer announced her age. Let's say he wrote both 22 and 30 and the girl said she was 28 years old. The operator would cover up 22 with his thumb and show 30, winning the game. If she said she was 24, he covered up 30 and showed 22, so he also won.

• Actually, very few carnival games nowadays are crooked. An operator who is caught cheating loses his contract with the carnival, and since he already makes good money running an honest game, why risk it? In a good week, a carnival scale can take in $10,000 of pure profit.

ber them well. So I judge some male customers as fighters. If I think he's a lightweight, I put him at 128–134 pounds; a welterweight is 142–148; a middleweight is 156–162. For another example, I go with a girl who weighs 141 pounds, and I can compare ladies of her height to my girlfriend and get a good idea what they weigh.

Look at people from at least three angles. Walk around to the side and especially the back. You want to see how much bulk—or lack of it—they have to them. Are their clothes stretching here and there? Are those pants just baggy, or are the legs filling them up pretty well? If someone is built thickly, that tells you to guess a weight in the upper end of the range. A guy of 5'8" can easily weigh over 200 pounds if he's built like a small tank.

There are funny lines to use with men who are *really* big, and I do get some 300-pounders. For a huge guy I might announce, "Okay, you weigh one hundred and," then I wink at the crowd and say, "That's his *left* leg." Another line is: "You weigh"—pregnant pause—"a *lot.*"

Look at arms and wrists. If a man is wearing baggy clothes or a woman has a loose-fitting dress, you can't get many clues about their bulk. But someone's arms and wrists will tell you whether this is a big or a very thin person, so you adjust your guess accordingly.

Store what you learn. You might get a tall, skinny man you've guessed at 160 pounds—but on the scale he turns out to be 20 pounds heavier. Store this information away so that the next time you face a tall, skinny guy, you'll remember how much the earlier one weighed. As this kind of information rolls around in your head, it becomes part of your instincts, helping you to guess more and more accurately.

HOW TO INTERVIEW SOMEONE

John Brady

The author of *The Craft of Interviewing*, John Brady has conducted hundreds of seminars on this skill for editors and journalists. Among his interview subjects have been Gloria Steinem, Joseph Wambaugh, Neil Simon, and William Goldman. He edits *The Interviewer*, a newsletter for professional interviewers.

1. Don't use the word "interview."

Interviews scare people. They think of police interrogations, or a Mike Wallace–style encounter, or a job interview. So never say, "I'd like to interview you." Instead: "I was wondering if I could spend a little time with you and gather some information."

2. Get intermediaries on your side.

Whomever you talk to first—a secretary, an executive assistant, a public relations representative, or a spouse—is screening things for the person you want to interview. Your job is to get that intermediary on your side. Ask his or her name and add it to your Rolodex. When you call a second time, use the secretary's name—"Hello, Arlene"—and you become a much more friendly factor in her life. Soon you have a person who's on your side conveying your interview request to the boss; it's two against one—so the boss is much more likely to say yes.

Remember, too, that if you don't treat a subject's employees with respect and courtesy, they can be powerful forces to block your way.

3. Don't think of an interview as a one-shot deal.

If a person can only give you an hour, ask to divide that time into two meetings—maybe fifteen minutes in the morning for coffee and forty-five minutes at the end of the day. Or half an hour today and the same tomorrow morning. Two interviews are better than one, and three are better than two. You develop rapport each time you meet a subject. And after the preliminary social call—which is what the first interview consists of—you can do away with the small talk and get to the heart of the matter.

4. Try to get the subject out of the office.

An office makes a pretty dull setting, and people are more likely to hold forth rather than converse openly there. Out of the office, subjects tend to be looser and more loquacious.

5. Never be on time for an interview—always arrive early.

If you arrive at least ten minutes ahead of time, you'll stay more in command of the situation. You are being somewhat aggressive, in a nonthreatening way, and have an edge. But if you arrive late for an interview, you lose any chance of taking charge. You're reduced to spouting schoolboy excuses—the traffic was terrible, I couldn't find a parking spot, the elevator was jammed—which leaves you at a psychological disadvantage. Furthermore, your late arrival says to the subject, "Something else was more important to me than this interview." The subliminal negative impression will be hard to overcome.

Arriving ten minutes early also gives you time to absorb the atmosphere of the subject's home or office for use as "color." Occasionally, you'll even get a bonus—an extra ten minutes with the person you've come to see, because the time is open.

6. Start with a strong question.

Your first question should make it clear that you've done your homework and are going to be an interesting person to talk to. It should be a door opener. Although some interviewers like to begin with small talk, an easy question, or background information ("Can you tell me a little about how you got started in the widget industry?"), that to me is sure boredom. It's better to say, "When you decided to leave medical school in 1972 and pursue a business degree at Harvard, what was in your mind?" Do a little advance digging into their résumé and read articles published about them; talk to people who have known them, perhaps a co-worker or spouse. Then you can open up a real avenue of communication from the start.

7. When the subject gives you a great quote, keep a poker face.

A dynamite quote might be a revelatory statistic ("We're gonna do a trillion dollars' worth of widgets this year") or something personal ("People around here think I'm a Harvard Ph.D.; hell, I didn't even graduate from high school"). Stay casual, because if you react strongly or start taking notes feverishly, some subjects will think better and say, "Oh, maybe you better not use that." Just let the statement roll around the back of your mind and throw out a diversionary question: "Well, a lot of people don't go to grad school these days—but if you were to choose a college, which one would you go to?" As he starts talking about the Ivy League or the Big Ten, you write down the bombshell quote. By taking notes a bit out of sync, you can get the quote without revealing how good it is or giving your subject the idea it will become the lead of your story.

THREE TRICKS TO MAKE TOUGH SUBJECTS TALK

Silence Silence is a great prod. When someone gives you an answer that isn't the whole story, mentally count to five before you respond. This creates an uncomfortable gap in the conversation, a space he often will try to fill with sound—perhaps by blurting out more than he intended.

Flattery If the subject gives you a short answer and clearly wants to move off the topic, follow his lead. Later, after a coffee break or a pause while he takes a phone call, you might say, "You know, you said something earlier that really intrigued me." Suddenly, he is all ears—what did he say that was so fascinating? Now you read back the subject's answer and ask for amplification by saying something like, "What do you really mean here?"

Repetition An editor of the *Playboy* interviews once told me that the magazine's interviewers ask the same question three, four, or even seven times in the course of several days with the subject. Most interviewers don't get that much time, but if you keep returning to the topic, you do have a much better chance of getting an answer.

8. If a subject gives monosyllabic answers, play "Twenty Questions."

You can't turn someone who is terse into a raconteur through your wily interviewing style, but you can elicit enough short answers and bring them together in an interesting way. An exchange might go like this:

"How did you meet your spouse?"

"In a bowling alley."

"Really, when was that?"

"Oh, about twenty-two years ago."

"Where was the bowling alley?"

"Des Moines."

"What were you doing in Des Moines?"

"I was there for a bowling tournament."

It's like pulling teeth, but after fifteen or twenty questions, you learn in a piecemeal way that this man met his wife two decades ago in a bowling alley when he was with a company team. They met somewhat by accident—a fierce storm had knocked out the electricity and canceled the tournament, so everyone went across the street for a sandwich. The impromptu blackout party went on till midnight. And so forth.

By tying together a string of short answers, you have constructed a good anecdote. It's like being an artist at an easel: He employs only little dabs of paint; but after a while, when he steps back, there's a picture.

9. Never write out sensitive questions.

If the subject happens to see your list of questions and notices that some of them are aggressive, he'll think you have arrived with an agenda and an attitude, rather than being objective. A friend of mine arranged an interview with Frank Rizzo when he was the mayor of Philadelphia, and one of the questions he wrote on an envelope was, "Why do you trample on the civil rights of Philadelphians?" When he sat down, Rizzo reached over, took the envelope out of his hand, and said, "Whaddya got here?" He read the questions—including the zinger—and went into a snit, tore the envelope into a million pieces, and threw the writer out the door.

It's far better to look for an opening so that he brings up the sensitive subject himself—or at least seems to. Wait for him to say something like, "You know, being mayor of a city like this isn't the easiest job in the world." Then you can respond sympathetically: "I agree, Mr. Mayor, it's a difficult office. But there are some people who say that you trample on the civil rights of Philadelphians in the course of your job. How do you handle criticism like that?" You've taken a fairly innocuous statement of his and used it as a transitional device for getting to your sensitive question. The idea is to leave the mayor with the impression that *he* brought up the topic in the first place. Once it's on the table, you can discuss it at length.

10. Ask really tough questions dead last—or even later.

Even routine interviews can become thorny if you stray into certain sensitive areas. There's sex, money, religion, and relatives— the major reasons for divorce in America. Then there's age; people don't like to feel they're getting old, on the job or otherwise. And there are business plans and strategies; companies know the competition will read the story, and if they're too candid, they sometimes pay a price.

If a touchy topic doesn't come up comfortably along the way, don't introduce it until the end. Then you can probe the rumors

TELEPHONE
INTERVIEW TIPS

Easily 60 percent of interviews for print are conducted on the telephone. Here are two helpful ideas:

Call at lunch hour. Usually you'll find your subjects out. Leave a prominent message for them to call when they get back— which they will usually do on their own nickel. I know a magazine editor who makes *all* his calls during lunch hour. It's also a good technique for the frugal writer on a budget.

Close your eyes. During a phone interview it's easy to become visually distracted—by the view outside the window, by another project on your desk. Knowing that the tape recorder is running, many interviewers become lazy listeners. (I've even seen a writer doing a crossword puzzle during a phone interview.) But if you shut your eyes, you'll find yourself listening closely to the other person without distraction. This is vital, because you can immediately follow up on his thoughts and ideas. If you don't follow up during the interview, you miss the opportunity—no matter what you have on tape.

about the third marriage and the disappearing spouse, since you already have 90 percent of what you need to write the story. Even if you get kicked out, you can probably go to press with what you've got.

One way to introduce a tough topic is to type up a critical quote from a trade publication or a newsmagazine and bring it with you. Hand it to the subject and say, "I'd like to give you an opportunity to answer your critics and set the record straight." You become a kind of moderator rather than an interrogator.

Another trick is to get information by offering information. If you want to know how many widgets he's got control of, give him a statistic you've found in your research. This quid pro quo approach implies, "Can you top this?"

If you *don't* get the answer you need, wait a day and then telephone again, saying, "I don't think I've got enough information on this particular area. Could we have a cup of coffee?" He might either agree or suggest, "Let's talk about it now on the phone." Regardless, once the ice is broken, he may be forthcoming with an answer.

SECRETS OF A FIVE-STAR WAITER

Tim Dewey

Tim Dewey works twelve hours a day during the tourist season, cramming a whole year of work into six months. He saves his money and spends the rest of the year traveling to such places as Paris and Bali.

I've worked in lots of different kinds of dining rooms, aboard an elegant cruise ship, in Continental restaurants where I flambéed specialties at the table—and most recently at a wilderness resort in Washington, where superb service comes as a pleasant surprise. I enjoy my work, and that's the biggest secret of surviving as a waiter. I won't kowtow or act subservient toward a customer, but neither will I act like a snob or a know-it-all; I won't match wits over a customer's wine choice. My goal is to make people feel comfortable so that their meal is a pleasant experience.

When I seat people, I'm aware that some tables are good and others aren't. So I expound on the virtues of that table. I never say, "Is this all right for you?" because naturally a lot of people reply, "Well, no, it's right next to the kitchen door." I say, "Here's your table, our best one for people-watching" or whatever good I can say about it.

The real secret of being a five-star waiter is alertness, awareness. When a group sits at one of my tables, the first thing I do is assess their attitude. In the pine woods of Washington most people feel happy, which makes my job easier; but in a city restaurant a customer may have had a rotten day and need careful handling. I try to get attuned to each table.

When customers are ready to order, they often ask me what's the best thing on the menu. It goes without saying that I have to be familiar with my menu so I can answer their questions intelligently. Is the Chinese chicken salad made with MSG? Are there onions in the quiche? But their questions only hint at what they *really* want to know; for example, when a woman asks whether the sauce on the filet of sole has shrimp in it, she might be allergic to *all* shellfish. That's something a good waiter should be aware of.

How far should you go in your menu recommendations? I can usually judge whether people may want to try a new dish by finding out where they're from. People from California experiment; they'll eat *anything*. People from Kansas or the Midwest usually like traditional food; they want their meat well done and their vegetables mushy. A lot depends on how you present things. Maybe one out of a hundred people eats sweetbreads, so when I worked on the Hawaiian cruise ship I wouldn't describe exactly what sweetbreads were; I'd explain that it was a beef item, prepared *paniolo* (Hawaiian cowboy) style in a delectable sauce—and almost everyone tried it. I didn't say, "It's a cow's neck gland," because nobody would have touched it. (Once people tried sweetbreads, they often really liked them.)

As I pick up my plates in the kitchen, I double-check to make sure the potato isn't missing, the garnish is there, and that things are done the way each person asked. If I get to the table and have forgotten something, it's great to have the kitchen or galley to blame it on, saying, "They're preparing it; I'll be right back with it." That way I don't look stupid.

It's simple to remember which person gets which salad, soup, entrée, and dessert—you write orders on the ticket in sequence from left to right. Let's say you have a party of eight and want to serve the four women first. When you organize your dinners on the tray in the kitchen, you look at your ticket and arrange the

> **At a dinner party one should eat wisely but not too well, and talk well, but not too wisely.**
> —*Somerset Maugham*

women's entrées on the front of the tray. That way you're not shuffling through all the plates—which in a good restaurant have domed covers over them—and saying to yourself, "Well, this one had veal, and this other one had steak." Everything is laid out in order.

RESTAURANT SLANG

Ned Foley and Jim Riley

All day—A single order, as in "all-day order for the cod"

Blanches—Food servers who don't know what they're doing

Blast—To heat up, as in "blast that sirloin"

Burn one—Cook an order right away, either because it's late, the customer is in a hurry, or the waiter forgot it

Campers—Customers who occupy the table too long; also "sitters"

Crumbs—Children (they leave crumbs on the floor under their chairs)

Deep-six—To throw out, as in "deep-six those french fries"

Dress it—Wrap it up

Deuce—Two diners at a table; "we're loaded with deuces" indicates a poor situation, because the restaurant serves fewer meals than it would to full tables

Duke—Tough customer who thinks he knows everything; also, "John Wayne"

Eighty-six—To throw someone out of the restaurant

Gummer—An older person who takes forever getting through a meal

In the weeds—The cook/waiter is buried, swamped; also, "under"

Julia Child—A customer who analyzes the meal at length

Leona—Difficult customer, as in Leona Helmsley

Lungs—Smokers

No commercials—No excuses why something wasn't done right

Send back—An order that was screwed up and has to be returned to the kitchen

Setup—Complete set of tableware and a napkin; "I need another setup on 4" means that one customer is being added to Table 4

To travel—To go; also, "with legs"

Yesterday—Right away; "I need that order yesterday"

Ned Foley started out in the restaurant business twenty years ago as a waiter and bartender; now he owns two Northern California "stores" called Steamer Gold Landing and Fairfield Landing. Jim Riley is the chief operating officer at the Hilltop Steak House in Saugus, Massachusetts, the busiest restaurant in the United States. On an average day, Hilltop prepares for its 4,000 customers more than 3 tons of raw beef and 1,000 pounds of seafood (some of which goes home in 3,200 doggie bags) and the kitchen washes about 34,000 soiled dishes.

When I train new waiters, their first question is what to do if they drop a plate of food. Answer: Ignore it; then have the busboy quietly clean it up. If you make a big production out of it, that only makes things worse. The biggest disaster I ever saw was a waiter carrying two trays, each stacked with a dozen entrées; he lost them, not once but twice, in front of the same people. The third time around he made it—and the dining room gave him a standing ovation.

The secret of not dropping things is to organize your tray properly. Put the stemware in the center, then add the plates so that their edges lie over the bases of the glasses; that way the glasses can't tip over and spill. Set a teapot on your tray with the spout facing inward; if the tray tips, the hot water will spill on the tray, not down you or on someone else. I'd feel terrible if I hurt someone with hot water.

Spillage happens because you're in too much of a hurry or are carrying too much. Even though I can load ten entrées on one arm, I'd rather make two trips from the kitchen than be overloaded and off balance. Also, I'm always using my peripheral vision and noticing the body language of customers. If it looks as if people are getting ready to stand up, I make a detour with my tray.

When you do spill something on someone, you quickly identify whether it's hot or cold and is going to stain. You offer to wipe it up or to bring them a cloth so they can do it themselves; some people don't like to be touched, so you don't force yourself on them, no matter what the accident is. Then you offer to buy them a cocktail or wine or to have their clothes cleaned or even replaced, depending on the circumstances. (The restaurant pays for this; I wouldn't work in a place where the waiter had to pay for such accidents.) If I can't smooth a customer's feathers, then I bring the restaurant owner to the table so the patron realizes that the restaurant is really concerned. After all, if I drop an éclair in your lap, then just pick it up and continue on my way, that would be terribly rude.

Once a table starts eating, you adjust yourself to the diners' eating speed. Some people eat as though they have two forks; they just shovel it in. Others eat very, very slowly. You have to be aware in order to keep all your tables moving along without either neglecting or pushing anyone.

Diners should never have to crane their necks searching for their waiter. Customers say to me, "Oh, you must have ESP." But I can anticipate their needs because I stand back there and watch them. I notice whether a person is a fast coffee drinker or a slow one, so I appear with the coffeepot at the right time. And when I walk through the dining room, I don't have tunnel vision. As I go by a table, I notice whether they're finishing their salad and are ready for the next course.

As a waiter you have to like walking—yet you want to economize your steps. Some customers will run you ragged making seventy-five trips to get them things; to prevent that, you must establish who's in control of the table. You can say meaningfully, "I'll be with you in a moment."

A good waiter doesn't run for just one item, either; he makes it a trip. When I check one table, I put their request in my mind, then check the next table. I might end up going to six different tables, getting six different items, and bringing them back to six different people—but I've only made one trip to the kitchen. Some waiters would make six trips.

> **A gourmet who thinks of calories is like a tart who looks at her watch.**
> —*James Beard*

At every stage of a meal, you try to make people feel comfortable. That means being sensitive to how people want things. Cabernet Sauvignon, for instance, is supposed to be served at room temperature, but sometimes people ask me for ice cubes to put in it. Among wine buffs that's considered gauche, but you don't want a customer to feel that way.

Some waiters are condescending, of course, and make diners feel stupid. I never do that. On the cruise ship I once set a finger bowl on the table in front of a man—and he drank it. So I asked him how he liked it. He said it was a little thin. I replied, "Well, that was to clean your palate; I'll bring you another one to clean your fingers, and then we'll continue with your meal." Never let someone feel he's done something wrong.

Another mark of a professional waiter is that he doesn't intrude. You can sense whether a customer doesn't want to be bothered or is inquisitive about the menu and wants to chat. Also, during the course of the meal you can learn whether people want coffee so you don't have to come up later and say, "Excuse me . . ."

I also remember the preferences of customers I've served before, so the next time I see them I can say, "Oh, Mrs. So-and-so, that dish has onions in it, so you won't care for it." It's a sensible approach: If I remember that you drink decaf coffee, that saves me time and also lets you know I'm aware of you as a *person* instead of just a tip. I'm lucky, because over the years I've learned to remember people and their orders automatically. Even if I serve eighty dinners in an evening, I can recall that a certain person at Table 6 had a Caesar salad and a medium-rare steak.

No matter how well you serve them, some customers are rude and abusive. One of my worst customers was a drunk in San Francisco. He ordered, then two seconds later demanded, "Hey, where are my eggs?!" I said, "Well, they're still in the shell. I haven't been back to the kitchen yet." He threw some jelly at me. When a person mistreats me, I absolutely ignore them; if they're way out of line, I kick them out of the restaurant.

At the end of the meal there's the matter of tipping. I don't look at people as tips, because that takes all the enjoyment out of it. But not all waiters are that way. Many look at their customers carefully to see if they're well dressed and well groomed, if they look like high rollers. (And some customers encourage this, pulling

---

One-Liners When You Send Something Back to the Kitchen

"Excuse me, waiter. I think this has already been eaten."
—*Chevy Chase*

My grandfather loved rare roast beef, but hated it to be over-cooked. He would innocently say:
"Tell me, waiter, is the chef on vacation?"
"No sir, he's right back there in the kitchen."
"Well, he *needs* a vacation. Apparently he doesn't know the difference between a piece of rare roast beef and a Mark Cross wallet. All this thing's missing are the stitches."
—*Jonathan Winters*

out a wad of money and flashing it around—usually one $100 bill wrapped around a bunch of singles.) Some waiters give much better service to those customers who look like potentially big tippers. But I don't believe in that. Senior citizens on a budget deserve to be treated just as attentively as somebody else who may leave a 25 percent tip.

There's no difference in how men and women tip. But people in the restaurant trade know that certain occupations are notoriously cheap—lawyers, doctors. And certain areas of the United States are cheap, like the South. People from New York tip no matter how bad the service is; but they're also the most aggressive about what they want and don't want. People who glad-hand you, who loudly compliment the food and service, usually tip zippo or a dollar. They feel as though they can spend their words, as if that makes the glow carry over into your pocket. Waiters and waitresses overtip, but are very picky about food and service.

I'd rather be aware of people than tips. By giving good service, by being sensitive to people's desires, you can make someone's dining experience enjoyable. And that's what makes me look forward to going to work.

SELL YOUR USED CAR WITHOUT ACTING LIKE A USED CAR SALESMAN

Richard DeVos

Richard DeVos is the cofounder of the Amway Corporation, which operates in forty countries with a network of more than a million independent distributors. Figuring an eight-hour work day, Amway takes in $1 million an hour.

I think most consumers have had it up to here with the "used car salesman" approach to selling—the gimmicks, the pressures, the tricks. That's not how I do business, and I've built a $2-billion-a-year company on selling. Yes, of course I want to sell products, but I want to be a decent person at the same time.

Few of us will work as professional salespeople. But most of us will need to sell something sooner or later. Very likely, it will be an automobile. So here are my principles, applied to this common situation.

To make a sale, first make a friend.

In my business, which is Amway, we build on the idea that you've already got friends; now sell to them. But what if you want to sell your used car to a stranger who answers your classified ad in the newspaper? The first step is to make a friend of him so that he's willing to listen to your presentation.

He has to trust what you say, which means he's got to trust *you*. Part of being a friend is to be open and willing to tell the buyer about yourself—who you are, your experiences, that you've lived in town for twenty years, and so forth.

As you converse—just two people trying to get acquainted—you kind of talk about the car. You mention its features; he talks about what he likes and doesn't like in a car. He mentions what went wrong with the last car he had; you assure him that with this particular model, you've never experienced anything like that. It's an easy, running conversation; it's not you hard-selling the car's good points and he looking for flaws or objecting at the end.

Establishing a warm relationship also helps you steer clear of the usual suspicions, like "Did you disconnect the speedometer, buddy?" You avoid that whole area of mistrust.

Create a positive atmosphere.

Imagine a used car sitting in front of a dilapidated house where the paint is peeling and the grass isn't cut. Consciously or unconsciously, the buyer is going to suspect that the car has been cared for in the same shabby way as the house. But a shiny car parked in the driveway of a home that looks like Donna Reed's will seem pretty wonderful. So be sure to create an atmosphere that puts your buyer in a positive frame of mind.

"Closing" a sale needn't be a hard sell.

The "pitch" is just a little incidental thing at the end of the conversation that says, "Hey, I've got something here that will really fit your needs." Let's say that a potential buyer has inspected your car carefully and

A TIP ON SELLING

Help the buyer arrive at *his* goal, not yours. Too many salesmen have something to push. At an appliance store where they've got too many toasters of a certain brand, they try to get those off the shelf, regardless of what the customer really wants.

A better approach is to help a buyer fulfill *his* desires instead of yours.

So most of your selling should consist of questions. Why? Because you want to pull information out of the prospect to determine his desires. As an example, I've bought several boats from one salesman. He spends most of his presentation finding out what my wishes are: How am I going to use the boat; where will I be going; how big is my family; in what style do we like to entertain; are we going to sail in rough water or smooth; do we plan to take long or short cruises; do I like a bathtub or can I get by with a shower? He spends his time gathering information. The final delivery of the boat is just a matter of fulfilling my wishes: "Now that we know what you want, here it is!"

you've talked at some length. He says, "Well, how much do you want for it?" Now you *know* he's thinking about buying, because he cares about the price. You just come back and say, "Well, this car is $5,000. I hope that fits your price range."

Now you try to lead him to a point where he can make a decision. Maybe you suggest, "There's only one way to find out if you want to go ahead. Why don't we get in the car, drive around the block, and see what you think?" Life is built on making decisions, so at the end you just ask him to make up his mind. It's not a trick; it's simply concluding the dialogue.

Enjoy the "horse trading."

If the buyer likes your car, he'll see how cheaply he can get it. I don't blame him. It's part of the game of trading, so don't be threatened by it. "Can you do any better on the price?" he says. You may respond, "Oh, I probably could do better—if you want me to make nothing on the sale. I paid a certain amount for the automobile. You've seen the maintenance records, so you know I've put a lot into it. My price is a fair one, and I'm sure you won't begrudge my getting a fair price for the car."

Most people ask a seller to lower the price just because they think they *ought* to. Don't treat it seriously; just move on from there. If he wants the car and you stay firm, he'll buy it at whatever you're asking.

Of course, there may be situations where you have to negotiate. If you're asking $9,500 for your car and someone offers you $8,500, you have to decide whether you really priced it so high that you *can* take $8,500. He may figure that you set a high enough price to leave some wiggle room. If that's true, go ahead and dicker.

**Q: What's two and two?
A: Buying or selling?**
—*Lord Grade, British TV mogul*

WIN A DEBATE

William F. Buckley, Jr.

William Frank Buckley, Jr., founded the *National Review*, the voice of the American conservative political movement. His television interview program, *Firing Line*, has made a large audience familiar with his witty control of the English language and his skill at debate.

If you want to come out on top in a debate, be sure to offer engaging examples to dramatize your case. When arguing for the idea of a flat income tax rate, for example, I had to come up with examples that would appeal to the audience. I couldn't say, "Look, I don't think Henry Ford ought to be taxed at a heavier rate than the local grocer." But I could say, "Who persuaded us that the taxi driver willing to work seventy hours a week should be taxed more heavily than the guy who's willing to work forty hours a week? Who slipped this by us?"

Incidentally, this argument demonstrates a useful stratagem: To strengthen your point, you can give the impression that "other people" have put one over on "us"—that we are all the victims of a shoddy philosophy.

To hit the other guy hard, you sometimes have to go ad hominem. The argument ad hominem attacks not the other person's case but the other person himself. Of course, you're not ad hominem about "this guy with the big nose" or anything like that. You direct it to "a man who would use this kind of rancid argument, which is beneath a respectable level." Then you show up illogical sequences in his thought.

Before a sympathetic audience, though, don't hit the other

guy too hard. If the audience didn't come in already determined to oppose you, then be careful not to attack the other guy so relentlessly as to earn him sympathy. Sometimes I've done that, even knowing all the while that I *am* doing it, and later I kick myself in the butt. It's an action that would not be forgiven in, say, an attorney—to beat up on an opponent simply for the sake of dramatic or dialectical satisfaction. When you have an audience well disposed toward you, the goal is to win them over completely.

Sometimes, however, you must be satisfied simply to demonstrate the weakness of the other person's case, but not to win the audience. Most of my life I have debated in front of audiences who wouldn't consider walking into my own tent, and therefore I have had to settle for something less than persuading them. My technique in such cases is primarily to say, "This guy over here who's spouting all this nonsense is terribly fallible, and if you are taken in, you ought to go home and wake up with an appropriate hangover." Now, this approach doesn't win you friends, but it leaves the other guy much deflated.

There are a few points of technique to keep in mind. One is to be sure the other person answers your question. Many times an opponent fails to answer, simply making his own point instead. In such a case you can say, "Now, here is what I asked, and here is what his answer was: Can you possibly find a link between the two?" Rub that in as much as you feel the situation warrants. Representative Patricia Schroeder, for instance, has never in her entire life answered the questions I have posed. Moreover, after she has finished speaking, you haven't the remotest idea what she *has* said . . .

> **Never argue with a fool— people might not know the difference.**
> —*from* Murphy's Law, *by Arthur Block*

You should also be aware of the "invisible man" ploy. During a debate, some people use the technique of never referring to you at all. It can be quite effective. They just say their piece, and when the time comes for rebuttal, they just say more of it—as if you weren't present. It's especially devastating if you are—as I once was—

twenty-four years old, debating against people who are sixty-five years old and eminent in their fields. In effect they say, "The guy over there is really not worth listening to."

You can defend yourself against this by making great fun of your opponent, which usually shakes him out of it. Tease him about your relative invisibility, e.g., "Not only am *I* invisible, but so are the arguments I am using—and also those of John Locke, and Montesque, and also Adam Smith." Shame him by suggesting that his failure to acknowledge your existence is also his failure to acknowledge some of the giants of political literature. This technique of invoking a group of notable minds around you acts as a bolster for your own position.

On my television program, *Firing Line*, I found that an exchange is successful, or not, with intense attention to timing. The guest who makes a bewildering point is often best treated by an instant's pained silence before you remark on what he has said or not said.

The opponent who never stops talking invites staccato interruptions—and, sometimes, conspicuous inattention. A young man on *Firing Line* who argued that there were no differences, really, between the United States and Nazi Germany I found impossible to keep from talking, either for the purpose of commenting on what he said or to ask for elucidation. He simply continued to talk. Finally, I picked up my bundle of notes, extracted from them an issue of *Time* magazine, and proceeded to read from it while he went on. Timing.

When possible, conclude with a punch line. If you can structure an argument so that you end with a bang, people are going to remember your point. It's the same as when you're playing music and need a resolution: In a debate you try to do one final coda that has the effect of destroying *his* coda. A memorable exchange of this kind took place in 1968 on *Firing Line* during a discussion with Alabama's Governor George Wallace, a partisan of racial segregation, who in 1963 had sent state troopers to the University of Alabama to block the entry of two Negro (as they were then called) students. I abhorred his action. On reflection, though, my judgment is that Wallace outpointed me by concluding with a punch line:

WALLACE: In fact, we *don't have* segregation in Alabama. . . . I've always made speeches in my state in which I said anybody's entitled to vote regardless of their race or color. And we had Negro citizens by the *thousands* who voted in 1958, when I first ran for governor. And, I might say, in the runoff for governor, they voted for *me*.

WFB: Is that because they didn't have the education you're talking about?

WALLACE: You reflect on the Negro voters of Alabama if *you* want to, but *I* won't.

If two people agree all the time, one of them is unnecessary.
—David Mahoney

HOW TO BE A
COUCH POTATO

Bob Armstrong and Jack Mingo

In 1976 Bob Armstrong and Jack Mingo founded the Couch Potatoes, a group whose name has passed into the American language and popular culture. Their books include *The Official Couch Potato Handbook*. Based in Northern California, cartoonist and illustrator Bob Armstrong draws during commercials. Writer Jack Mingo lives in the San Francisco Bay area; besides two books on the Couch Potatoes, he has written *Prime Time Proverbs: A Book of TV Quotes* and *The Whole Pop Catalog*.

Do you enjoy excessive amounts of TV viewing? If you know all the words to the theme song from *The Patty Duke Show*, if your body conforms to the shape of your overstuffed sofa, you're already well on your way to being a Couch Potato. To guide you onward, we'll answer the most common questions about Couch Potatoism.

Where did the name "Couch Potato" come from?

The name is perfect. Potatoes have many eyes. They're tubers. It came to us in a cosmic revelation.

But aren't Couch Potatoes vegetables?

Why are vegetables considered in a negative way? Vegetables are good for you! Vegetables are firmly rooted, always growing. If people call us vegetables, we take it as a compliment.

What are a Couch Potato's basic needs?

The television set itself ranks number one. Spare no expense, even if you must scrimp on luxuries like food and rent. Remember that a Couch Potato without a television set is just an indolent buffoon staring at the wall. We elders of the Couch Potato movement have lots of sets in our homes. Most of them are old black-and-whites, some with a sepia-tone picture that evokes nineteenth-century TV. These televisions were cast off by our friends—an act incomprehensible to a true Couch Potato.

The Couch Potato's second-best friend is the toaster oven. As a tubeside treat, try this recipe from our own Chef Aldo, the Station Break Gourmet: "Little Chocolate Doughnuts: Pour a single layer of Cheerios on an old pie tin. Carefully place a chocolate chip upside down in the hole of each Cheerio. Pop into toaster oven and melt lightly." Remember, prolonged viewing requires stamina. In a week, the typical Couch Potato eats his or her own weight in snacks. Always eat from all five major food groups: sugar, salt, grease, carbohydrates, and alcohol.

You'll also need a couch chosen strictly for comfort. The center of activity at Couch Potato headquarters is a 1930s sofa upholstered in bologna pink corduroy. Avoid vinyl, which feels weird and can emit embarrassing noises whenever you shift position. You may want a stain-repellent fabric, allowing you to wait until a commercial to clean up spills—or you may prefer a fabric that's absorbent, so that if you spill something you won't have to get up at all.

Other necessities for your viewing module: A copy of *TV Guide*, which not only tells you what's on but doubles as an oven mitt. And some TV trays, which Couch Potatoes have judged "arguably one of the twenty most significant inventions of this century."

How can I maintain the TV set in optimal viewing condition?

Wipe the screen and knobs every few years. Timing is important; no use cleaning your screen before absolutely necessary. One way to tell when that time has arrived is the day you can no longer tell if the TV is on or off.

To dust the top of your TV the easy way—buy a cat.

Please explain some do's and taboos of proper viewing.

Many people ask, "When is it okay to talk during a TV show?" Answer: Almost never. To avoid disturbing others, conversation should be restricted to requests to pass food or drink or to comments of interest to all ("Isn't that Sonny Tufts there behind the fat lady in the back of the crowd?").

Among the Ten Commandments of Couch Potato etiquette is the important "Thou shalt be wary of anything educational or British." Of course, many of our members enjoy reruns of *Benny Hill* and *Fawlty Towers*, but we do not recommend that anybody look at *Masterpiece Theatre*, since watching public television causes the same sort of brain damage as reading. TV isn't something you watch because it's good for you! That's like putting vitamin C in candy bars; it just doesn't make sense.

How can we train younger viewers properly?

The Couch Potatoes have an auxiliary for youngsters, known as the Tater Tots. Small fries are encouraged to view, and we scoff at the notion that watching TV causes violence. It's when you make kids *stop* watching TV that they get violent.

As youngsters, did the Couch Potatoes watch a lot of TV?

We fondly remember the family television as an electronic hearth, with everyone gathered around for magic moments. Some of us preferred historical programming (*Yancy Derringer, Davy Crockett*). Others loved *Lawrence Welk*—the white man's *Soul Train*. Many members never missed *My Mother, the Car* or *Gilligan's Island*. Some enjoyed amateur talent shows

---

TV Facts for the Couch Potato

• If you want to enjoy an extended viewing session, ask your favorite station to broadcast *The Longest Most Meaningless Movie in the World*. This 1970 British film ran . . . and ran . . . for forty-eight hours.

• More Americans have TV sets than indoor plumbing.

• In 1941 the Bulova watch company paid $9 to broadcast the first TV commercial.

• A poll asked children from four to six years old, "Which do you like better, TV or your daddy?" More than half answered, "TV."

like Ted Mack's, with orchestras of elderly ladies playing tunes on eggbeaters. From the seemingly insipid to the profound, the important thing is to watch—view it all.

Are there deeper political or psychological meanings in TV shows?

Sure. Just look at the political ramifications of *I Love Lucy*. Lucy symbolizes the United States, and Ricky, of course, symbolizes Latin America. She never understands him. Although well meaning, everything she does screws up his life in the end. They finally got a divorce in real life. Today in politics you can see the same thing happening.

What about sex and TV—do they mix?

Remember that a marital encounter on the couch could very well cause you to miss something interesting on the tube, something you may regret missing for the rest of your life. As our bumper sticker says, "Couch Potatoes Don't Do It—They'd Rather Watch."

But if you seek company in your viewing module, here are some surefire pickup lines for meeting potential Couch Tomatoes (the ladies' auxiliary):

"I love your perfume. Isn't that Channel No. 5?"

"Want to come up to my apartment and see my 26-inch Zenith?"

But what about the spiritual side of TV viewing?

We Couch Potatoes see ourselves as televisionaries. An adept viewer can stay in position on the couch for days at a time, adopting a position that may look like a slouch, but is a spiritual pose comparable to a yogi's lotus position. The couch is a great place to relax your body and allow your orbs to absorb the mystic blue light.

We strive to reach a state of "at-one-ment" with the tube. Some of us achieve inner peace through Transcendental Vegetation. Some read the Couch Potato scriptural reference, the "Book of Changes"—*TV Guide*. Others take a Zen approach: They don't watch because they *like* what they're watching; they like it because it's there; they watch because they watch. To unlock television's deepest mysteries for novices, Couch Potato elders may pose paradoxical riddles, called Zen Koans, with distinct video overtones. They'll ask, "What do you want, good grammar or good taste?" or "Wouldn't you really rather have a Buick?" Wrestling with these problems helps young Zen viewers achieve Enlightenment.

Although it would appear that Couch Potatoes just sit around and watch TV, there's more to television than meets the eye. May we all find our own inspiration through prolonged viewing.

> **Television is more interesting than people. If it were not, we would have people standing in the corners of our rooms.**
> —*Alan Corenk*

MASTER OF THE UNIVERSE

HOW TO COOK THE PERFECT EGG

Julia Child

Julia Child brought French cooking into American kitchens through her pioneering cookbooks and programs on public television.

Boiling

You want to boil an egg so that the yolk is set through and is a clean, beautiful yellow, with no ugly dark ring where it joins the white. The white should be tender, not the consistency of rubber. Here's how.

Prick the shell. At the large end eggs have an air bubble, which expands as the egg heats and will crack the shell unless you provide an escape valve—by pricking a little hole in that end. Use something like a drafting push-pin, going down ¼ inch through the shell and into the egg itself.

The simmer method. Because the mass cooking of hard-boiled eggs can be tricky, I rarely exceed a dozen to a batch. Lower the eggs into boiling water, bring the water back to a simmer, and set the timer—12 minutes for "large" chilled eggs and 13 for "extra large." Keep the water at a slow simmer, which means very small bubbles and slight movement.

Remember you're all alone in the kitchen, and no one can see you.
—*Julia Child*

The coddle method. To ensure a set-through yolk for "jumbo" eggs of 2½ ounces plus, I think coddling is more reliable. Place the chilled eggs in a pan of cold water. Use 6 cups of water for one to four eggs and an additional cup of water for each additional egg. Bring the water to a boil, set the pan aside, and cover it. Time it exactly 17 minutes, or 18 minutes for "jumbos" of 2½ ounces plus.

Prevent that dark ring around the yolk. Overcooking eggs or letting them stay warm after proper cooking creates a chemical reaction between the yolk and white, causing discoloration. To avoid this, chill the eggs—the faster the better. Have a tray of ice cubes at the ready. As soon as the eggs are done, drain the water, turn the ice into the pan, and run enough cold water over the eggs and ice to cover them all.

Peel eggs the easy way. Tap an egg gently all over to break the shell. Start peeling from the large end under a thin stream of cold water. If it won't peel cleanly, bring a pan of water to the boil, take the eggs three at a time from the ice water, and drop them into the boiling water for exactly 10 seconds; then return them to the ice water. This often helps, the theory being that the boiling water expands the shell while the ice water shrinks the body of the egg from it.

Store the eggs properly. Always refrigerate the eggs submerged in cold water in an uncovered container. They will keep for several days without altering either flavor or texture.

Poaching

Use very fresh eggs. As an egg ages, the white begins to turn watery. But when an egg is very fresh—ideal conditions few of us are so fortunate as to encounter—the white clings around the yolk, so the egg can literally be dropped from the shell into simmering water.

Or use the "10-second boil." Store-bought eggs can be helped by pricking a hole in the large end of the shell before lowering it for exactly 10 seconds into a pan of boiling water. This sets a film of white around the egg body. Then break the egg into simmering water and leave it for exactly 4 minutes.

Or use a perforated metal egg poacher. An even better solution for store-bought eggs is the perforated metal, egg-shaped cup you see in gourmet shops and catalogues. Arrange a set of cups in a wide pan containing enough simmering water to cover by 1 inch. After the 10-second boil, break an egg into each cup and simmer for exactly 4 minutes. Carefully scoop out each egg with a soup spoon. If it is to be served immediately, dry it off by rolling it back and forth in a clean, folded towel.

Storing and reheating poached eggs. Submerge the eggs in an uncovered bowl of cold water and refrigerate. They will keep perfectly for two to three days. When you want to reheat them, lower them into a pan of lightly salted, simmering water for exactly 1 minute.

Scrambling

Break four to six eggs into a bowl. Add a tablespoon of cold water, along with a few grinds of white pepper and a good pinch of salt, and whip them with a fork just long enough to blend the whites and yolks.

> **Life is too short to stuff a mushroom.**
> —*Shirley Conran*

Use low heat. Low heat is the secret to beautifully cooked scrambled eggs. Take your time so that the eggs coagulate slowly into a tender, broken custard. If you've not tried them cooked this way, it may well be a revelation.

Set a 10-inch, no-stick pan over moderately low heat and add a tablespoon of butter. When it has melted, pour in all but 2 tablespoons of the egg. Nothing happens for a minute or two as you slowly scrape all over the bottom of the pan with a spatula. Gradually, the eggs begin to thicken as you keep scraping a little more rapidly and moving the pan off and back onto the heat to slow down the cooking. When the eggs are the consistency you wish, remove them from the heat and fold in the reserved egg, which will stop the cooking and cream the curds.

Add finishing touches. If you wish, fold in a spoonful or two of softened butter or heavy cream plus minced fresh herbs (parsley or chives). Serve at once on warm (not hot) plates. *Warning:* Don't stir anything like a sauce into the eggs before cooking, or you'll make a messy scramble. Instead, spoon it around or over the finished eggs.

Frying

Preheat the broiler. In a frying pan of reasonable size pour 1/16 inch of butter, olive oil, or bacon fat. (If you've fried the bacon, use the same pan, but first decant the bacon fat into a small glass bowl and wipe the pan clean before spooning in the clear fat.) Set the pan over moderately high heat on the stove, and when hot, break in as many as six or eight eggs. Cook a minute or more, until the white has set nicely on the bottom. Baste the eggs with the fat in the pan, then set the pan closely under the hot broiler, moving it in and out under the heat and basting several times. The eggs will film over on top and will be perfectly cooked both top and bottom.

Bon appétit!

How to Shoot the Sky Hook

Kareem Abdul-Jabbar

Called "history's greatest basketball player," Kareem Abdul-Jabbar is the NBA's all-time regular season scoring leader, with 37,639 points; he has been featured on the cover of *Sports Illustrated* twenty-five times.

I worked on this shot a lot, but I was lucky: As early as seventh and eighth grades a coach worked with me on big man's moves, because I was so much taller than everybody else. I worked out the coordination and muscle memory, so that by the early part of my career I had a tremendous advantage.

My best student in the sky hook has been Magic. It's a perfect shot for him to use on little guards. They can't do anything; he's too big for them.

How to shoot it

To sink a regular shot, you line your eyes up with the goal and put the ball up along the same vertical line. But to shoot a hook shot, you have to turn your shoulder toward the basket; your head turns sideways, and you hold the ball away from the basket. The triangulation is askew—the relationship between your body, the ball, and the basket. Some people can't deal with that; they feel uncomfortable with it. If you keep practicing, though, it will seem more natural.

It helps to remember that the sky hook is actually a regular hook shot, except that the ball isn't kept out at arm's length. You actually hold it in pretty close, just off your shoulder, with your elbow bent. Now you want to get elevation. The hand holding the ball goes up at an angle slightly *away* from the hoop, while your body leans *toward* the basket. Your arm goes up, and at the top you release the ball with an arch. Naturally, you're aiming to get the ball up and over the front of the rim.

Defending against the sky hook

If the person shooting the sky hook is adept at it, it's impossible for a single defender to block the shot.

Nobody roots for Goliath.
—*Wilt Chamberlain*

FIND WATER BY DOWSING

Gordon Barton

Dowsing is not something you do; it's something that happens. Nobody really knows how it works.

After all, our objective mind can't tell where water lies under the ground and doesn't know how to locate it. Dowsing goes beyond that, in my opinion, to a higher level of awareness. I think everyone has the ability.

The proper state of mind

I've taught a lot of people to dowse, and the very few who couldn't do it had a belief system that just wouldn't accept the possibility; their preconceptions or fears stopped them cold. So try dowsing with an open mind. It's also important to be relaxed, to just have your mind blank. Most people can't make their minds a blank, so a good approach is to keep your mind focused on the target—water. Concentration is required: If you're walking around a piece of land with dowsing rods and you trip, for instance, your mind immediately jumps to thoughts of your stumble. You lose concentration, so you have to go back to the quest again.

I feel that one should dowse with a humble attitude toward the universe; I might even say a spiritual attitude. You're making a link with the earth and with something far beyond our understanding. It's sort of like prayer: Usually it will respond, although sometimes it won't (and when it doesn't, you're not supposed to get what you asked for, anyway).

The dowsing rods

Although most people picture a dowser holding a forked stick, an easier device to use is L-rods, or angle rods. These are two lengths of round metal stock, each bent at a 90-degree angle near one end to form a grip. Typical dimensions might be 12 to 18 inches long with a 6-inch grip, but L-rods can be as short as an inch or as long as you want. I slip plastic sleeves over the grips so that the rods can rotate freely in my hands.

You hold the rods in what we call the search position: Your hands form loose fists around the grips; the rods are 8 to 10 inches apart, held level and pointing forward; the tips are slightly down so that the rods don't fly around.

First, you have to learn to recognize your "yes" signal from the rods. The "yes" response is a physical movement of the rods—they may swing outward, or the tips may move inward and cross. You determine which it will be in your case by asking the rods to give you a "yes." (You can say this aloud or, as I do, just keep it in your mind.) For me, the rods cross; for many people, they swing out. If nothing happens, don't worry. You can also find out what a "yes" signal is by going out onto a piece of land where you know there is some underground water; this can be a buried pipe leading to a hose faucet or lawn sprinkler. Holding the rods in search position, walk slowly toward the location of the pipe. When you pass over it, the rods will either cross or spread out; that will be your "yes" signal.

Finding water

When I go to a piece of property to seek underground water, I first pose a series of questions for the rods to answer about that

The American Society of Dowsers

• For information about dowsing, about the American Society of Dowsers' national membership and local chapters, or about the society's dowsing school, write to:

• The American Society of Dowsers
P.O. Box 24
Danville, Vermont 05828

dowsing session: "May I? Can I? Should I? Am I ready? Is it in the most compassionate interests of the Cosmic?" (I add the last question because I want to make sure that my dowsing is right on every level, beyond what I could even conceive of.) If the answers are yes, I proceed.

I ask, "Is there good, potable water on this site for this person at this time, year round and twenty-four hours per day?" That's a formula I've put together, partly from other dowsers. Each part is important; if you don't mention twenty-four hours a day, for example, sometimes you find water that doesn't flow around the clock.

Now you walk forward, with the rods in search position. When you cross over a vein of water, the rods will move to indicate "yes." As you walk past the vein, the rods return to their original position. By backing up and walking forward, you can pinpoint exactly where the vein lies.

Getting details

The water you locate may not be a very wide vein or even a vein at all, but just a column of underground water. You have to ask questions to find out. The form of these questions is very important, because you receive answers only to what you ask. It's like programming a computer: "Garbage in, garbage out."

You must pose the questions separately, and they have to be framed as yes or no questions, so you get yes or no answers. I stand at the place where I've located water and say, "Please indicate to me now the depth of the water. Is it over 100 feet?" If the answer is yes, I'll go deeper. (If no, I try lower numbers.) Next I ask, "Is it over 150 feet?" If the answer is no, the water lies somewhere between 100 and 150 feet down. I keep asking questions, bracketing the numbers until I get the actual depth.

Find Your Lost Car Keys by Dowsing

• You can ask the L-rods to help you locate any item you've misplaced—perhaps your car keys. Hold the rods in search position, walk slowly around the room where you think you may have mislaid your keys, and wait for the rods to move to your "yes" position. This tells you that the keys are right near you. (However, you should be aware that when you lose things, there is often an intention involved. Subconsciously, you really don't want to go to the opera, let's say, so you put your keys away somewhere. This can cloud your search.)

• Over the years I've found lost jewelry and many other items for people by dowsing.

The same system works for volume of flow. I ask, "All right, is it over 10 gallons a minute?" If it says yes, I go higher; if no, I go lower. Either way, I keep asking questions until I determine the rate of flow.

I recommend that people write down the questions and responses. If the search isn't successful, they can go back over their list and see where they may have asked the wrong questions or not enough of them. This way of narrowing things down is much like a game of "Twenty Questions."

In dowsing, I feel that the questions—and the search itself—should be undertaken in humility. We are being granted the ability to dowse, and it's something very worthwhile.

MAKE AN EFFECTIVE SPEECH

Art Buchwald

> For the past twenty-five years, humorist Art Buchwald has been one of America's most popular and highly paid speakers.

At some time or other, everybody's going to be called upon to make a speech. So we may as well learn to do it well. At a dinner gathering, I'm usually the dessert. My listeners really don't care what I say; they just want me to make them laugh—and that's fine with me. Here are my rules for making a good speech.

Outline your speech first.

If you're organized, you won't go floundering. Get your facts together, then arrange your speech as a story. Once I helped someone who was to speak at Alcoholics Anonymous. For AA you first admit that you were an alcoholic, then you tell stories about how it was, and finally you talk about how much better it is now. There's a beginning, a middle, and an end. In this case, it was a happy ending—which is the best kind.

Don't speak from a manuscript. Use 3-by-5 cards.

When you use 3-by-5 cards, you're giving a talk. When you use a manuscript, you're giving a speech. People like talks, but they don't like speeches.

Know your audience.

For any group—supermarket executives or lawyers or whatever—I do about ten or fifteen minutes referring to what they do

> **Hell is a half-filled auditorium.**
> *—Robert Frost*

and what they're interested in. Then I've got them on my side—and I can do no wrong when it comes to the rest of the speech.

Always check the microphone ahead of time.

Do not trust anyone else.

Work the room before you speak, if possible.

Gag writer Bob Orben told me, "Everybody whose hand you shake at the cocktail hour is your friend when you give the speech."

Don't worry about stage fright.

> The human brain starts working the moment you are born and never stops until you stand up to speak in public.
> —*Sir George Jessel, English politician*

It's normal to have stage fright. Even very successful people live in deathly fear of making a speech. I've worked with guys on speeches to the Gridiron Club—guys who want to be president of the United States—and they're more afraid of talking at the Gridiron than they are to the Russians. What you want to do is relax yourself. I tell speakers to pretend that everybody out there in the audience has no clothes on. That thought in your mind is funny, and it loosens you up a little bit.

There's no rule against being funny.

But you have to be aware of what's going on in the audience's mind. If you're me or Mark Russell or someone like that, everybody already thinks we're funny, so we don't have to persuade them. But if you're an unknown or the president of General Motors, nobody thinks you're funny. It's going to take you five minutes to win them over. So get your laughs right at the beginning.

If you are given a long introduction—and there are people who give long introductions, and who also think they're supposed to be funny, and it goes on endlessly—what you do is get up and say, "And in conclusion . . ." That always gets a very big laugh.

But don't try to be Bob Hope. It doesn't work for most people. The best way to be funny is not with gags but with something

anecdotal. A funny story that's true is the best kind of humor—
and we all have anecdotes. If you're willing to work on being
funny, it's kind of heady, because everybody loves to make people laugh. It's even better than the dough they pay you.

Don't start listing things one by one.

Never say: "Now I have five proposals. Number one . . ." And
the people in the audience say to themselves, "Oh, Christ!" You
go on, "Number two . . ." And by the time you're at the fifth one,
everybody's snoozing.

Talk to the whole room.

You're trying to win over anywhere from a hundred to a thousand people. You have their attention at the beginning, and your
job is to keep it. That means swinging your head around like a
swivel. If it's a big room, talk to the left, talk to the right, and talk
to the center; then talk to the left again. Don't address your
remarks to just one side.

Take your time.

The reason that people rush when they're giving a speech is
simple: They want to get it over with. If you take your time, you'll
have everybody's attention—and you'll end up enjoying yourself.

Believe in what you're saying.

You can always tell when a speaker doesn't feel it. You know—
he's talking about what a great country America is and everything, but he's just putting in time. The best speakers know
what they're talking about, and they really mean what they say.

Don't go on too long.

No audience ever got angry at a speaker for talking short.
Some groups, like conventions and conferences, might give you
an allotted time; if so, stick to it. For a lunch or dinner where
people have had a four- or five-course meal, I don't speak longer
than twenty-five minutes. If I'm in an auditorium, I will go forty

to forty-five minutes and then open it to questions for another fifteen minutes, so my entire program is an hour. People are sometimes nice enough to say they wish I'd gone on longer, but I've never been criticized for cutting it off, because I didn't bore them and everybody walked away happy.

You don't have to leave them laughing.

A person who isn't noted for being funny doesn't have to try to close with humor. The best thing would be to get your laugh at the beginning, then end on a good note—which is a serious note, possibly, and something that will stay with them. If you can, you want to work your way up to a standing ovation. That's the highest accolade you can earn.

Don't forget, you're being judged when you get on your feet. But once you make a few speeches, you'll really get to like it. Since you're the one who's talking, you're the leader. And if you can hold people's attention and make them laugh, it's a hell of an experience.

If you cannot say what you have to say in twenty minutes, you should go away and write a book about it.
—Lord Brabazon

BARGAIN FOR THE BEST PRICE IN THE BAZAAR

Tony Wheeler

The publisher of
Lonely Planet
Publications' highly
regarded guidebooks
to travel in exotic
places, Tony Wheeler
has bargained his way
from Afghanistan to
Zimbabwe. An
Australian, he started
his publishing compa-
ny eighteen years,
many hundreds of
thousands of miles,
and a hundred guide-
books ago.

Bargaining is most necessary and most fun in the colorful back blocks of Asia. (But bargaining isn't restricted to exotic bazaars. Ever hear of anybody buying a new car without negotiating the price?)

Where to bargain

It isn't always easy to tell where you should bargain and where you shouldn't. Just because a big fancy shop has price tags on every item and a sign saying "fixed price" doesn't mean the price won't become instantly negotiable if you appear hesitant about buying. Even hotel rooms are fair game. During most of the 1980s, Singapore had a real glut of hotels, and if you walked into any hotel—it didn't matter whether it was a back-street fleapit or a Hilton—and asked "How much is a room?" you'd find that a further polite inquiry about any "special price" available would likely cut the room rate in half.

In some places, of course, the price is the price; no negotiating takes place. Pacific islanders, for instance, usually don't bargain. I've seen places in Papua New Guinea, where, in order to accommodate visitors who were used to dickering, the handicrafts were neatly labeled with "First Price" and "Second Price." That way the vendor could arrive instantly at the knocked-down price without having to engage in any distasteful negotiations along the way! Local knowledge is the only way to tell where you should or should not bargain.

How to bargain

Remember that there's no point in knocking the price down by 50 percent if the price was 100 percent too high in the first place. So before you start bargaining, find out what the price really should be. The last time I was in Hong Kong I needed a new suitcase. Some back-street luggage shops had the suitcase I wanted for $120 to $150. (One even had a sign offering a "special price," reduced from $180 to $140.) I went into a regular department store and found the same suitcase at a fixed price of $100. Then I returned to the back-street shop that had it for $120, told them the department store was selling the suitcase for $100, and knocked the price down to $75.

Once you've found something you want, the number one rule of successful bargaining is to appear uninterested. Act as if you find the object of *possible* interest, but you don't really care whether you get it or not. As long as it looks as if you may lose interest and wander off, you've got the upper hand.

The corollary: Once the seller knows that you positively *have* to have the item, you've lost.

Don't let the vendor force you to make the first move. Why? Once you've started bargaining, you're committed to your offer. Get his (or her) price first. Ideally, you want to get his second price as well. You do that by asking, "Can't you do any better than that?" or "Is that your best price?"

MY FAVORITE BARGAIN

The best bit of bargaining I've seen recently was one I played no part in. I was in the south of Egypt at Tutankhamen's Tomb in the Valley of the Kings. Rather than take a taxi to the Valley of the Nobles, my wife, Maureen, and I decided to climb over the hills that divide the two valleys. "No way!" said our children. "We're on strike until you provide transportation with wheels."

"Then sit by the path and die," we announced, marching off up the hill. Halfway up the slope we sat down to wait for them to give in. Not thirty seconds later they appeared—riding donkeys!

"I asked how much to ride one of the man's donkeys to the top of the hill," announced my son, age six. "He said ten Egyptian pounds [$5]. But don't worry," he went on. "I knocked him down to one pound. See you at the top of the hill!"

Once you've got the seller moving in the right direction (i.e., down), then you can start moving in the other direction (up). Do that by making a real offer, but a low one. (If you offer *too* little, though, you won't appear to be a real buyer, so your offer must look as though it may lead somewhere.) There are all sorts of rules of thumb for making a first offer, like one third of the initial asking price for handicrafts in Indonesia, or two thirds for electronic gear in Singapore. But they're just that—rules of thumb.

If it's an old-fashioned, colonial-era bargaining session, there are plenty of standard lines of negotiating chatter for each side to roll out. The seller can legitimately say things like: "Your offer is less than the wholesale price I paid! There's no profit left for me. Think of my poor children." You can respond: "I'll have no money to pay my departure tax. I'll be broke when I get home. I guess I'll have to buy it next trip." An especially effective line is, "Omar's place around the corner has it cheaper."

Moving gradually, you dicker back and forth until a mutually acceptable midpoint is reached. Remember that you're never going to match the price the locals pay. In Indonesia, for instance, they say there are three prices—the local price, the price for other Indonesians, and the price for you. Aim to get that third price, and you're doing fine.

How do you know when to stop bargaining? There are three logical times. One, of course, is when you've bought the item. Another is when you just can't reach an agreement—you don't want to buy the thing badly enough to meet his price, and he doesn't want to sell it badly enough to meet yours. But the most important time to stop is when it's no longer fun. Buying something in a bazaar in Asia is not like bargaining for your life. Getting the lowest possible price is not a question of personal honor. Bargaining should be a mutually enjoyable sparring match, a pleasant interaction with the locals. When you start getting utterly fixated on saving the last 20 cents, you've taken bargaining too far, and it's time to quit.

Here are a couple of general tips to remember: Don't make frivolous offers. Lots of people have tried to get rid of a persistent street vendor by offering a ridiculously low price, only to find out they've just bought some item like an alarm clock in the shape of the Buddha. Also, don't bargain just for the sake of bargaining. Travelers buy lots of things they don't need simply because bargaining can be such fun, and before they know it, their bags are full of terrible souvenirs and handicraft "bargains" that they really have no interest in. Finally, if you're buying items to resell at home, remember that nothing is a sure thing. Even though a semiprecious gem dealer in India promises that you can make a fortune on his stones back home, ask yourself: If this is such easy money, why isn't everyone doing it?

HOW TO RUN A (PHONY) SÉANCE

Leo Kostka

Leo Kostka has presided over more than twelve hundred séances at the Magic Castle, the famous Hollywood conjurors' club, where he is resident medium.

In a dark room, a fake medium can make the "spirits" move objects, blow trumpets, and write spooky messages—all by trickery. You can, too. So let's gather in a psychic circle, dim the lights, and try some "spirit writing" that's guaranteed to give people a pleasant chill down their spines.

What you'll need

A candle, two pieces of cardboard, two rubber bands, a pen, and a cigarette lighter. Background music is optional; something in the "new age" style works well.

The setting

Seat four or more friends around a table with a glowing candle in the center; all the room lights are off. The cardboard, pen, and rubber bands lie on the table in front of you. The lighter is in your right pocket.

The medium in action

"Let us form a psychic circle," you say in your best spooky manner, "and find out if the spirits are with us tonight."

Show the pieces of cardboard to be blank on both sides. Hold them stacked and wrap the rubber bands around them, about an inch from each end. Place this package on the table with the pen on top. "Perhaps we will get a message from 'the other side.' We shall see."

Now you are going to execute a subtle bit of trickery known in the trade as the "medium's grip." Ask everyone to place his hands palm down on the table. As you talk about spirits and such, casually slide your hands until they are about two inches apart. Now instruct each person to lift his right hand and grip the left wrist of the person next to him. When this has been done, your neighbor to the left will be holding your left wrist; your right hand grips the wrist of the person to your right. Say, "This assures us that nobody—including myself—can do any funny business."

Announce that you will now snuff the candle. Here's where the trickery comes in. Remove your right hand from your neighbor's wrist, reach toward the candle, and snuff the wick between your fingers. As you lean back in the darkness, slide your left hand a couple of inches to the right and use it to grip the wrist of your neighbor on the right. He will think you're holding on with your right hand.

This little subterfuge leaves your right hand free! No one can tell, because the room is pitch black. It's simple for you to feel around gently for the pen, pick it up, and locate the open area of the cardboard between the rubber bands. Write "*I am here*" in fairly large letters. (You'll find that with a little practice you can easily write in the dark—and it doesn't matter if your writing isn't entirely legible; after all, spirits don't necessarily write with perfect penmanship.) Silently turn over the cardboard package so that the writing ends up on the bottom, facing the table, and replace the pen.

Background music will drown out any slight noise made by your writing. You can also cover the sound by talking about the "energy of the psychic circle" and encouraging everyone to concentrate on the query: "Are the spirits with us?"

After half a minute say, "I believe we've been in the dark long enough; let's see if there has been a message. Let me light the candle."

Now you will undo the "medium's grip." Slip your left hand off the wrist of the person on your right. Go to your pocket with your right hand and remove the lighter. As you reach forward to light the candle, slide your left hand (which is still being gripped by your other neighbor) a bit more to the left. The person on your right (and everyone else) will believe that you simply lifted your right hand, got the lighter, and lit the candle.

Use both hands to remove the rubber bands from the cardboard. Lift off the top piece and display both sides. This reveals the blank upper side of the bottom piece, but don't turn it over; you don't want to reveal your spirit message yet. Say, "Apparently, our energies weren't focused enough; there's no message. Let's try again."

Place the bottom piece of cardboard on top, which puts the writing on the inside of the "sandwich." Replace the rubber bands. As you return the cardboards to the table, casually flip them over. Place the pen on top.

All your dirty work is done, and from now on it's all theater. "Let's do it differently this time," you say. "We'll all lay our hands on the cardboard. My hands will be on top of everyone else's, to be sure I can't touch the cardboard or indulge in any trickery."

When this is done, snuff out the candle. Ask everyone in the psychic circle to use all their strength to ask for a message from the spirit world. After a short time relight the candle. "I don't want to touch the cardboard," you say. "Will someone else take off the rubber bands and find out if we received a message from beyond?"

People will gasp when they see "*I am here*" written by a ghostly hand.

Here are some extra tips for your séance:

1. You can conduct the séance even if you don't have a can-

dle. Just be sure to sit where you can easily reach the lamp or light switch, which should be behind you and over your right shoulder. When you execute the "medium's grip," instead of snuffing and relighting the candle with your right hand, reach behind you and turn off and on the light. Except for that, there's no difference in the way you secretly substitute one hand for the other in the dark.

2. Your spirit message will be even spookier if you can secretly learn a snippet of information about someone at the table ahead of time—anything from his social security number to a bit of romantic gossip. The spirits can then mysteriously divulge it.

3. You can create other mysterious effects by using an inverted drinking glass as a "spirit chamber." Place some small object like a gold locket beside it, and in the dark have the spirits transport it under the glass.

Or secretly remove something from your pocket—a rose, perhaps—and lay it on the table as a "spirit manifestation." It's surprising how much you can do with one hand and in the dark.

THROW A BOOMERANG—
AND HAVE IT COME BACK

Doug DuFresne

Doug DuFresne has
held the world record
for "fast catching"—
throwing and catching
one boomerang five
times in the quickest
time—and shares the
Australian record for
hunting-stick accura-
cy. Based in Portland,
Oregon, he manufac-
tures Outback
Boomerangs, in right-
and left-handed mod-
els, for both beginners
and experts.

It's a thrill to throw a boomerang that sails out over an open field, makes a curve, and returns so you can catch it. And it's not hard to learn how.

Grip

Form your hand into a loose fist, with the ball of your thumb against the middle joint of your forefinger; then place the *end* of the boomerang between these two points. The flat bottom side goes against your finger, the curved top side against your thumb. Grip it tightly enough so that the boomerang won't twist in your hand, yet loosely enough so that it will spin freely when you release it. (If the end of the boomerang hits the base or web of your thumb as it spins out of your hand, you're holding it too far up the wing; grip just the tip.)

Tilt

A boomerang should be held almost vertical, with just a slight tilt. In terms of a clock face, it should be tilted between 12:30 and 1:30. You can adjust this depending on how the boomerang flies (see *Troubleshooting*).

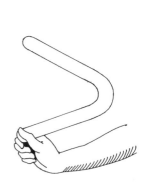

12 ← Correct tilt
1
2
Too much tilt
3

Aim

Check the wind direction before you throw. You can drop some dry grass and see how it falls, or hold up a stick with yarn or strips of Mylar attached. Imagine the wind as coming from 12:00 on a clock face; you'll want to throw the boomerang toward about 2:30.

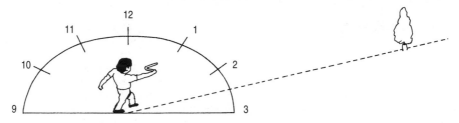

Throw at some distant object, like a tree; if it's 50 yards away, aim directly at a point on it about 5 yards off the ground. Be careful not to throw the boomerang as you would a ball, with an arching flight to reach the target. Throw it almost level.

Throw

There's nothing mysterious about a boomerang throw. You use the same overhand motion a baseball pitcher does. Skill counts more than power. Stand with your left side facing the direction of the throw; your weight is on your right foot. Both feet are facing about 90 degrees from the direction you're throwing. Cock the boomerang back in your hand until the wing you are holding is parallel with your forearm, but don't twist your wrist. You will want to keep the boomerang cocked back until the last possible moment before the release. Extend your right arm behind you, so you'll have a long throwing motion. To start the throw, lead with your left elbow, swinging it around level with your shoulder. This should pull your chest around; the right arm follows. Aim directly at the distant object and throw, flipping the boomerang with your wrist as you release. The boomerang should be spinning as it leaves your hand. Be sure to follow through, and finish with your weight on your left foot.

Catch

The boomerang should be slowing down, floating, hovering when it reaches you; it's almost like a helicopter landing when it settles down gently for the catch. If it's moving fast, you haven't thrown it correctly.

The boomerang should be spinning in a horizontal plane when it returns to you. As it rotates, there is one side coming toward you and one side going away; it looks like a ring. Rather than trying to catch it in the middle, where there's only air, catch the side that's coming toward you, which would be the left side. Hold one hand below and one above, and trap the boomerang between your palms.

BOOMERANG SENSE

Safety My throwing instructions are for a right-handed person throwing a right-handed boomerang. If a left-handed person throws a right-handed boomerang, the results are unpredictable and potentially dangerous.

Once you throw a boomerang, you can't take it back. So be sure it's not going to fly (or bounce) into anything or anyone. The ideal place to throw is a large grassy field—no sidewalks, backstops, trees, or people—with at least 60 yards open in every direction.

Be sure you and your friends keep your eyes on the boomerang as it flies. If it appears that anyone might be hit, warn him loud and clear.

Get out of the way if the boomerang returns *at* you instead of *to* you. (If it slows down and hovers, it's coming "to" you; if it returns as if it wants to take your head off, it's coming "at" you.)

Don't try to catch a boomerang that is coming in above chest height; it may take an unpredictable bounce off your hand and hit you in the face.

Don't throw in winds over 5 miles an hour or in the dark.

Care and Feeding A beginner often buys a cheap boomerang, figuring that if it works he'll get a good one; but many cheap boomerangs don't return properly. To avoid discouragement, buy a good one at the start.

Store your boomerang flat, with nothing resting on it, or hang it on a wall.

Avoid storing a boomerang in excessive humidity, sunlight, or heat, which can cause warping.

If your boomerang gets wet from rain or damp grass, wipe it off. In wet weather use a leather glove (goatskin works best), so the boomerang won't slip as you throw it and fly out of control.

Troubleshooting

The boomerang should fly about half its range straight away from you, then turn rather abruptly to the left and curve back toward you.

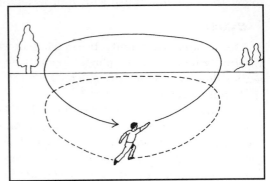

Correct flight pattern

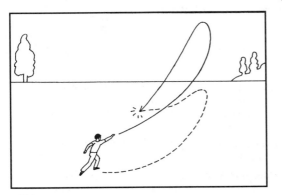

Sidearm

Problem:

The boomerang turns up and to the left shortly after it leaves your hand.

Solution:

Tilt the boomerang less; don't throw sidearm. Don't twist your wrist at release.

Problem:

The boomerang dips downward as it turns left.

Solution:

Tilt the boomerang more.

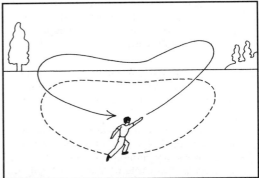

Too little tilt

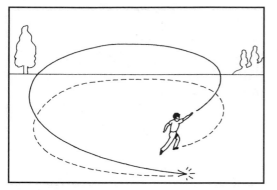

Too far left

Problem:

The boomerang goes by on your left side and lands beside you.

Solution:

Turn more to the right when you throw.

Problem:

The boomerang crosses its original flight path in front of you.

Solution:

Turn more to the left when you throw.

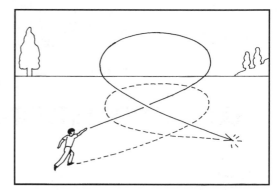

Too far right

Problem:

The boomerang flies over your head.

Solution:

Reduce the power of your throw.

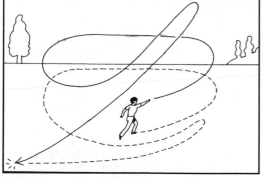

Too hard

Problem:

The boomerang returns toward you, but doesn't come all the way.

Solution:

Throw with more power. Don't twist your wrist; use your whole body. Be sure to follow through.

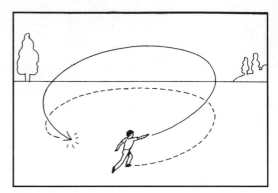

Too soft

THE AMAZING BOOMERANG

Ted Bailey

The world's oldest known boomerang was made from a mammoth tusk in Poland about 23,000 years ago.

Barney Ruhe of Brooklyn, New York, duplicates the feat of William Tell *in reverse*—by placing an apple on his own head and throwing a boomerang that returns to crack the apple in half.

The world record for most consecutive throws and catches of a boomerang is 801, set by Stephane Marguerite. Dennis Joyce set the record for "maximum time aloft" when he threw a boomerang that hovered in the air for 2 minutes and 59.94 seconds.

In King Tut's tomb (2000 B.C.), archaeologists found boomerangs with golden caps.

In *How to Steal a Million*, Peter O'Toole robs a museum by throwing a boomerang through the protective light beams surrounding a million-dollar statue. This sets off false alarms that prompt the guards to shut off the alarm system—allowing O'Toole and Audrey Hepburn to come out of their hiding place, grab the statue, and escape.

Australian aborigines use boomerangs for hunting animals as large as kangaroos. A blow to a kangaroo's leg from a 1.5-pound hunting boomerang will bring the animal down.

By attaching a burning coal to a boomerang, the aborigines of Queensland created a night-flying toy.

A former president of the United States Boomerang Association, engineer Ted Bailey designs and makes boomerangs that set world records for maximum time aloft.

Relax Your Whole
Body with the Yoga
"Salute to the Moon"
111

RELAX YOUR WHOLE BODY WITH THE YOGA "SALUTE TO THE MOON"

Lilias Folan

After Lilias Folan intro-
duced yoga to public
television in 1970,
Time magazine
dubbed her the "Julia
Child of Yoga." Her
new PBS series is
Lilias! A resident of
Cincinnati, Ohio, she
has made three
videos, including
Energize with Yoga,
and is the author of
*Lilias, Yoga and Your
Life*.

The Salute to the Moon (or Chandra Namaskar) is restful and nurturing for the body and the mind, so it's enjoyable to do before bedtime. I learned it from my colleague Richard C. Miller. In 1990 I went to Moscow and introduced it to yoga students and teachers in the Soviet Union—yoga *perestroika!*

To learn the sequence, study the illustrations keyed to the instructions below. Then speak the instructions into a tape recorder and play them back as you do the salutation. You should wear comfortable clothes, with no shoes.

Each posture is linked with the breath. As you practice, you'll feel the easy, restful flow of the Salute to the Moon.

1. Standing pose: Stand with your feet apart, at hip width. Keep your spine long; pull your shoulders down from your ears. Take three breaths, imagining that they come up through the soles of your feet.

1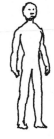

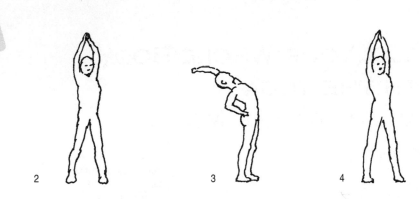

2. Arm raise: Inhale as you raise your arms over your head.

3. Lateral bend right: Place your right hand on your hip. (Your left arm is toward the ceiling.) Exhaling, bend and stretch to the right side.

4. Return to center: Inhale as you return to an upright position, with both arms over your head.

5. Lateral bend left: Place your left hand on your hip. Exhaling, bend and stretch to the left side.

6. Return to center: Inhale as you return to an upright position, with both arms over your head. Now exhale.

7. Arc back: Lift your rib cage and contract your buttock muscles. Inhale; then gently arc back. *Caution:* Do not drop your head or hold this position; there should be no pain or pressure in your lower back.

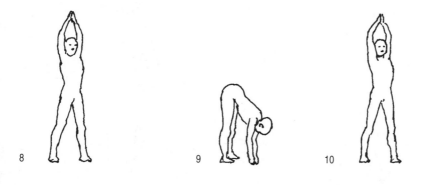

8. Return to center: Exhale as you return to an upright position, with both arms over your head. Now inhale.

9. Fold forward: As you exhale, fold forward at the waist, bending your knees slightly.

10. Return to center: Inhale as you return to an upright position, with both arms over your head.

11. Arms in T: Extend your arms in a T and place your legs 3½ feet apart. Turn your right foot out 90 degrees; the left foot points slightly to the right.

12. Triangle right: Exhaling, bend your upper body to the right. Your right hand touches your shinbone while your left arm points toward the ceiling.

13. Return to center: Inhale as you return to an upright T position.

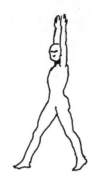

14

15

14. Triangle left: Exhaling, bend your upper body to the left. Your left hand touches your shinbone. Your right arm points toward the ceiling.

15. Return to center: Inhale as you return to an upright position. Turn both feet toward the right. Raise your arms over your head.

16. Fold right: Turn your whole torso to the right. Exhaling, fold your torso forward over your right thigh. Bend your right knee comfortably. Your forehead is toward your knee; your arms are relaxed, with your hands on either side of your right foot. Don't strain.

16

17

18

Relax Your Whole
Body with the Yoga
"Salute to the Moon"

115

17. Change sides: Inhale as you return to an upright position, with your arms raised. Turn your feet toward the left.

18. Fold left: Turn your whole torso to the left. Exhaling, fold your torso forward over your left thigh. Bend your left knee comfortably. (No pain, please!) Your arms are relaxed.

19. Return to center: Inhaling, return to an upright position, with your arms raised over your head. Your feet are spread at hip width.

20. Return "home": Exhaling, lower your arms. Close your eyes. Enjoy how your body feels. Take three breaths, imagining that they come up through the soles of your feet. Let the day's stress and strains flow out your shoulders and down your arms into the earth.

Repeat the moon salutation six to eight times. Enjoy!

**You Too Can
Have A Body
Like Mine**
—*Charles Atlas
(Angelo Siciliano),
advertisement*

19

20

Play Serious Checkers

Gil Dodgen

Gil Dodgen codified
the rules of checkers
to write a computer
program called
Checkers for the
Software Toolworks.
At the U.S. National
Checker Champion-
ships, his program
battled to a tie for fifth
place in the masters'
division.

Many players who play both games seriously
consider checkers to be more difficult than
chess. Although the rules of checkers are
very simple, it is a tactically very precise and
complex game. When one considers that
moves cannot be reversed until kings appear
on the board and that jumps are forced, it is
clear why a player must analyze the conse-
quences of each move precisely to great depth. It is actually possible to lose a checker game before the fifth move. To plan a
strategy, an expert player must look ahead at least fourteen
moves (or "half moves" in checkers jargon); the world champion
is reputed to be able to think ahead thirty to forty moves. A computer program that plays checkers must analyze roughly
400,000 positions in the midgame when looking ahead fifteen
moves.

Despite the game's complexity, basic play is guided by certain
principles. Their observance can help players of any skill level;
in fact, masters have lost championships through simple over-
sights.

General strategy

These tips apply to any stage of the game.

1. Learn to spot shots (see Illustration 1). A "shot" is an opportunity

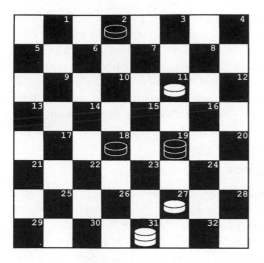

Illustration 1: Spotting Shots
White to move and win by a "shot." If white moves 27–23, either way black jumps, white gets two for one. White can also get three for two and win instantly with 11–7, 2–11, 27–23, 19–26 (or 18–27) and white cleans up the board with 31–8.

to give up *n* pieces in exchange for winning back *n plus 1* pieces or more. Here's an illustration (remember that in checkers you have to jump if you can): After an opponent jumps one of your pieces, you may be able to make a double jump back—which means that although you've lost one piece, you have taken two back. Such opportunities abound in the game; there are "two for ones," "three for ones," "three for twos," and so forth. It's important to notice these opportunities, because overlooking a shot can cost you the game immediately. (Many books contain shot problems, which help you learn to spot them.)

2. Look for chances to immobilize your opponent's pieces (see Illustration 2). You want to hold *n plus*

Illustration 2: Immobilizing the Opponent
On the right side of the board, one black king holds two white pieces. On the left, two hold three.

1 of your opponent's pieces with *n* of your own pieces. For example, let's say your king is in a position to trap two opposing pieces against the side of the board. (A king can move backward and forward, but the opponent's pieces can only move forward, so the one king can pin down two pieces.) This is called a "cramp"—any situation where pieces are immobilized. Another illustration: You move two pieces so that they effectively immobilize three of his pieces. Any such situation is almost like having an extra piece of your own on the board.

Opening and midgame play

1. Develop out of the single corner. To "develop" means to advance pieces across the board. If you look at a checkerboard, you'll see that at the lower left-hand corner there is a black square all by itself; this is called the single corner. At the lower right side of the board there are two black squares; this is the double corner. A piece in the single corner has only one square to move to. At the double corner, there are twice as many options.

However, the double corner is easier to attack, because there are more ways to get at it. Early in the game you want to keep the double corner intact, to avoid weakening it further. This means it is generally best to develop out of the single corner, moving diagonally toward the center of the board.

2. Try to control the center of the board. Try to occupy or control as many of the four center squares as possible, forcing your opponent to the side of the board. You'll have many more options than he does, because pieces trapped on the side have only one square to move to, whereas pieces in the middle of the board have two squares to move to.

3. Exchange into the center of the board. If you're going to make an "exchange"—where you give up one piece and then jump to get the opponent's piece (or pieces) back—it's best to exchange toward the center of the board instead of the side. This helps you maintain control of the center. If your opponent is taking over

> **Victory goes to the player who makes the second-to-last mistake.**
> —*Savielly Grigorievitch Tartakower*

the center, you can trade those pieces out and replace them with your pieces.

4. Avoid exchanges out of your king row early in the game. The "king row" is the row closest to you. Whenever an opponent's piece moves into that last row, it becomes a king—a very important and powerful player. Early in the game, especially, avoid letting your opponent exchange in any way that forces you to jump a piece out of your king row, allowing him to move in and be crowned.

5. Know how to defend your king row. The first three squares starting on the double-corner side—numbered 1, 2, and 3 on the checkerboard—are the strongest guard positions for the king row. In general, try to keep these pieces in place longest.

Sooner or later, you'll be forced to evacuate the king row. Be careful which pieces you move out first. If you have pieces on 1, 2, and 5, it's generally best to move the piece off 1 rather than 2; the remaining pieces on 2 and 5 are still very capable of guarding the king row. Many people believe it is generally best to keep the pieces on squares 1 and 3 in place the longest, moving off 2 first. However, this may allow your opponent to plant a piece on 10, forming a "bridge" through which he can get an early king. (The bridge piece on 10 is very strong early in the game but becomes a liability later, when the opponent has kings with which to attack it from behind. At this point try to free it by exchanging out one of the pieces on 1 or 3.) In addition, leaving the piece on 2 may prove advantageous in the endgame, since it can hinder the mobility of the opponent's newly crowned kings.

Generally, moving 3 to 7 is better than moving 3 to 8; it gives you more mobility and greater ability to control the center.

6. Prevent your opponent from getting kings—especially the first king of the game. If having a king gives a player an advantage, then having the *first* king means an even greater advantage. An opponent can use that king to harass you and immobilize your pieces.

7. When you get a king, put it into play immediately rather than trying to get more kings. Let's say you have a king, with two more pieces in position to become kings. If you crown these two, meanwhile allowing your opponent to get a couple of kings, his position will grow relatively stronger. It's wiser to move your king into the center of the board as soon as possible, where it will be in a position to immobilize your opponent's pieces, and to delay getting your other kings.

8. Use the "time" strategy. This approach goes contrary to intuition: Early in the game, don't develop too many pieces too quickly. It's dangerous to move lots of pieces far out on the board too soon, because if your opponent holds back and plays a waiting game, you're likely to run out of moves; you'll end up in his lair and lose pieces.

However, when the number of pieces on the board drops to seven or six per side, then the strategy reverses: Now you want to start developing pieces as quickly as possible, because you don't want to enter the endgame with your pieces stuck on your side of the board, where they could be trapped and never become kings.

9. If you're playing black, try to occupy square 19. This is an exception to the rule about not developing a piece far forward too early in the game. Square 19 offers a strong attacking position on the opponent's double corner (which tends to be weaker than the single corner, because there are more ways to attack it). Since you can anticipate getting your first king on the double-corner side of your opponent's board, square 19 is a strong outpost, as long as the piece can be defended.

Endgame play

Let's define "endgame" as the time when kings have appeared on the board and the population has dropped to four or five pieces per side. The theory underlying your strategy now is mathematical: As the ratio of your kings to your opponent's kings increases, so does your chance of winning.

1. Try to pin your opponent's pieces against the side of the board by using your kings. You want to prevent his pieces from becoming kings. While you hold his pieces trapped, you go get *your* pieces crowned. This strategy often involves a "changing of the guard." You might hold his piece on the side of the board with one of your pieces, go down and crown a king, and bring the king back; now hold his piece with your king while you go down and crown your other piece.

2. When you are ahead, try to exchange the opponent's pieces. Again, it's mathematical. Let's say you have five pieces and your opponent has four, which gives you a strong advantage—exactly 25 percent. If you can exchange, losing some pieces but recovering them when you jump in return, you will alter the ratio even more in your favor. Say you end up with two pieces to his one; now you have a 100 percent advantage! By the way, two kings against one is a guaranteed win (with one extremely rare exception). You chase his king across the board, force him out of the double corner, and pin him to the side, winning the game.

A corollary to Rule 2: If you are behind, *avoid* exchanges.

3. When you're behind, try to get as many kings as you can. Let's say that you and your opponent each have four pieces, that two of yours are pinned, and that your opponent is going to get two or three kings. Make every effort to get two kings yourself, even if it means allowing your opponent to get three, because you'll be in a much stronger position with a ratio of three kings to two than with a ratio of two to one. The two kings can work together to defend each other. Whenever

THE GAME OF
CHECKERS

Checkerboards and pieces were placed in Egyptian tombs as long ago as 3,500 B.C.

Of 17 million Americans who have played checkers, no more than 100 have attained the level of master or grand master.

When grand masters face each other across the checkerboard, they endure both mental and physical exhaustion in daily sessions that last twelve hours; the rules require thirty moves to be made each hour.

World champion checker player Dr. Marion Tinsley has not lost a match in thirty-five years and is considered by many the best player who ever lived.

you're behind, try to keep the ratio of kings as low as possible and maximize your total number of kings.

4. Consider the power of "the Move" (see Illustration 3). Having the Move can be decisive in the endgame. Having the Move means that you can always force your opponent to retreat. To illustrate, put a white king in one single corner and a black king in the other. Note that whoever moves first wins, because he can reach the center of the board first, keep the opponent from getting to a double corner, and force him to retreat to the side of the board where he is pinned and captured.

The principle of the Move applies with more pieces on the board as long as each side has the same number of pieces. If you do not have the Move, you may acquire it by making an exchange.

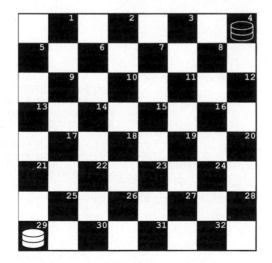

Illustration 3: "The Move"
Whoever moves first will have "the Move" and can force the other up against the side to win.

GET IN TOUCH WITH FAMOUS PEOPLE

Michael Levine

Michael Levine heads
an entertainment PR
firm based in Los
Angeles; his best-
selling "almanacs to
the inaccessible"
include *The Address
Book, The Music
Address Book*, and
*The Corporate
Address Book.*

Mail addressed to "Barbra Streisand, c/o Hollywood, California" ends up in the dead letter office. To reach a celebrity, you need a complete, correct address—which can be as elusive as a butterfly and just as hard to collect. While compiling my address directories of famous people, I've looked everywhere for leads. When Richard Nixon moved to Manhattan, for example, I knew he lived on Sixty-third Street because it was mentioned in the media, but I didn't know which building. One day in a taxi I asked the driver, "Do you happen to know which one is Richard Nixon's building?" He pointed: "I think it's that one." Later I walked up to the doorman and asked, "Does President Nixon come down very often?" "No," he replied. "Not very often." Now I *knew* I'd found the right building. I had Richard Nixon's address!

Another example: How would you get a letter to author Salman Rushdie, who's under death threats from Iran and is in deep hiding? I telephoned Scotland Yard, because it was issuing statements on his behalf, and asked if it forwards mail. "Absolutely," was the response. That's where you can reach Salman Rushdie.

Tenacity and common sense work wonders, but you don't

always need to go to such lengths to get the address of a famous person. My search starts in the library, in reference books like *Who's Who in America*, Standard & Poor's business directory, *Current Biography*, and so forth. They often list celebrities' work addresses; you can write to them there. Also, cartoonists can be reached through their newspaper syndicates; pop stars through their record companies; movie actors in care of the Screen Actors Guild. (In fact, any time there's a union associated with a celebrity's employment, you can write c/o the union.)

If people have been written about in a magazine article, send a letter to the magazine; if they appeared on *Good Morning America*, write to the producer of the program. Publications and TV shows won't give out famous people's addresses, but they will often forward mail.

Celebrities like to hear from the public, and many find their mail to be critically important—second only to money. Enter-

HOW TO GET CELEBRITIES
TO RESPOND TO YOUR LETTERS

To improve your chances of getting a personal response:

1. **Send photos of yourself.** These supply a human face to go with your letter, making it more personal, powerful, and hard to resist.

2. **Include a self-addressed, stamped envelope.** Celebrities have an unusually high volume of mail. Whatever makes it easier for them to respond helps tip the odds in your favor. Include your name and address on each page of a letter and on photos or anything else you enclose.

3. **Keep it short.** Notables are very busy people. Long letters tend to be put aside for future consideration . . . which never comes. If you're asking for an autographed photo, don't write four pages of prose.

4. **Make your letter easy to read.** Type if you can, and stay away from pencil and crayon.

5. **Be sure packages are easy to open.** Don't wrap gifts with yards of string and tape.

6. **Never send food.** If you mail brownies for a celebrity's birthday, they'll get thrown away for obvious reasons of security and spoilage.

7. **Set yourself apart from the flood of similar letters,** especially if you ask for an autograph. Don't mail a form letter; make your request specific. If you admire someone, say why. Flatter. Demonstrate your own creativity; if you write poetry, for instance, send a poem. Make your request original.

tainment figures, especially, keep a close watch on their letters as a real indication of what people are thinking and feeling; they use the mail as a private Gallup Poll. Corporate heads and politicians believe that for every letter they receive, a hundred more people feel the same way but didn't take the time to write, so the influence of your letter is multiplied by 100. You have a powerful voice.

I don't have a photograph, but you can have my footprints. They're upstairs in my socks.
—*Groucho Marx*

REMOVE THE "BIG FIVE" SPOTS AND STAINS

Don Aslett

Best-selling author
Don Aslett appears
often in the media with
his cleaning advice.

Blood

Keep the stain wet. Blot up the excess. Flush and rinse with cold water. (If the stain is old, soak in salt water.) Then use ammonia, the best general solution for getting bloodstains out. For a stubborn stain, soak in digestant for 30 minutes. (One brand of digestant is Biz.) Don't use digestant on silk or wool, though. The washing machine works wonders. As a last resort, apply rust remover or bleach.

Coffee

Don't let it dry! Blot it up by sponging with cool water for as long as any stain is coming out. Do not use ammonia. Vinegar is the best all-purpose solution to lift out coffee. As a last resort, use hydrogen peroxide, working up to chlorine bleach if the fabric will tolerate it. If the coffee had lots of cream and sugar in it, use dry solvent spotter after the area has dried.

Grease

Food: Remove the bulk, then hold a cloth on the material long enough to absorb or transfer out as much grease as possible. Use a laundry pretreatment and

---

Stain Removal Tips

• There is a 75% better chance to remove stains if they're caught fresh.

• Use a white cloth. You can see if the stain is coming out and if the color is fast.

• Remove the excess first. Blot or scrape to get the bulk of it.

• Remember: You blot, lift, *absorb* stains out—not rub and scrub.

wash with Wisk Power Scoop. Dry cleaning solvent can be used on old stains, especially on dry-cleanables.

Automobile grease or oil: Dry cleaning solvent and paint thinner both work well.

Ink

There's no one kind of ink. One third will come out with pure alcohol (from the grocery store). One third will come out with dry spotters and plenty of blotting. One sixth will come out with water and detergent. One sixth will come out only with a pair of scissors. Which is which? You won't know. Always try dry spotters first, then alcohol, then water and detergent; bleach and scissors are last. A white cloth will tell you what's coming out.

Kool-Aid and Other Red Drinks

Catch them quickly. Diluted ammonia is the best neutralizer and solvent. Rub salt into the stain, let it absorb, then vacuum it out. A new product called Red Out or Red Ease does a good job. Work it in and place a towel over the area; place a steam iron (cotton setting or 300 degrees) on top for 20–30 seconds for heat transfer. For any light pink that remains, use bleach (red is tough).

TEACH YOUR ELEPHANT TO WATER-SKI

Cheryl Shawver

Cheryl Shawver has been training animals for twenty-five years and is the general manager of Animal Actors of Hollywood; the company trains animals—from parakeets to elephants—for movies, TV, and commercials.

The director of a movie called *Honky-Tonk Freeway* wanted to film a sequence of an elephant waterskiing. He came to Animal Actors of Hollywood, where trainer Wally Ross taught an elephant named Katy how to do it. Later I worked with Katy when she water-skied in Japanese television commercials.

To teach *your* elephant this useful skill, follow these simple steps:

Get an elephant.

Your elephant should know the basic commands: to move over, to back up, to lift her foot, and (most important for water-skiing) to stand still and not move; the command for this is "steady." Your elephant also must be willing to load into a truck and travel to the lake.

Get elephant-size water skis.

Our skis were mounted solidly on a little barge, which was hidden underwater, out of the camera's vision. Given Katy's weight—she's a 7,000-pound pachyderm—the skis had to be carefully engineered so that they neither sank nor rode too high in the water. An elephant can water-ski about half as fast as a person, and to make it look as if Katy was going faster, the engineers put ridges on the underwater section to churn up a bigger wake. The skis cost $80,000 to design and build.

Start the elephant on dry land.

Before we actually took Katy out on the lake, we built a prop the same size as the skis but mounted on wheels. She learned to step up on it, to place her feet in the right positions (which we marked with paint), and to stand still. If you've ever tried to make an animal stand still for a long time, you know it isn't easy, so you do it in many short sessions over a long period. This conditions the animal gradually.

After a while, we began to roll the prop a short distance. When Katy moved one of her feet, we'd tell her "no!" and place the foot back. If she behaved correctly, we'd pay her an apple or a doughnut. (Elephants' main diet is hay, but they love all kinds of fruits, vegetables, and sweets. Because elephants are bottomless pits, a goodie makes a nice reward.) Pretty soon Katy could roll 20 or 30 feet, and she stood still whether her trainer was standing nearby or a short distance away.

Then she got on the water skis, but without floating yet—just standing at the edge of the lake. She had to learn to accept that even though water was all around, she couldn't jump in and play. (Elephants *love* water and are great swimmers. They can even let out all their air and walk on the bottom, with their trunks sticking up as snorkels.)

Elephant Training Tips

• Because an elephant is such an intelligent animal, she can get bored easily. You don't want to make her do something over and over again and get sick of it. Instead, train her in lots of short sessions, with just enough repetitions so that she understands and learns the behavior solidly, but not enough to make the routine tedious and unpleasant.

• Use lots of positive reinforcement—praise and goodies—so she enjoys her work. She'll soon realize that she's going to be paid well, that the trick is fun and doesn't hurt.

• It's important never to let an elephant perform a behavior the wrong way, because it will be very hard to undo. When she makes a mistake, correct her and go over it again until she does what she's supposed to; then give her a nice reward.

• Always intersperse training sessions with exercise and play periods. When Katy was learning to water-ski, she got free time at the end of each day's sessions to do the things *she* enjoyed—go for a walk, have a bath, play in the mud. Without this Katy may have figured that to have any fun, she'd have to jump off the water skis and go swimming on her own.

Go out on the water.

The speedboat would slowly pull Katy for short distances on the wobbly skis. After a while came the first big loop out from the dock and back. Two trainers sat on either side of her with a basket of goodies, handing her one about every 25 seconds and making sure her feet didn't move—which would have thrown the skis off balance and dumped everyone in the water. As the days went by, we worked down to one trainer. Finally, Katy was ready for her solo turn in the movies.

When the camera was set to roll, the trainer told Katy "steady," hopped in a little boat just out of the frame, and traveled right alongside her. As soon as a take was finished, the trainer stepped back up on the ski. (It's much easier to control the animal when you have a person riding on the ski or on top of the elephant—and it looks good, too. That's what we did for the Japanese commercials.)

It took Katy just four weeks to learn to water-ski—that's faster than some people I know.

How to Raise Money on the Telephone

David Levy

Direct marketing and telephone fund-raising specialist David Levy offers his expertise to such groups as the Grantsmanship Center, where he presented his telemarketing strategies.

I specialize in fund-raising efforts for non-profit groups like the American Red Cross and the Sierra Club. I always advise my clients to do a direct-mail campaign first, and after that to phone all the people who didn't respond. This way you can maximize your direct marketing efforts, since a telephone campaign can get those tougher dollars.

In a typical campaign, you start with a test list of 1,000 names and numbers. (These are preferably members, donors, or former donors.) Take the data from 50 to 100 hours of phoning and look at the dollars per hour pledged. If it's a long-distance campaign, to be successful you need $80 in pledges for each hour worked by your callers. Remember, only 70–80 percent of that money will come back; this leaves you $55–$65 per hour. Then you have to subtract the cost of doing the campaign.

When you prepare a telephone script, get on the phone and say it to someone. You want to sound like a real person, not like somebody reading a script. You're a person talking to another person who shares a common concern. Make whoever is on the other end of the line feel as if this is the only call you're going to make that evening.

When you get on the phone, the first thing you always say (after verifying that you're talking to the person named on your list) is: "Hi, this is Dave Levy, and I'm calling on behalf of the Campaign Against Drunk Driving," and then pause. This is uniform in all scripts. Make sure the other party gets your name and that of the organization. At that point, the person may not want to take the phone call. You'll respect that right. The pause is short, because you don't want people to hang up on you, but at the same time you have to be aware that often people are offended by solicitation calls. That's why it's important to be extremely professional and courteous.

After the pause, thank the prospect for past support. That's the number one rule in telephone fund-raising. Use such phrases as "Thank you for signing the petition" or "Thank you for your past support." It's very important that you say this as if you really mean it.

Now you need to create an emotional appeal with a sense of urgency. When you're creating a plan of action, think in terms of "good news" and "bad news." For example, the good news: "With your support, we were able to raise $100,000 and educate ten thousand schoolchildren about the devastating effects of drunk driving." Then the bad news: "Unfortunately, statistics show that one out of two people will be involved in a drunk driving accident in their lifetime."

Depending on your organization's issues, you have to create some bad news based on reality and to tell some good news based on what you're going to do with their contribution to make things better. Your strategy should relate to what your prospect is hearing about the issue on television and in the press.

When you begin the body of your script, go right into an action word, such as: "Right now" or "Currently." This is how a typical script might go:

> Tonight we are contacting all our supporters to first thank you
> for your past support and to update you on our current activi-

ties. Right now Bread for the World is asking our senators to support the Child Immunization Act. With the tireless efforts of Bread for the World members and supporters, we were able to get the House of Representatives to pass it into law. Now we need Senate approval. We need your continued support. We need you to write to your senators and let them know you feel this law should be passed. And we need you back as a member in 1992 so we can continue our efforts to fight hunger and social pain. Can we count on your support with a contribution of $100?

It's very important in this whole process to personalize your approach, and you can do this by using the prospect's name. But don't do this on a first-name basis; use Mr. or Ms. or Mrs.

This relates to another issue regarding your opening line, when you say, "Hello, this is Dave Levy calling on behalf of Bread for the World." Often, the next line is: "How are you?" Everybody knows what that question means. It means that a telemarketer is calling. I don't recommend this. The prospect is not somebody you know personally, even though you are going to speak in a personal manner. I think it's a little too informal to say "How are you?"

A better line is: "Can you hear me okay?" This tells you that the party can hear you and accepts your right to give the rest of the presentation. It also gets your prospect in a positive frame of mind. If you're friendly and nice, he or she will want to listen and be friendly. When you say, "Can you hear me?" you hope the response is: "Yes, I can hear you" or "Uh-huh."

Then, when you give your pitch (asking the prospect to volunteer time or write to a senator), he or she will say "Uh-huh" again or "Sure." And when you get to the close and say, "Can we count on your support with a contribution of $100, so we can help starving children here and abroad?"—and then pause and say "Okay?"—the potential donor will say "Okay" back.

The "okay" close is the most powerful close in telemarketing. Some callers like to say "Would it be okay?" or "Do you think it's possible that you could help us out?" That's not okay. That's not a commitment. That's not fund-raising. You need to close for a specific pledge, and you can do that with the "okay" close. By using it, you force the prospect to say yes or no.

We all use "okay" in our daily life as a way of letting someone know that we understand or that they can go on to the next issue. But if you aren't comfortable with the "okay" close (and some callers aren't), there are other ways to do it. For example, "Can we count on your support with a contribution of $100? It would mean a great deal to us." That gets the person thinking. It asks a question. It does work. But the very best telephone fund-raisers all use the "okay" close.

Always ask the prospect for a specific gift. The rule of thumb is to look at the date and amount of the last gift and ask for more than that. I feel you should ask for twice the amount. If you have a lot of people saying "yes" to you right away, then you know you're not asking for enough, because they could probably give more.

Always try to get a specific pledge if you can, because specific pledges come in at a rate four to six times higher than open pledges. An open pledge is someone who says, "Well, I'm not sure how much I can give, but I'll try to give something," or "I want to give, but I have to check with my husband (or wife)." If you get a specific pledge, you're going to get 70–80 percent of those people to send their money back. But if you get an open pledge, only 10–20 percent will send in their money.

The fulfillment device you use to secure your pledge corresponds directly to how you leave the phone conversation. When you get a pledge, immediately offer your thanks: "Thank you for your pledge of $100 for the Campaign Against Drunk Driving. Let me just confirm your address." Then say, "Great. What we'll do is send you a specially marked gift envelope in the mail in the next few days. It'll be stamped with a red telephone, to remind you that we spoke this evening. All we ask is that you send back your gift of $100 within two weeks after you get this letter. Okay?"

This confirms that you have the right address and the correct amount of the pledge. Remarkably enough, just having a red telephone on your fulfillment letter will raise your response 2–3 percent. It's an association device; that way donors can distinguish your letter from all the other mail they get, and it will remind them that they spoke with someone and made a commitment to someone.

Get the fulfillment letter in the mail *the next day*. Every day you wait to send it will cost you 5 percent in returns. So don't start any project before you have your fulfillment letter written, your stationery ready to go, and a mechanism in place to send letters out in a timely manner. If you don't get your letter out quickly, why should they respond to you quickly? By sending the letter the next day, you are showing that it's important for donors to get the money back to you right away.

The fulfillment letter should be short and consistent with what you said in your phone call:

Dear Mr. Jones:

Thank you for speaking with one of our representatives a few nights ago and for agreeing to make a $100 contribution to the Campaign Against Drunk Driving. Your support will enable us to continue our lobbying effort to focus attention on this national crisis. With your support we will work at the state and local level to ensure the maximum penalty for drunk driving violations. Your contribution of $100 will be used immediately. Please return your contribution in the enclosed envelope. Again, thank you for your support and continued generosity.

Sincerely,

(Signed by the executive director or another figure with great name recognition)

Only about half of the people who pledge will send their money back after this letter. Wait three to four weeks, then generate your first reminder letter. This will bring in another 15–20 percent. Then you will probably do another reminder, which will bring in another 5–10 percent. This will get you to the anticipated 70–80 percent response rate.

Get the Cheapest Rate and the Best Room at a Hotel

Peter S. Greenberg

Peter S. Greenberg, an award-winning journalist, writes an investigative travel column called "The Savvy Traveler" that is syndicated in more than sixty newspapers; he travels 250,000 miles a year.

To get the cheapest rate on a hotel room, you should never, never call the toll-free 800 numbers that are advertised by hotel chains like Hilton, Hyatt, and Sheraton. Those 800 numbers are nothing more than clearinghouses for blocks of rooms, which are put on the market at the highest rate they think they can get away with.

It's almost always cheaper to spend a dollar or two, call the individual hotel long-distance, and negotiate your own rate. There may be thirty-five separate rates that can be used for any room—corporate rates, weekend rates, senior rates, student rates, auto club rates, and so forth. The "rack rate" is the highest possible tariff published for that room. It's what they charge people who don't know any better.

Because hotels tend to be overbuilt in today's travel economy, there are plenty of opportunities for bargaining. An unsold room is the last thing a hotelier wants; it represents revenue the hotel can never recoup. (It's like an airplane flying with an empty seat; the fare is lost forever.) The hotelier will figure that earning something is better than nothing. As an example, in some big-

> There are two classes of travel—first class, and with children.
> —Robert Benchley

city hotels, the weekend rate may go as low as $69 a night. Suggest cutting a deal in which they'll extend that rate throughout the week if you'll stay in that hotel.

The factors that count here are not only supply and demand but also location and season. A special rate at a hotel in Hawaii over Christmas? Forget it. However, getting a rate in March may be easy, because there are empty rooms.

You need to know how to cut the deal, which you can do either before you get there or when you're in the lobby. Let's say you've actually arrived at the hotel. A lot of times the desk clerk will throw out a room rate just to see if it will fly; it's like the "first price" in an Arab bazaar. So you should remember the primary rule of bargaining: "Know when to walk out of the stall." If the hotel is 50 percent full (or, to look at it another way, 50 percent empty), it's ten o'clock at night, and the clerk says that rooms are $159, you simply respond: "I'll give you $79 or forget it." I've seen clerks leap the counters to make that kind of deal as the potential guest was heading for the door. Again, for the hotel, something is always better than nothing.

What about calling ahead? If it's a convention hotel, it's the beginning of the week, and you're in New Orleans or Chicago and the town is packed, of course you're going to call the hotel before you go there. The question is, whom do you ask to speak with? The reservations agent? No. Ask for the director of sales. You want to let him (or her) know you're a corporate person just like he or she is, not some yokel off the street. You might say: "Listen, I was going to talk to the reservations people, but I'd rather talk to you, because I'm going to be coming to Chicago quite a few times over the next several months, and I'd like to work out a rate with you."

Can You Trust a Wake-up Call?

• The general manager of the Willard in Washington, D.C., once gave me some good advice: Never count on a wake-up call, because there's no assurance you're going to get it. You're leaving it to the human factor. Don't trust the clock-radio or alarm clock in your room, either. What he suggests as a backup is to order coffee from room service the night before. After all, when the waiter comes banging on the door in the morning, you've got to open it. Now you're up!

If you look like your passport photo, you're too ill to travel.
—*Will Kommen*

(*Note:* Call the reservations desk ahead of time and find out its prices, just to get a basis of comparison.) Then see if you can cut a deal with the director of sales.

If so, (a) you've got a deal with someone who's highly placed in the hotel, (b) you've got a contact at the hotel, and (c) you've got a rate substantially below what you'd get if you walked in off the street or telephoned for a reservation. A hotel—just like an airline frequent flyer program—wants your loyalty and repeat business. And if you can give it that loyalty, or at least a perception of it, you'll get some deals.

Now, how can you get the best room? First, you should remember that you actually spend very little time in your hotel room, and most of that is in the bathroom or in bed. So what do you really want in a room? The main thing (after cleanliness) is quiet. Hotels tout their rooms with views, but these tend to be noisier, because you can hear all the activity from the street. Avoid rooms over the ballroom or under the disco. And stay away from rooms above loading docks; they're quiet during the day, but at three o'clock in the morning, when the garbage trucks arrive, you're in trouble; those guys love to throw bottles and bounce trash cans. Finally, you don't want to be right next to the elevator shaft, where there's mechanical noise and people talk at all hours.

When you check into a hotel, be sure your room is far from all these noisy features. However, don't ask if there's construction going on—there's *always* construction going on in any hotel. Ask if your room is *near* the construction; then the clerk will see that you know what you're talking about.

I tend to like rooms on lower floors. This is partly for safety; after all, there's not a fire department in the world that can get above the eighth floor in any building. But what I really like about the lower floors is that you can get the elevator faster and—most important!—you have better water pressure in your shower.

How to Get the Best Deal on a Rental Car

Don't call the toll-free 800 number for Hertz, Avis, National, and the rest. What people don't know Is that most rental car dealers are local franchises and can set their own rates. If you call the 800 number, you're quoted the national rate, and that's what you'll pay when you get to the counter in Boise or Des Moines. But if you call the rental car location in Boise and say, "I'm coming in tomorrow. What's your best rate?" it might offer you lots of good deals that the national office doesn't even know about.

STAMP OUT COCKROACHES

Michael Bohdan

Professional exterminator Michael Bohdan runs the Pest Shop, Inc., in Plano, Texas, and has appeared on many television programs, including *The Tonight Show Starring Johnny Carson*, discussing roaches and other pests.

I'm known as the Marlin Perkins of the bug world. Cockroaches—the number one pest in the United States—interest me particularly. Theirs is a strange and somewhat frightening world, but I'll be your guide. You can call me "Cockroach Dundee."

First, let's get to know the cockroach. It has been on earth for 350 million years, a hundred times longer than human beings. About four thousand species have evolved, and it's no wonder that cockroaches are so successful. A large one can live for three weeks without food or water. It can swim, staying underwater for fifteen minutes without drowning. It is immune to radiation levels that would annihilate reptiles, birds, and mammals. In one year a happy cockroach couple can bear 130,000 offspring—so if Noah had invited a pair aboard the Ark, they would have needed only two years to repopulate the world with roaches.

Cockroaches will eat almost anything, from cinnamon rolls and apples to cigarettes and toothpaste. A dozen roaches could live for more than a week on the nutrients in the glue of a single postage stamp. An adult roach can hide in a crack as thin as a dime. Cockroaches can start to run in fifty-four thousandths of a second, faster than you can blink an eye, so you can't easily catch them.

Cockroaches can carry lots of gross bacteria on their feet,

which is one reason why you should get rid of them. Here's how, in three easy steps.

1. Identify the species.

In the United States, the three most common types of cockroach are the small German and the larger American and Smoky Brown. Their droppings look something like rodent droppings, but with ridges. If you spy these droppings in your kitchen, you've got trouble. One cockroach running on your countertop probably indicates hundreds or thousands more living inside the walls.

2. Choose the right weapon.

Most people get a can of bug spray and apply it to the baseboards. But sprays are not all that effective, because cockroaches spend 99 percent of their time in cracks and crevices, where sprays can't reach. For the same reason, foggers also are not so effective—and who wants to leave the house for up to four hours?

> **Men should stop fighting among themselves and start fighting insects.**
> —*Luther Burbank*

The newest anti-cockroach technology is the bait station. I recommend a brand called Combat; there's a small size for German roaches, a larger size for American and Smoky Brown types. The active ingredient is a chemical that roaches feed on, but it doesn't kill right away; it's a time-delayed product. After discovering the bait, roaches eat some of it and then return to the nest to share the bait with others; within twenty-four to forty-eight hours they start dying. It's a passive way to get rid of roaches, and compared to spraying, it's better for the environment and your health. These bait stations are odorless and child resistant, and they last for three months.

3. Use the weapon properly.

Studies show that 75 percent of Americans handle their own pest control—but a mere 2 percent of these people read the label on the products they use. Take time to read the label entirely and follow the instructions.

Use a flashlight to inspect cracks and crevices under the sink, behind drawers, and so on. Look for bugs or droppings. Check behind the microwave oven, because cockroaches like both crumbs and heat.

Place the bait stations strategically, using the double-face tape that's included. Stick one bait station behind the microwave; tape another to the porcelain on the underside of the sink. Because cockroaches love to live under dishwashers, you should remove the bottom plate on the front of the machine and insert a bait tray. Do the same thing under the refrigerator.

Large roaches often live outside. To keep them from coming inside, fill any cracks and holes in your outside walls with pieces snipped from plastic kitchen pot scrubbers. Try to build these pests out. Keep woodpiles away from the side of the house, since a woodpile is a common "roach motel."

HOW TO TELL IF YOUR HOUSE HAS TERMITES

There are many kinds of termites, but 90 percent of the damage done in the United States is caused by subterranean termites—over $1 billion a year. Termite work is definitely not for the do-it-yourselfer; contact a reputable pest control specialist if you find any of these signs.

1. Look for mud tubes, about the size of pencils, running up your outside foundations; also, little globs of dirt on your inside bathroom walls. Termites need a humid environment, and the moisture in the bathroom attracts them. They build their mud cases inside the walls and feed on the wooden structure of your house. Not a pretty picture.

2. In the spring, check windowsills for what look like black ants. If, on close inspection, they resemble black grains of rice and have straight (not elbowed) antennae, thick waists, and two pairs of wings of equal length, they aren't ants but most likely termites. (See illustrations.)

3. Look for physical damage to your house. In the sheetrock you may detect tunnels, faintly visible behind wallpaper or paint. Termites avoid light and are silent invaders, usually hollowing out wooden materials (baseboards, rafter tails, ceiling boards) to obtain their diet of cellulose.

Ant

Termite

LOOK AND ACT YOUR BEST ON TELEVISION

Arnold Zenker

During his fifteen years in broadcasting, Arnold Zenker was a talk-show host on radio and TV and once substituted for Walter Cronkite on the air. He heads Arnold Zenker Associates in Boston, a firm that prepares executives, professionals, and officials for public and media appearances. He is the author of *Mastering the Public Spotlight*.

Whether you're a businessman who has a TV crew from *60 Minutes* banging on the door or a concerned citizen appearing on your community cable channel, you must remember one thing above all: Television is show business; it is not the real world. On TV you're an image, not the three-dimensional you.

Novices confuse television with reality. They think that an interview with a reporter is a genuine conversation. They feel, "I just want to be the real me." But no viewer can get to know the "real you" in fifteen seconds—or ten minutes, for that matter. You're onstage, and to be effective you must give a performance, just like an actor.

Americans have their TV sets on about six hours a day, and they half-watch while they read newspapers, change diapers, cook meals. You must say your piece in a way that will cause a person to look up. Your goal is to break through the glass and reach them! As a media skills trainer, here's what I tell my clients as I prepare them to go on television.

Appearance and delivery

On TV you're dealing with image more than substance. So

your image on the screen must be the image you want to communicate. Don't worry if you don't look like Robert Redford or Farrah Fawcett. What counts is that your appearance match your intended message. As an obvious example, let's say you're a physician talking about medical matters; it's probably helpful to be in a white jacket. This visually identifies you for the viewer, and it also implies "compassionate person."

But things are not always so cut and dried. I often work with CEOs before a television crew comes. "Instead of having you sit behind that huge desk in your gray suit," I may advise, "why don't we go into the plant and have you roll up your sleeves? Be a workingman." That way the executive will appear more down to earth and accessible—one of "us" instead of one of "them."

A classic contrast to that is the old shot of Richard Nixon walking along the beach in a three-piece suit and wingtip shoes. That's exactly what you *don't* want to do. Make your appearance enhance your image.

> **No TV performance takes such careful preparation as an off-the-cuff talk.**
> —*Richard Nixon*

Technically speaking, you shouldn't wear white or other light-colored clothing; it reflects, forcing the camera to compensate and making your skin tones look muddy and uneven. I'm opposed to very dark outfits for the same reason; dark colors recede, causing your face to pop forward too dramatically. Choose tans and medium blues and favor warm colors—as opposed to grays and greens, which can make you look like a cadaver.

Always think of what your face is going to look like to the viewer. You are being shot close up, so if you can do without your glasses, get rid of them. A face blocked by frames can't communicate as well. If you must have your glasses, watch out for frames that don't fit well (you'll have to adjust them constantly on camera), are too severe, or have big lenses (they reflect).

Since most interviews are done in three-quarter profile, you'd rather have your best side facing the camera. Most of us have a profile that appears younger, prettier, more pleasing. Look at snapshots or home videos of yourself; it's often easy to tell. If you have a mole or other blemish on one cheek, you'll want to show the other side.

Makeup is a must—for both men and women. Television lights are hot, and every blemish and stubble of beard is going to show. A large commercial station will probably have a makeup artist, while a small one or a cable station won't. So always be prepared to put on your own makeup. Men can get by with pancake. Women can use regular makeup as long as it has a matte finish; nothing shiny. Women who make up their eyes heavily should watch out; what looks good from 10 feet away at a cocktail party may look ghoulish on the screen in a closeup.

Don't let your eyes move around a lot, because if it's a tight shot and your eyes move, it looks as if you're hiding something; you appear "shifty-eyed." Move your head rather than your eyes.

When amateurs get uncomfortable during an interview, they start twiddling; under tough questioning their legs start to swing, their hands flutter and wave wildly. The camera exaggerates this movement, and on such a small screen it's very distracting. So move slowly. If you turn your head fast (or even at a normal speed), it makes people at home cringe. If you turn your head slowly, it looks normal.

A general rule is to forget the camera and talk to the interviewer. For the audience, this creates a belief that they're eavesdropping on a real conversation. There's nothing more awkward than a person who's asked a question by a reporter and then his head spins, as in *The Exorcist*, looking for the camera.

As you get more experienced, you may want to play to the camera a *little*. But the only time an amateur should look at the lens is when the opportunity arises to say, "If you want to buy my book, the address is . . ." Then you're selling to the people at home.

Don't look around for the monitor, either, because if you watch yourself on it, you're liable to get a "Gee, I'm on television" expression on your face. What you want to do is drop an opaque curtain between you and everything else outside that interview—forget the monitors and microphones, forget the technicians, forget the lights and camera.

Television is an intimate medium. We watch it one or two at a time in the privacy of our homes. So try to stay conversational and easygoing. Instead of thinking that you're doing a television appearance before ten million people, pretend you're talking to one person. (This is an old trick from radio days.) Ask yourself, "If I were just having a cup of coffee or a beer with this reporter, how would I talk?" I often say to clients during practice interviews, "Talk the way you'd talk to your wife at three o'clock in the morning in bed." Television is intimate. Avoid being "the speaker."

Be careful about exaggerated facial expressions, too—the dramatic frown, the broad laugh. A closeup can make you look like a gargoyle. In fact, always be aware that the camera may be on a tight shot of your face. That means no twitching, and if you have to straighten your glasses or wipe perspiration off your brow, try to do it during a commercial break. (If you're sophisticated enough to catch a glimpse of a monitor out of the corner of your eye and you see that the shot is on someone else, that's also a good time to do it.)

Remember, people don't listen to television; they watch it. What you're trying to do in your brief time on the air is to present an appealing image that in every way reinforces the message you want to get across. But what is your message?

Content

About 99 percent of any successful TV appearance takes place before you ever go near the camera. It's a matter of preparation. When you go on television, you're really not much different from Johnny Carson or Diane Sawyer. How would they prepare? Well, clearly they'd have a script. It's too late when the camera's on them; if they're not ready, they begin to stumble and say the wrong thing.

To control the situation you must have an agenda of your own—three or four points you want to get across. In a taped interview, the audience won't ever see all your answers, only the one or two that are selected for broadcast. Your goal is to make sure the answer that ends up on the screen contains the message you want to convey.

It doesn't matter whether you're talking about a sensitive political issue or about gardening; you want your message to be clear. This means you must speak in sound bites—short, effective blurbs of information. Each answer should be 10 to 20 seconds long. (In the last presidential campaign, the average length of a sound bite from Bush or Dukakis on network news was only 9 seconds.) Why this length? If you give a TV crew a one-minute answer, they'll cut it. If you give them a five-second answer, they'll have to link two or three answers together. Cutting and splicing can be done in ways that make you look uninformed, evasive, and so forth. But if you give the reporter a sound bite that the tape editor can take right off the reel, you have some control.

The way to guarantee good sound bites is to think them up in advance. Don't wait until the questions are asked with the camera in your face. Start strong by stating your sexiest, most attention-grabbing point first; you can't build to a punch line on television. And be sure each sound bite has what the pros call a "gee whiz" in it—meaning that the tape editor will say, "Gee whiz, that's got to be on there," and the audience will say, "Gee whiz, that's right; I didn't know that."

It also adds interest if you vary your sentence length. After a twenty-word answer, give a short one; it adds punch and keeps people listening.

If you've only got 15 seconds, then by definition the words you choose are important. Make them memorable by using metaphors, alliteration, attention-getting statistics, and anecdotes, and look for words that immediately convey an image to people.

> **The most important thing in acting is honesty. Once you've learned to fake that, you're in.**
> —Sam Goldwyn

If viewers later repeat something you've said, you know you've done a good job. A good example is when Lloyd Bentsen looked at Dan Quayle during their debate and said, "I knew Jack Kennedy. Jack Kennedy was a friend of mine. Senator, you're no Jack Kennedy."

Controlling the situation also means handling questions properly. Amateurs, in the belief that they're having a real conversation, spend their time answering the reporter's questions, no matter which questions are asked. What you should be doing is thinking, "Ah, this question allows me to give Answer A from my agenda."

To brush off a negative question, look within it for a word or phrase or idea that allows you to spin the answer back toward your agenda; you then deliver a packet of material that you have rehearsed and want to convey. Watch politicians; they do this all the time. If a reporter asks about abortion, they don't want to talk about abortion; it's a no-win situation because no matter which side they're on, people will be angry. So a politician says something like, "The real issue is, have we provided enough money in the budget for health care"; then he spins off abortion and back to something *he* wants to talk about.

At the same time, you have to give the reporter something he can live with—an anecdote, fact, or great quote he can use on the air. If you give it to him and also get across your agenda, then both of you are happy with what ends up on the screen.

Your goal in any television appearance is to leave as little to chance as possible. The illusion should always be one of spontaneity. The reality is that you're doing exactly what you were prepared to do. For better or worse, television is a business of illusion.

How to Make It in Show Business

Steve Martin

• Be so good they can't ignore you.

ESCAPE FROM A HEDGE MAZE

Adrian Fisher

Adrian Fisher is the chief executive of England's Minotaur Designs, the world's leading firm of maze designers, which is heading a revival of mazemaking in Europe. His book, *Labyrinth—Solving the Riddle of the Maze,* traces mazes and labyrinths from their ancient mythical origins to modern landscapes.

A hedge maze is a garden puzzle, a walk-in enigma made up of convoluted paths and blind alleys. Within winding walls of greenery, a person can lose himself in delight. But a maze is also more; it is a profound symbol whose path represents the path of life itself, with its inevitable wrong turns and dead ends, all leading toward a mysterious goal.

Hedge mazes were created during the Renaissance, and by Victorian times they were fashionable diversions in the gardens of the wealthy and in public parks. Over the centuries a great game of chess developed between maze makers and the public, in which designers created new patterns for the citizenry to solve. In this endeavor, certain principles of good design apply. For example, a good maze packs the most pathway into the least space—like putting a gallon into a pint pot. And a long alley should always disappear around a corner so that a person can't tell whether it's a dead end until he gets there—whereas a dead end that you can see is particularly inept.

There are keys that unlock a maze's secrets. With these in mind you may find your way to the goal—and, more important, back out again.

Hampton Court, 1690

The simplest type of maze is a continuous hedge folded and refolded upon itself; this means that the perimeter hedge is continuously connected to the central hedge, or goal. To find your way through, just place your hand on either the right or left hedge and start walking. Although you may have to follow the hedge into every dead end, you will always come out again. In time, you will inevitably reach the goal.

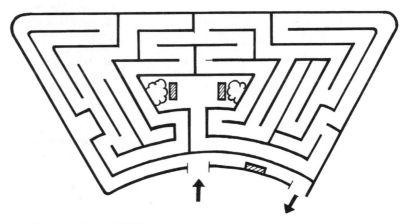

Chevening, 1820

When designers realized that the public had solved the simple Hampton Court type of maze, they came up with a more devious plan. In the maze at Chevening, keeping your hand on one hedge leads not to the goal, but back to the entrance again. Why? The designer placed the goal in a separate island of hedge, floating within the maze; this island is not attached to the perimeter hedge you have been following with your hand.

To solve this maze, proceed as you did for the simpler type, but when you come to a place where only one hedge separates you from the goal, transfer your hand to that hedge. Following this hedge leads you to the center.

Longleat House, 1975

The maze at Longleat House introduced a new element in maze design—a third dimension—by adding bridges. These over-passes create a complex situation in which the two halves of the same hedge are topologically two different paths. There really isn't a logical solution to it. To add further confusion, along the path at Longleat there are identical curves with identical benches in them, causing you to think, "I've been here before . . . or have I?" On average, it takes an hour and a half to thread through Longleat's maze.

TAKE BETTER
LANDSCAPE PHOTOGRAPHS

David Muench

The landscape photography of David Muench appears in a number of recent large-format books, including *Nature's America*, *Utah*, *Eternal Desert*, and *Colorado II,* and in countless magazines. His arresting images, which always reflect a spirit of place, have made him one of the premier photographers of the American landscape.

Don't eat breakfast and dinner at the usual time.

Mealtimes are exactly the times you should be outside taking pictures, because the best light for landscape photography happens in the early morning and evening. Warm, low light brings out earth tones, creating an earthy feeling. And it's more inviting to the eye than the flat, overhead light of noon. In Alaska you have the ultimate, with a three- or four-hour sunset possible.

I also try to avoid the standard summer-trip syndrome. From October through March is a more exciting time for landscape photography. The light direction is lower all day, which is much more appealing to the eye.

Stay on the edge.

There's an edge between day and night that triggers excitement in a photograph, and also between seasons of the year. I like going out during the off-seasons—on the edge of autumn and winter or of winter and spring. When wildflowers appear on the Arizona desert in March or April, for instance, it adds something if there is still snow up above in the high country. The strong feeling of winter plays off the springtime flowers and gives the photographs an edge.

Don't shoot likenesses.

I have a hard time with likenesses of nature. A straight recording of the Grand Canyon won't provoke your mind at all, because it just shows the surface of things. A photograph of the surface won't evoke the mystery, the power and majesty of the world. I go more for the essence of things. I want to show the sense of place. Even with a subject as well known and often photographed as Half Dome in Yosemite, I still hope to accomplish something that speaks of its greatness.

I remember once being in Shenandoah National Park along Deer Hollow Trail, a very popular trail. It had rained considerably and the fog became dense; you could hardly see in front of you. The trees just sort of suggested themselves, looming out of the fog. There was a sense of genesis, of being there the first time anything had happened. It created a feeling of the primeval. The resulting photographs were exciting to look at, because they were such a change from the more typical overhead-sunlight view of things, so much more than mere likenesses.

Suggest other dimensions.

Nature is always changing, and a photograph that implies the passage of time can have a fourth dimension. You can use a tripod and make a long exposure of water flowing around some still object, maybe a stream rushing around a particular rock. In this kind of time exposure, the motion of the water creates its own soft, flowing form, and that suggests the passing of time—or possibly something timeless. (It's interesting to visualize the photograph before you take it and later see how well it matches what you imagined.)

Another way to add an extra dimension to a photograph is by doubling the image. I love hiking in the slot canyons of southern

Utah, and often my photographs will include reflections in a pool. Incredibly, the flow of the canyon is dramatically enhanced by the reflection of the steep rock walls that appear in the water.

Or I may focus on eroded rock—some beautiful, convoluted design that's dramatic in itself—to imply the raw activity that has been going on for ages, long before man appeared on earth. I often think of how we're here for only a blink of time.

Have more than one subject of interest in a photograph.

One of my goals is to portray the complexity of nature, to blend various elements within the unit of a photograph. If I'm photographing, say, the ancient, twisted bristlecone pines high in the Sierras, I may bring in mountains as a distant spatial factor. The photograph then becomes complex as it mixes wood, rock, and sky.

Or simplify.

Another strong urge of mine is to simplify a scene. With some places there's so much going on that I will restrict myself to a simple subject—a lone cactus, a rock, one tree—to identify the place and put you there. Don't bring in other elements that just confuse the eye. Instead of a mountain range with various textures and forms and lines running everywhere, you can photograph just a single mountain.

Use soft or ambient light to bring out a subject.

When the sun is directly on a subject—rock, open desert, pine forest, mountain—it can be brittle, especially in a closeup. And this direct light, with its dramatic quality of light and shade, may alter the real forms of things. Softer or overcast lighting situations, though, can be more rewarding. With soft light you start to see the subject's own form, and its character comes out in a show of detail. I enjoy photographing in the rain, because it enhances rock and wood and makes subtle colors more rich.

(Various films, especially Fuji Velvia, will bring out very rich colors in lower-light situations.)

Make your photographs physically sharp.

To obtain very sharp images I prefer a large-format camera, primarily a 4-by-5; but I also work with a 35mm Leica. And I use a tripod, especially in longer exposures. Should I be photographing the ocean waves as they break on the beach during a storm, I'll place the tripod right in the water. I have to keep the camera from wiggling because I'm standing on shifting sand in moving water; it's a little dance out there. You can go through quite a few tripods this way.

Return more than once.

Places are just like people; after the second or third visit you begin to know them better. You feel at home; you have a sense of the place and begin to get involved. That's when exciting things happen. You haven't reached the point where you know the place so well that you're bored with it (which is why photographing the place you've lived all your life can be hard unless you can trigger yourself into fresh responses).

Wait.

Sometimes I'll wait all day for a single photograph, just hanging on until the light is right or the weather changes or the feeling is strong. And there are places where I'm still waiting to get that photograph I'm happy with—like Mount Shasta, one of the great mountains in the Cascade Range. I've come close to something that expresses its strength and evokes the feeling of what that mountain is all about, but I'm not there yet. And I've been by there twelve or fifteen times.

Sometimes I actually visualize a photograph and then wait to capture it. In New Mexico, for instance, at Taos Pueblo there's a famous church made of earthy adobe; it's a classic and has been photographed a million times. I envisioned it in heavy snow to see what forms might emerge, maybe toward evening when it's snowing. And a big snowstorm came in, *just* the way I'd imagined; it was uncanny. The snow shapes rising from the ground made a totally different design from the usual architectural image we're used to. It transformed the whole thing, turned it a different direction. Those photographs were a matter of visualizing something exciting, waiting for it—and throwing in a lot of luck.

In fact, when it comes to photographing landscapes, luck is the biggest trick of all.

A PERSONAL APPROACH TO FROG TRAINING

Professor Bill Steed

As the dean of Croaker College, the world's only institution of higher learning for frogs, I'm proud of our complete training regimen for students who want to compete in jumping contests, like the famous Calaveras County competition held in Angels Camp, California.

Bill Steed, the founder of Croaker College in San Francisco, has been featured with his students in newspapers, magazines, and on television programs around the world.

The course of study includes plenty of pumping iron and exercise. Each morning I take the frogs out for roadwork in their

CROAKER COLLEGE CELEBRITY GRADUATES

Many famous people sponsor scholarships for Croaker College students, who tour the nation making personal appearances at shopping malls, state and county fairs, and other festivities. Meet the stars:

"Jellybean" This is Ronald Reagan's frog. He's twenty-one years old now—the oldest member of the student body—and doesn't have a gray hair on his head. When he jumps, he veers a little to the right; we figure it's the Republican influence, but we haven't been able to correct it. Outside of that, and a few little lapses of memory, Jellybean is a good frog.

"Dolly Do" Dolly Parton's frog wears a blond wig and a gold glitter dress with red bows and trimmings. During the show she slips out of this to reveal a bikini with a size 38DD bra.

"Doc Holliday" Willie Nelson's frog has a costume of red, white, and blue overalls, with a matching hat that has two braids hanging down from underneath. Willie's right proud of him.

"Miss World Hopper" A true star! She rides a toy motorcycle down a 10-foot ramp, sails out over four semi trucks, and lands upright in a little wading pool. Then she hops off. The audience looks at this stunt bug-eyed.

TEACHING YOUR FROG TO JUMP

Choosing your frog The best place to find a frog is in a running stream or irrigation ditch. Living here (rather than in a pond) keeps the frog exercised. That's because every time he plops in the water, he has to swim against the current to get back to his special spot on the bank.

You don't want a real big frog, because they're too heavy to jump. Your average bullfrog, when he gets up to 3 or 4 pounds, is just like a person who's overweight trying to run the 100-yard dash. So choose a frog that's no more than a pound.

Hold him up and look at him. If he seems to be all legs, with long, sinewy muscles like a high hurdler, he's got potential. Believe it or not, there's even a certain look, just like a person with determination in his eyes. A few frogs appear downright mean, like rodeo horses, and when you turn them loose, they're bound for the skies.

Measure how far your frog can go in three hops. If he jumps 12 or 14 feet, that's good. Warmed up, he'll probably jump 16 or 18 feet. But if your frog sort of shuffles and hops sideways, he'll probably never be a winner; it's back to the stream for him.

Feeding In nature frogs will eat just about anything that moves. In captivity they don't eat as well, so you often have to force-feed them. Just stick a bit of food down their throat. (Actually, they don't have a throat, only a diaphragm between their mouth and their stomach, so force-feeding isn't as gruesome as it sounds. You just pop it down.) The frogs' training table might feature a chicken gizzard cut in four pieces.

Hypnotizing your frog Put the frog on his back, rub his stomach gently, and say, "Look deep into my eyes. Your eyelids are getting heavy. You're getting very sleepy . . ." He'll just lie there with his front feet sticking up. Then you implant posthypnotic suggestions in his mind, such as: "You will start fast and jump straight to victory."

Physical training Regular exercise is vital. At Croaker College the frogs pump iron every day. For the bench press, they lie on their backs and lift little barbells. They also do chin-ups. Just hold your frog so that his front feet can grasp the bar, and he'll pull himself up. He must develop strong front legs, or every time he lands he'll skin his chin.

Handling The less you handle your frog, the better he'll perform. A good way to carry him is inside a wet burlap sack. Put him in and roll him up gently, so he can't jump around and expend too much energy. He'll be comfortable and stay quiet. Now lay the sack in a tub or container that has an inch or two of water in the bottom. Big-time frog coaches put the sacks into electrically heated boxes for jumping contests, to warm the frogs up to an ideal 81 degrees. A warm frog jumps much farther, but a cold frog won't jump hardly at all.

At a contest, don't fool with your frog before it's time for him to jump. Don't even take him out. When you get to the starting line, unroll the sack, lift him out, drop him to the ground, and let him go. All of a sudden, he discovers that he's in the daylight and escape is possible—which is all a frog is interested in. (In the woods, his only way of avoiding danger is to hop.) If you've got a good frog, when you set him down he's going to leave this planet!

sweatsuits; I've got leashes for them, and we walk about five blocks. Then they hit the sauna bath, bubble bath, and massage pad. (Heck, they've got a better lifestyle than I do!)

At night I pull out my projector and run some training films. These home movies, made at jumping contests where the students have competed, help them avoid making the same mistakes again.

In training winners, we feel that the psychological aspect is just as important as the physical. So we work on the top end of the frog. A frog's brain is about the size of a pinhead cut in half four times, which makes training him an uphill battle all the way. Added to this handicap is the terrible inferiority complex that frogs carry around. All their lives they've heard that they're dirty, ugly, slimy, and cold, that they're down in the mud, the lowliest of low.

To overcome this problem, every frog that matriculates in Croaker College is first hypnotized and then psychoanalyzed, freed of his hang-ups and inhibitions. Then we fill him plumb full of positive thinking. All the frogs' little waterbeds are wired for sound, with pillow speakers that play a pep-talk tape. It repeats suggestions, à la Norman Vincent Peale's "positive thinking," while the frog is asleep. A soft voice says: *"You're a great frog. Your skin is soft and moist like damp velvet. Your beautiful eyes reflect your effervescent personality. You like people; people like you—but most important of all, you like <u>yourself</u>."* We play the tape over and over. It ends with: "You can win, you *will* win, you MUST win—for dear old Croaker." The frogs are brainwashed until they believe it. (People ask, "How do the frogs understand the tape?" Well, how does a dog understand commands in English?) The next thing you know, the frog springs forth with a new self-image. That's the reason our graduates from Croaker College are the winningest frogs in the world.

GET HUNDREDS OF CREDIT CARDS FREE

Walter "Mr. Plastic Fantastic" Cavanagh

Walter Cavanagh's collection of credit cards has been displayed at the Ripley's Believe It or Not! Museum. He originated and still dominates the "largest collection of valid credit cards" and "world's longest wallet" categories in *The Guinness Book of World Records.*

I have 1,214 different credit cards—more than anyone else on earth, according to *The Guinness Book of World Records*. The cards give me $1.6 million in credit, and I've seldom paid a cent in fees. They include a sterling silver card issued by a casino in Reno, Nevada, and another one that's good only for charging an ice cream cone at a store in Texas. I have credit at Harrods in London, where the Queen of England shops. With a card I got from a mortgage company, I can walk down the street, see a house I like, and just whip out my credit card and buy it.

I also have the world's longest wallet. Unfolded from the top of a thirty-story building, it touches the ground 300 feet below. My wallet weighs 35 pounds.

How can a person get so much credit? When I started I had no credit at all. I was just out of the Peace Corps and had one credit card to my name; I thought there were maybe ten or twelve different cards in the entire world. Then I made a bet with a friend: Which of us could collect the most credit cards in a year? I won, so he took me to dinner—paying for it, of course, on a credit card. Here are my secrets for amassing credit.

The key, I discovered, is to get "single-purpose cards." These are issued by retail stores, airlines, car rental companies, and so forth. I went to the library and got out the Standard & Poor directory of American businesses that earn over $1 million annually. There was a category for department stores, complete with mailing addresses. So I photocopied those pages, cut them up, pasted them on envelopes, and sent out form letters requesting their credit card applications. When they arrived, I filled them out—which is, admittedly, boring. And back came hundreds and hundreds of credit cards! (The only store that ever turned me down was J. J. Newbury's, the dime store, which said I had too much potential credit.)

Applications for retail stores often ask if you have accounts at other establishments in that city. So I wrote to every single store listed on the applications, and this multiplied my cards rapidly.

Most important, these single-purpose cards have no annual fees. It costs nothing to charge your purchases at Bloomingdale's, Saks Fifth Avenue, or Neiman Marcus; nor to charge phone calls with the new AT&T card; nor to charge your travel expenses at United Airlines and Hertz.

As for general-purpose cards, the Discover Card issued by Sears charges no annual fee; you can use it just about anywhere. Also, most savings and loans offer no-fee Visa or MasterCard if you have an account there.

Many businesses are downright eager to give you a card because they want you to buy their goods or services—and pay them interest. I discovered a sure way to tell which stores are anxious to extend credit: When you go in and ask for a credit card application, if the clerk puts a number or initials on it, it means the store is having a promotion, and for each application

> **When you are in love with someone, you want to be near him all the time, except when you are out buying things and charging them to him.**
> —*Miss Piggy (Henry Beard, in Miss Piggy's Guide to Life)*

turned in the clerk gets a commission. In this situation, you know it's going to be easy to get a card.

Sometimes stores will actually give you things to encourage you to use their credit cards. At 90 percent of the places where I have an established line of credit, I've never even been inside the store. After a while they often send what I call a "hurt letter." They say, "Mr. Cavanagh, why haven't you come in and used our card? If you come in, we'll give you a free gift just for using it." I've gotten steak knives and Corningware; I even won a color television set in a promotion. All because they begged me to come in.

Credit cards serve a good purpose. But just be sure to pay them off in a short time. In my work as a certified financial planner, I tell clients that they couldn't safely find an investment with a return of 20 percent, so it makes no sense to pay a credit card company that much interest.

Credit cards also can be lots of fun. I have a long trench coat, and the whole lining is filled with credit cards. You ought to see people's faces when I flash my cards.

Don't let your mouth write no check your tail can't cash.
—*Bo Diddley*

WRITE FICTION

W. Somerset Maugham

There are three rules for writing a novel. Unfortunately, no one knows what they are.

HOW TO WRITE
A MYSTERY STORY

Raymond Chandler

When in doubt, have two guys come through the door with guns.

Juggle Two Balls and an Apple— While Eating the Apple

Dave Finnigan

The author of the definitive text *The Complete Juggler*, Dave Finnigan has personally taught more than half a million people to juggle. His Edmonds, Washington, company called Jugglebug makes and sells juggling equipment. (He advises people wanting to find juggling balls, rings, clubs, and so forth, to check a nearby magic store.)

Eating an apple while juggling looks impressively difficult but is relatively easy—and it's a very entertaining stunt. Let's proceed step by step. First, we'll learn the basic juggling move with three balls. Then we'll substitute an apple for one ball and chomp it as we juggle.

First Ball

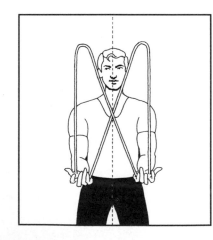

Let's begin with a single ball—easy enough! Hold each hand palm up, like a scoop, and toss the ball from hand to hand. The ball traces a figure 8 in the air. You catch the ball toward the outside of your body, scooping it back toward the center to throw again. Each toss reaches a peak a foot above your shoulder.

Tips: Your hands should stay lower than your chest. Look at the peak of each throw, not at your hands.

When you can do the figure 8 easily . . .

Add a second ball

The "basket" exercise Hold one ball in each hand, pressing them against the heels of your hands with your fourth and little fingers. This leaves a "basket," created by your other three fingers, where you can hold another ball.

Add a third ball. Pick it up and toss it from hand to hand—from basket to basket—in the figure 8 pattern you learned earlier.

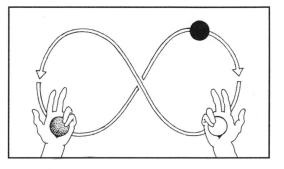

Swap two balls In your right hand (or whichever hand you favor) hold two balls; the left hand holds one ball. Toss the ball from the "basket" of your right hand. When it reaches a peak, toss the ball from your left hand. The balls land in opposite hands, having crossed in the air. The first one you throw is the first one you catch. Practice until you're able to repeat this ten times without dropping a ball.

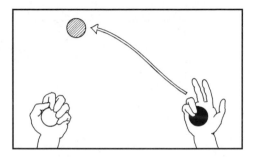

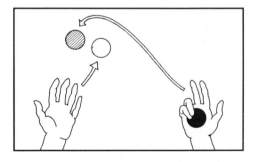

Juggle all three balls

To begin, repeat what you did to swap two balls: Throw the ball from the right-hand "basket" and wait till it reaches a peak. Now toss the ball from the left hand. When the second ball peaks, throw the third ball from your right hand. When the third ball peaks, toss the ball from your left hand. When the next ball peaks, throw the ball from your right hand. Now just keep going. Alternate your hands—right, left, right, left. One ball is always aloft, with another ball going up. Guess what: You're juggling!

But wait—how do you stop? Simply catch the final ball in the "basket" of one hand. And then take a bow.

While you practice, here are some tips to remember: First learn to throw consistently to the same height on each side; then

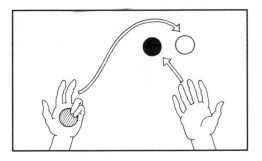

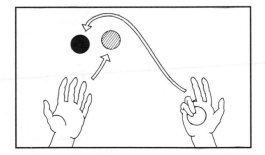
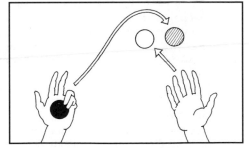

HOW TO JUGGLE BOWLING BALLS

Bob Whitcomb

"Look, he's juggling bowling balls. How does he do it? And, more important, *why* does he do it?"

Because it's a great challenge, it's something none of my friends can do, and it looks amazing. You're dealing with objects that are (1) bigger and (2) heavier than regular balls, so the way to learn how to juggle them is by tackling these two elements separately.

Bigger size Start by juggling three regular balls. Open up your juggling pattern—toss the balls higher and wider—so that the balls can clear each other. Then move up to juggling three basketballs. Don't grip them with your fingers; just catch them underneath. Basketballs help you master objects of large size without the encumbrance of extra weight.

Heavier weight Practice juggling shotputs; each should weigh about 8 pounds. (Bowling balls weigh 8 pounds and up.) Juggling shotputs will teach you to handle heavy objects.

Tips *To start* Hold a bowling ball in each hand and a third one on your right arm at your crooked elbow. When you toss the first ball from the right hand, the second ball will just roll down into place.

To stop Toss the last bowling ball extra high, to give yourself time to catch the other two balls. Catch one in each hand, letting them roll up your arms into your crooked elbows. Then catch the third one between your hands.

To stop with minimum finesse, just let the balls hit the ground. This method is not recommended if you have neighbors living downstairs.

To practice The best place to practice is outside on the grass.

What about dropping things on your toes? Try to avoid that. There's enough time when a bowling ball misses your hands for you to move your feet. (I always tell people to learn tap dancing first . . .)

If juggling three basketballs or shotputs gives you trouble, start with just one of them plus two regular balls. Slowly build up to more basketballs/shotputs. Then move to one bowling ball and two regular balls, to get the feel of it. Even if you never get any farther, this feat looks amazing in itself. You can also try juggling a grapefruit, an egg, and a bowling ball.

Juggling bowling balls close to you improves your leverage and is less of a strain on your arms. I arch my back and lean back so that the balls are up over my body, as opposed to standing straight and having the balls way out in front.

To add showmanship In my performances I start with a bowling ball in each hand and another on my foot; I kick that one up into the air, then start to juggle; it looks impressive—but it takes quite a kick to get going.

To get laughs Once I have all three bowling balls in the air, I say to the audience, "Now comes the tough part—trying to figure out how to *stop*."

As you juggle the bowling balls, look out at the crowd and say, "Remember, kids, don't try this at home. Try it at your *friend's* home."

Bob Whitcomb has juggled three 16-pound bowling balls for forty-seven consecutive throws—the unofficial world's record—and performs at festivals, fairs, colleges, and aboard cruise ships.

learn to throw in different patterns—high, low, wide, and narrow. Imagine an invisible wall about a foot in front of your body and keep the balls moving in that plane; don't propel the balls ahead of you, forcing you to walk forward to catch them.

Eating an apple in midflight

You'll need two balls and a ripe apple, which you're going to eat as you juggle. The secret is simple: Bring the apple to your mouth *before* you toss it, and take a bite. For starters, try just kissing the apple. You can buy time by tossing the previous ball extra high. That gives you more time to bring the apple to your mouth and back down before tossing it. After you can kiss the apple, then move on to biting off little pieces and eventually— especially if you favor a quick, sloppy style for this stunt—to chomping off big juicy chunks. Learn to do this with either hand; then you can stuff the apple in your mouth with both hands. Audience reaction is guaranteed.

> **I am interested in everything so long as it is well done. I would rather see a good juggler than a bad Hamlet.**
> —*C. B. Cochran*

FOR MEN AND WOMEN ONLY

HOW TO DECIPHER A WINE LABEL

Robert Mondavi

Robert Mondavi operates the Robert Mondavi Winery in the Napa Valley of California, where in the 1950s he originated the tradition of public wine tasting.

Oenologists do extensive scientific research to understand and improve the fundamentally mysterious process of winemaking. Let's unravel another mystery—what the wine label tells you about the contents of the bottle.

Appellation

This indicates the area a wine comes from. A California appellation means only that it comes from somewhere in the state, while a Napa Valley appellation indicates that it was made in this one highly regarded region.

Varietal name/regional name

If an American wine label says "Cabernet Sauvignon," federal regulations require that at least 75 percent of the wine must be made from cabernet grapes; for "Chardonnay," at least 75 percent of the grapes must be chardonnay; and so forth. In other words, the label indicates the varietal name. But French wines are labeled by area. If it's called a Bordeaux, you could have a Merlot, a Cabernet Sauvignon, or a Cabernet Franc. You know it comes from Bordeaux, but as for the types of grapes, they are blended in the proportions the individual winery has determined appropriate for the vintage and the style of wine it wants.

Sometimes too much drink is barely enough.
—Mark Twain

"Estate bottled"

On the label of a French wine, the term "estate bottled" guarantees that the grapes were grown on the estate—meaning the vines grow next to the winery—and that the wine was produced there. If the label says "Mouton Rothschild," for example, the grapes were actually harvested and the wine made on the Rothschild estate. In the United States, "estate bottled" means that the grapes have to be grown within a single county. A winemaker may have two pieces of vineyard, one next to the winery and one a mile or two away.

A wine that isn't estate bottled can come from various locations, some good and some not so good; that leaves you uncertain. The advantage of drinking an estate-bottled wine is that it comes from a certain place whose quality is known. It's easier to predict: If you've tasted that wine before, you can pretty much bank on what it will taste like this time.

"Produced and bottled by"

The phrase "produced and bottled by" means that the wine has to be produced by the winery and bottled by the winery. Although this seems obvious, it's easy to confuse the term with "made and bottled by." That designation means that all a winery has to do is make 10 percent of the wine, buying the balance from various producers and blending it. You never know how wines will react when they are blended; sometimes the result isn't good. So you're better off when a wine label says "produced and bottled by," because it usually indicates a winery that watches its wine-making much more carefully.

REMOVING RED WINE STAINS

Don Aslett

Catch the stain quickly! Use a good towellike material and cool water. Absorb—don't rub! Vinegar is the best all-around "solution" for a wine problem. Rubbing salt (as a poultice to absorb the stain out) has some benefit. If the stain remains, sponge with 91 percent pure alcohol from the grocery store. As a last resort, bleach the material to its tolerance level.

Cleaning expert Don Aslett has written a number of books, including Do I Dust or Vacuum First?

WINE TASTING MADE EASY

There is no reason to be intimidated by a mere bottle of wine—especially when you can unlock its secrets very easily. Just use your senses.

Sight A wine buff holds his glass by the stem, with the base flat on the table, and swirls the wine. Why? When the wine runs down the sides of the glass, it shows its "legs"—a term referring to stripes or columns of liquid. A wine with "good legs" is thicker and has more substance than wine that slides down the glass in sheets (an indication that it is thin and lacks interest for the oenophile).

Because there is an ideal color for each wine variety, we can learn a lot about wine from visual clues. Chenin Blanc should be the color of pale straw, for example. The more complex Chardonnay should be a richer gold, and if it's pale, it probably tastes weak or watery. A wine merchant can tell you the ideal color for each variety.

Smell Another reason for swirling the wine is to mix it with air, which volatilizes the alcohol and releases chemical compounds you can smell. Our noses can detect thousands of different odors in wine. As for wine terms: "Aroma" is the smell of the grape itself. "Bouquet" refers to the fragrances created in winemaking (the yeast used in fermentation, the type of oak used for barrel aging, and so forth). The sum of all the aromas in a wine is called its "nose."

Before you drink a bottle of wine, don't forget to sniff the cork: If the wine has turned sour, you'll have an early warning.

Taste Our taste buds detect just four flavors—sweet (front of tongue), sour (edges), salty (middle), and bitter (back). To taste sweetness, draw a sip of wine up the middle of your tongue; wine tastes sweet at a level of .7 percent residual sugar; below that, "dry" (which means free of sugar, not to be confused with astringent or tart). Roll another sip around the edges of your tongue and notice the acid, which gives a wine tartness and life; a wine without acid components is called "flabby." If the wine has an agreeable proportion of acidity, sugar, and other elements, it is said to have "balance."

To serve a bottle of wine properly, uncork it a while before serving it. This airing gets rid of chemical vapors and also adds oxygen to mellow the flavors and allow them to meld.

Feel Warm a sip of wine in your mouth for a moment, then judge its weight, or "body"—how thick or thin it feels. Some wines have a lush feel that tasters try to capture with words like "velvet." In red wines, especially, you'll detect the dry, puckery feeling of tannins, which are natural preservatives produced by the skins of grapes. The term "big" is used for wine that fulfills the senses.

No two people have the same proportion of taste buds, so no wine tastes the same to everyone. If *you* like it, nothing else matters.

—*J. D.*

Contents

The label indicates whether the bottle contains 750 milliliters, a fifth of a gallon, or some other amount. Since 750 milliliters is less than a fifth, you should consider the size of the bottle when you compare the prices of various bottles of wine. Wine also comes in larger sizes; a magnum holds about 1.5 liters, and table wine often comes in 3-liter bottles.

Percentage of alcohol

Not all labels indicate this information. The range for table wines is from 10.5 to 14 percent alcohol; dessert wines run 17 to 21 percent. Legally, a wine can be within 1.5 degrees of the percentage on the label; in other words, if the bottle says "12% alcohol," the actual amount is somewhere from 10.5 up to 13.5 percent. If a wine has a high alcohol content, you know to take it a little easier when you drink it.

How Much to Tip the Wine Steward

• I'm in the wine business, so I usually tip 20 percent of the cost of the wine. Most people, though, put down 10 or 15 percent, depending on how helpful and informative the wine steward, or *sommelier* (sum-ul-*yay*), has been. I think most wine stewards prefer to receive cash, discreetly tendered from hand to hand, but if you don't have the change, just include the tip on your credit card slip on a separate line from the tip for the waiter.

> My grandmother is over eighty and still doesn't need glasses. Drinks right out of the bottle.
> —*Henny Youngman*

DRIBBLE A BASKETBALL BETWEEN YOUR LEGS

James "Twiggy" Sanders

Delighting fans with his hilarious antics on the court with the Harlem Globetrotters, Twiggy Sanders is known across the world as the "Clown Prince of Basketball." He has perfected an awesome repertoire of trick passes, fakes, shots, and dunks.

If you're dribbling with your right hand, do this trick when your left foot is forward. You want to have a comfortable stance. Don't spread your legs too wide—or else your opponent will know the ball is going between them.

Bounce the ball directly between your legs. The ball hits an imaginary line drawn from the middle of your body down to the floor.

Your left hand is held on your buttock, ready to catch the ball when it bounces up. There should be enough bounce on the ball so that it comes up to meet your hand; you shouldn't have to bend down to catch it.

What to do next?

Drive. After catching the ball with the left hand, it's easy to change direction and drive left. You've got your body between the defensive man and the ball, so he can't get to it.

Bounce back. If the defensive player tries to go around you, bounce the ball back through your legs to the right hand and move forward, eluding him.

Bounce-pass. Instead of shooting the ball, bounce-pass it back through your legs to a teammate. Then . . .

Fake. After the pass, serve as a decoy by continuing to drive to the basket as if you still had the ball and were going to take a shot. The other team's attention is on you—leaving your teammate wide open to shoot a basket.

Practice drill

Walk forward while bouncing the ball from hand to hand between your legs—one bounce for each step. This takes practice, but it gives you a good feel for the ball and helps you perform the trick with either hand.

FAKEOUTS AND TRICK MOVES

Defense Know where to look. With all the shake-and-bake moves that players have now, you can easily get faked out. But my high school coach taught me the secret of guarding someone. He said, "Watch the guy's belly button." No matter where he shifts his head, and despite all his fancy moves, he can't go anywhere without his belly button; he's got to take it with him. So concentrate on it, and move in the direction it goes.

Offense When you handle the ball, never look at it; always look straight ahead. This is very deceptive, because your opponent doesn't know where you're going or what you're going to do next. (Looking down at the ball puts you at a disadvantage, because you can't see where you're going.) To dribble without watching the ball, you have to imagine in your mind's eye where it will bounce.

Master the head fake. Let's say you snag a rebound under the basket, but your opponent is on you and you're afraid he's going to block your shot. Here's how to fool him with a head fake: Starting from a crouch, lift up your head strongly, like a pump; your shoulders follow. Raise the ball over your head as if you're really going to shoot

it. Make a face, grunt—be really convincing. Then bring the ball down quickly and crouch. Throughout this fake you never leave the floor; everything goes up but your feet. Your goal is getting the defensive man to commit himself—to jump high trying to block the "shot." If he jumps, you're in a great position: You can wait until he's coming down and then go up for a clear shot. Or once he's up in the air, you can pass the ball to a teammate. Or you can just step into him and make him foul you.

Dunk the ball without looking at the basket. Most players think that when you get ready to shoot, you've got to look at the goal. But you can learn to dunk or do a layup "blind." Here's the secret: In basketball one thing that never changes is the location of the lines on the floor—the lane, baselines, and foul line. By looking at the floor, I can determine where I am in relation to the basket. I just dribble along, looking down, and my opponent thinks I'm concentrating on something else. Then suddenly I go up—and usually I find that rim. I figured out this trick in college, when I was 6'8" but only weighed 170 pounds and couldn't dominate many players. Instead, I had to deceive them.

How to Tie a Bow Tie

Gene Shalit

Gene Shalit has been a
commentator on
NBC's *Today Show*
since 1969.

Great men wear bow ties.

Lincoln. Churchill. Roosevelt.

Evil men wear long ties. Hitler.

A bow tie is elegant. It is always neat: You can never spill gravy on a bow tie (unless you dine while standing on your head).

A bow tie is economical. If it wears out, simply turn it over.

INSTRUCTIONS FOR TYING A BOW TIE

1. Put on a shirt (important). Raise the collar.

2. Select an appropriate tie.

3. Place it under the shirt collar and around your neck. (Professional wrestlers who do not have necks should eschew bow ties.)

4. Professional wrestlers should look up *eschew.*

5. Now allow the two ends of the bow tie to hang down so they are even. (If the tie has three ends, it is not even, it is odd.)

6. Oh, one thing. Before you drape the tie around your neck, adjust the thingamajig on the back so that it conforms to your neck size.

7. If you wear a size 19 or larger, discard the bow tie and apply for a job as a professional wrestler (see No. 3).

8. Grip the right end and gently pull down so that the right end is 2–3 inches longer than the left end. (Note to football players: I mean the right and left ends of your *tie.*)

9. Cross the right end over the left end, making an X. Then take one of the ends and loop it under and pull it through the loop (there, you've got it), and then yank both wings with a short sharp motion, uh-huh. Now fuss with it just . . . a . . . little . . . bit . . . and then shape it—careful, careful— just the way you want it—and *voilà!* Finito!

10. Nice going.

Next week: How to Put On Your Socks

There are two sorts of bow ties.

One is Real: You tie it yourself.

One is False: You clip it on and apply for a job as a waiter.

How to Tell:

If a bow tie looks perfect, you can bet it is False.

A Real bow tie should look slightly askew. It should flop slightly at one end.

It is impossible to make a Real bow tie look perfect, because if it's perfect it's False, and if it is False it isn't Real (i.e., False).

A bow tie's pattern should reflect the personality of the wearer.

Attractive patterns are *In.*

Patterns your wife's cousin selected for you are *Out.*

Solid colors are *Out* (unless you are going to a funeral).

Funerals are *Out.*

An elegant individual is a person who can tie a bow tie without looking into a mirror.

Checking yourself in a car window just before you enter the party is *In.*

If you are caught at it, it's *Out.*

About the Necktie

• In a store the necktie department is usually right in front, because ties are impulse items. Women buy 60 percent of all ties.

• The 100 million neckties sold each year, knotted end to end, would circle the globe three times.

• When a Spaniard wishes to insult another man, he points to his own necktie, a gesture indicating, "Your wife gave me this."

• "The great advantage of wearing bow ties is so no one will mistake you for a lawyer," observes columnist George Will, who wears them regularly. "The bow tie wearer is an independent thinker; no wonder lawyers don't want them on juries."

• Suave and stylish Fred Astaire sometimes used a necktie instead of a belt to hold up his pants.

—J.D.

GET RID OF RATS AND MICE

Michael Bohdan

Exterminator Michael Bohdan runs the Pest Shop, Inc., in Plano, Texas, and often appears on television.

As a rule of thumb, for every rat or mouse you see, there may be six to twelve others in your house. Once they get in, there is no humane method of coaxing them to move out. You have to do away with them. If you understand them, you can do it more effectively.

Traps

Don't use cheese as bait. Use cotton; the female mouse will think it's nesting material. Or try peanut butter, because mice are always hungry—and who doesn't like peanut butter? One trick is to rub the wooden base of the trap with bacon grease; a rat tries to lick it and gets zonked on the head.

Place traps against walls. Rodents always move along a wall, with their whiskers touching it for security. A trick for catching a really wiley old-timer is to place a 3-inch board perpendicular to the wall; then set a trap 4 inch-

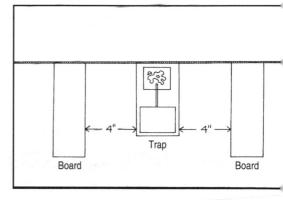

es away, with the bait tray toward the wall; leave a few inches of open space; then place another 3-inch board, and another trap. When the rat scurries along the wall, it will see the board and jump over, landing on the trap (see illustration).

Attach a trap to a vertical pipe, using duct tape. Rats are very good climbers. If a rat crawls up the pipe to get from one part of the house to another, he'll be caught.

Glueboard

Sold in hardware stores, glueboard is like very sticky flypaper. To make a trap with it, cut two entry holes in an inverted shoebox and place the glueboard under the box. A mouse or rat will go inside, seeking security, and get nailed by the glueboard. Or you can form the glueboard into a tube and stick it inside a length of 3- or 4-inch-diameter PVC plastic pipe. Put this infernal device in the bushes alongside the house, or against the wall behind the sofa if you see a mouse in your living room; the mouse will run along the wall, duck into the pipe for security, and get stuck.

Rodent-proofing

Rodent-proofing could prevent 90 percent of rats and mice from getting into your house. Walk around outside and caulk cracks or holes where they might enter. (Remember, mice can squeeze through a mere ¼-inch hole.) If your house has a crawl space, check ventilation openings and replace any deteriorated screens. Don't put cat or dog food in your garage or outside at night, because it attracts rodents.

CATCHING RATS AND MICE

It's important to know whether you've got mice or rats, which you can discern from their droppings. Mouse droppings are ¼ inch long, while rat droppings range from ½ to ¾ inch long and are fatter. A mouse travels up to 20 feet from its nest, while a rat roams 100 feet. So if you see mouse droppings, you know the nest is within 20 feet and you can lay your traps accordingly; if it's a rat, you will have to cover five times as much distance from the droppings.

Rats and mice are opportunists; don't give them a free meal or an easy way to get into your house.

THOSE AMAZING RATS

The United States has an estimated 200 million rats.

Rats can squeeze through a hole of just ½ inch. If a rat's skull will fit through a hole, it can elongate its body to pass through.

Rats can chew through aluminum sheeting, cinder block, lead, concrete, even glass. (Rodents' incisor teeth grow continuously, and to wear them down, they have to gnaw—even when they're not hungry.)

Without suffering serious injury, rats can fall from a height of 50 feet. They can jump 3 feet straight up and leap 4 feet horizontally.

Rats can swim half a mile and tread water for up to three days. They have been known to swim up broken sewer lines, surfacing in toilets.

Each year 45,000 people—mostly children under age six—suffer from rat bites. A quarter of all fires of unknown origin may be caused by rats gnawing the insulation off electrical wires and creating short circuits.

YOU CAN CARRY A TUNE

Seth Riggs

> Seth Riggs, a vocal instructor in Los Angeles, has taught seventy-six Grammy winners; he coached Michael Jackson for the best-selling album of all time, *Thriller*. His opera pupils are singing major roles with the Metropolitan Opera, Covent Garden, La Scala, and other companies.

Singing isn't as hard as most people imagine. We think of it as a special action, but singing is really just sustained speech. So the secret is simple: Don't do anything different than when you speak. You don't need to raise your shoulders, extend your arms, wrinkle your brow, stand on tiptoe, or do anything else unnatural.

To sing, you need just four things: *proper pitch* (hitting the right note), *duration* (holding the note), *proper breathing* (so you don't get choked up by a rising larynx), and a *nice quality* (which comes from having *vibrato*, or oscillation, in your voice). If you can't sing on key yet, or if you can but want to improve your voice, try this method.

Warm up.

Before singing, you need to get your voice active and stretch its range. Here is a simple exercise—the same one I use in coaching Michael Jackson, Julie Andrews, Stevie Wonder, Anita Baker, Julio Iglesias, Natalie Cole, opera singers, and all my other students.

1. Do a trill. One way is by rolling the tip of your tongue against your upper palate, just behind your teeth, as if you were saying "B-R-R-r-r-r-r-r-r-r." If you can't do that, you can make

a trill with your lips; it sounds like a horse or a motorboat: "puh, puh, puh, puh." While you do the trill, your voice can make a sound at some comfortable pitch.

2. Slide the pitch of the trill smoothly up and down. It sounds kind of like a siren, rising and falling. (The *loudness* of your voice doesn't rise and fall, only the *pitch*.) Extend the pitch as high and as low as you can without straining.

This simple exercise brings several benefits. It gives you the ability to hit many different pitches up and down the scale. It lets you sing a greater range of notes than if you sang syllables, like "Mi-mi-mi-MI-MI-MI-mi" or "oh-oh-oh-OH-OH-OH-oh." And singing a trill is so totally silly that you won't get discouraged and think, "I'm not doing it like Pavarotti or Streisand." You won't be intimidated. You're just warming up your voice with a funny exercise. (If you prefer to practice the trill in private, you can do it while driving the car with the windows rolled up—that way the men in the white coats won't take you away.)

Match pitches.

If you can get to a piano or guitar, play notes at random and try to match them with your voice—either trilling or using vowel sounds like *oh* or *oooh* or *eee*. Pick pitches that are within a comfortable range for you—which means close to where you talk. This is called your "optimum pitch range." To find it, say, "Hi, how are you?" in your regular voice; that's the range where you should start singing. If you have trouble telling if you are matching your voice to the piano, use a tape recorder and play it back.

Another good exercise is to sing along with someone on the radio or with a recording whose voice is in your general range. Don't copy Janet Jackson if you have a low

TWO TIPS FOR NOVICE SINGERS

1. Don't use body English: If standing on your tiptoes helped you hit a high note, you could stand on a ladder and *really* get up there. Stay physically relaxed, without pushing or straining your voice.

2. Sing in front of a mirror: You can make sure you're not frowning, grimacing, raising your eyebrows, or doing anything else you're not aware of. Avoid continuous smiling, which raises your larynx and starts to choke off your voice. You should look conversational as you sing.

voice or sing along with Lou Rawls if your voice is high. You'll know that a singer is in your range when you don't have to strain or push your voice to hit the notes. With practice, you'll be able to sing along and stay right on pitch.

Breathe properly.

Correct breathing involves the diaphragm—the muscle in the pit of your stomach that causes you to inhale and exhale. First, you must stand comfortably—which means your rib cage is up; your shoulders are back and down; your pelvic area is flat; your backside is turned under. This isn't a military brace, just a comfortable stance that opens up your airway. Now just drop your diaphragm—which you do simply by pushing out your stomach. That creates a vacuum, and air rushes in to fill it. Instead of your "taking" a breath, the breath just drops into your lungs. To sing, expel air through your vocal cords by pulling your stomach (diaphragm) up and in.

As you sing, a steady stream of air should flow out of your mouth. You don't want your Adam's apple to rise, as if you were swallowing, because that will restrict your air flow and make you feel choked and strained. To test this, put your finger on your Adam's apple as you sing; it shouldn't come up much.

Another point: Don't gasp for breath, which tightens your throat. You'll notice that when you inhale properly and your diaphragm drops, the larynx seems to relax, too.

> **I can't stand to sing the same song the same way two nights in succession. If you can, then it ain't music, it's close order drill, or exercise or yodeling or something, not music.**
> —Billie Holiday

Add quality to your voice through vibrato.

If you sing "Mary Had a Little Lamb" straight and flat, that's how it will sound: flat. This is the way children sing it—almost yelling, with no expressive quality. But if you allow some vibrato (oscillation) in your voice, it gives the sound a nicer quality and adds overtones, making your voice more pleasing.

To "find" your vibrato, sing and sustain the word "she" on a descending scale (so-fa-mi-re-do). Look for a little shake in your voice. That oscillation is what you want to encourage.

To develop it, try this exercise: On a piano, play up and down the first five notes of the scale (do-re-mi-fa-so). Sing along, saying the syllable "ghee." Each time you sing "ghee," give it a little sob sound. You sort of cry up and down the scale. That should kick off some oscillation. (The best vibrato, by the way, is about six or seven oscillations per second.) I teach this exercise to the most sophisticated singers, and it really works.

Adopt this practice method, and you, too, could sound like a real singer.

The Italian language is peculiarly suitable for singing, having no awkward diphthongs and virtually no final consonants.
—*Frank Muir*

BUSINESS TRAVEL WITHOUT A HEART ATTACK

Robin Leach

Robin Leach, the host
of the widely syndicat-
ed television program
*Lifestyles of the Rich
and Famous*, once
flew to Peking for six
hours, did his work,
and took the plane
back, all in the same
day.

I travel more than an airline crew, logging nearly 300,000 miles on the road annually, and am home only about twenty days a year. So I had to learn how to travel properly or go berserk. Here are my tips.

Travel light.

You don't want to be your own Sherpa. A man can get through a week on the road with just one suit, slacks, and a sport jacket (a blue blazer works well). As for the rest, why do businessmen on a ten-day trip carry ten shirts, ten undershorts, ten pairs of socks? It's madness. Just pack a couple of each and use the laundry facilities at your hotel.

Don't pack at the last minute.

You don't want to be rummaging through your closet in a panic when there's only an hour left before the flight. I always have a couple of hanging bags ready to go, each holding the basic sport jacket, slacks, and suit. After I get home, I give the whole bag to the cleaner's. Later, the bag of clean clothes goes back in my closet, ready for the next journey.

Arrive at the airport 40 minutes early.

You have to treat traveling as a priority and schedule your day with the trip as the most important part. How often have you seen someone running late for a plane, flailing with his luggage, sweat pouring down his face, his chest heaving? It's heart attack material. Allow yourself extra time to get to the airport; once you're there, sit in the bar, restaurant, or airline club and have a quiet glass of juice or an evening glass of wine, with no wear and tear on your body.

Sleep on the plane.

Flying can be therapeutic and relaxing if you do it sensibly. Don't work, watch the movie, or eat. Instead, sleep whenever you can. This way you'll arrive more refreshed. When traveling east, there's nothing wrong with flying all night and sleeping; you can use a sleep mask, an inflatable neck pillow, and a mild sleeping pill if you need one. Be sure to get a window seat, so the passenger next to you won't be climbing over you to reach the aisle.

Stay in a good hotel.

Just because you're on a budget, you don't have to stay in a $6 motel. Every "best" hotel has a small room, even if it's the size of a broom closet, that isn't terribly expensive. You can use all the "best" facilities, just like someone paying $1,000 a night— and a bed is a bed!

The scientific theory I like best is that the rings of Saturn are composed entirely of lost airline luggage.
—*Mark Russell*

Refresh yourself on arrival.

If you arrive tired and thrashed and have to do some business right away, revive yourself with exercise and a shower. Ten minutes of jogging outdoors or running in place in your room, some push-ups, fifty stomach crunches—any of these will get your blood flowing and your juices pumping. Then take a shower and put on fresh clothes. It's amazing how good you'll feel, even after a long, hard day of travel.

Use the guest services at your hotel.

Many hotels will pick up guests at the airport, shine their shoes free, provide copier and fax services, and so on. Take advantage of them. And why not do things you wouldn't do at home? Get up half an hour earlier and have breakfast in bed— that's what room service is all about!

Stay on your hometown schedule.

At the same time I'm upside down in Australia, I still have a business to run in New York. So if my trip is fairly short, I try to stay on New York time. (I wear a second watch with local time on it.) This system allows me to do all my business back at my office as well as all my business in the place I'm visiting. I do stay up longer than usual and get up earlier. But I still get my normal amount of sleep by taking a nap in the late afternoon and early evening.

Have yourself driven.

You don't have to be a supersnob with a stretch limousine. Use a private car-hire service or town cars. The taxi fare from Kennedy Airport to Manhattan is $24; a private car is $32. For eight bucks, why not travel the last part of your journey like a king?

In the end, my main rule of business travel is to stay relaxed. I don't want to die running through an airport with an overweight hanging bag.

Anyone seen on a bus after the age of thirty has been a failure in life.
—Loelia,
Duchess of
Westminster

HOW TO BLUFF AT POKER

London Haywood

London Haywood
maintains that he was
the youngest nuclear
scientist on Britain's
H-bomb team, was one
of London's leading
sales promotion men,
and retired at age
forty-one; maybe he's
bluffing. It is indis-
putable that he has
three times reached
the final table in the
seven-card stud event
at the World Series of
Poker in Las Vegas,
winning purses as
high as $33,000, and is
a world-rated stud
tournament poker
player. He writes a col-
umn on poker in *The
Card Player* magazine.

The mysterious art of bluffing is obscured by a veil. To pierce it, you must understand that bluffing in a "no-limit" game (where you can bet everything you've got) is quite different from bluffing in a limit game.

Here's why: Let's say you're playing with a $30 limit on bets and a $60 limit on each raise, and there's $1,500 in the pot. Trying to bluff at the end of the hand with a $60 raise isn't likely to deter somebody from calling you, because he's paying only $60 against $1,500 for his odds. But consider a no-limit game where there's $15,000 in the pot and a guy bets $200,000 at you: You're going to have to think very carefully about what to do. Let's look at both types of games:

Bluffing in limit poker

Though you don't get much opportunity to bluff in limit poker, it can be done. Actually, "representing" is probably a more accurate term than "bluffing," because you falsely represent a hand rather than push a pile of chips into the pot in an outrageous raise.

Steal the antes now and then. As an example, let's take seven-card stud, where you start with two cards face down and one card up. You have an ace showing and you raise; unless another player has a hand with some potential, he's not even going to call. In this situation you can, as they say, "steal the antes."

Represent your hand early. At an early stage of the game it's possible to bluff, because there aren't that many chips in the pot; also, the other player isn't likely to risk his money drawing blindly against a raise.

Let's say that on the fifth card in a game of seven-card stud you have a king, queen, and jack of clubs showing. The other player bets his hand and you raise; you're representing a possible royal flush, although the likelier probability is that you've got two pair, maybe a straight, or even a regular flush. This is a good time to raise, because you give the convincing appearance of a strong hand and it's early enough to force the other players out. Whether or not you actually *have* a strong hand doesn't matter if the other guy is persuaded and folds.

Bluffing in no-limit poker

You have a huge opportunity to bluff when there's no limit on how much money you can wager. You use chips like bullets; big bets and heart-stopping raises naturally intimidate the other players.

The basic principle of bluffing in no-limit is simple: First, figure out what the other person has, then behave as if you have something better. Your figuring is based on his visible cards, the odds, his bets, his position at the table, what you've observed about his strategy, and a hundred other hints that add up to an instinct about the hidden cards he holds. Your bluffing is based on various principles.

Use reverse psychology, but only to set up a future bluff. Reverse psychology is simple: You put your chips into the pot very hesitantly when you've got a good hand and secretly hope to be called. You toss in the chips fast and loose—as if to say, "This is no trouble;

POKER PLAYERS' LINGO

Aces up—Pair of aces and one other pair

Advertise—To intentionally be caught bluffing on a poor hand in order to set up a win on a good hand later in the game

At the river—Seventh and last card dealt in stud; "We're at the river"

Babies—Two small pairs

Bean—Dollar, poker chip; also "clam"

Boat—Full house; also "full barn," "full tub," "saloon"

Boys—Jacks

Bullets—Aces; also "oil wells," "American Airlines"

Bump—To raise

Chip dip—Adhesive applied to the palm of the hand, helping a dishonest player to steal a chip from the pot as he places his own bet or shoves the pot across the table to the winner

Coffee house—Deceptive chatter and false assertions at the poker table

Cosmetics—Cheater's markings on the back of a card, including ink, daub, and tint

Cowboy—King

Dead Man's Hand—Aces and 8s; legend says Wild Bill Hickok was shot in the back while holding these two pairs

Dolly Parton—Two pairs, 9s and 5s, from the song "Nine to Five"

Four flush—Four cards of a single suit (five are needed for a flush); a "four-flusher" bluffs when he lacks the fifth card of a flush

Friend—Card that makes a hand better

Gut shot—Card that fills an inside straight

Inside straight—Straight filled by drawing a card to the middle of a series; i.e., drawing a 9 to a 7, 8, 10, jack

In the pocket—Cards face down in a stud hand

Jackson Five—Jacks and 5s, from the pop group

Judge Bean—Three 10s (perhaps refers to "30 days in the county jail")

Live one—Poor player, loser

Mop squeezers—Queens; also "dames," "hookers," "ladies"

Mortal nuts—Hand that can't be beaten; also "Brazilians"

Pee wees—Low cards

Pocket aces—Pair of aces face down in a stud hand

Rake—Cut of the pot taken by the casino as a fee for use of the poker room

Rat hole—To pocket some of one's stakes or winnings during a poker game; also, "go south"

Rats and mice—Two pairs consisting of 3s and 2s

Rolled up—The third card in stud; for example, two aces face down and one face up would be "aces rolled up"

Street—Synonym for card; for example, "fifth street" is the fifth card dealt in a hand

Subway tickets—Cards dealt from the bottom of the deck

Trips—Three of a kind, or "triplets"

Wheel—Hand consisting of ace, 2, 3, 4, 5; the best hand in lowball

Wired aces—One ace showing, one face down, in a stud hand

Yard—$100; also, "a bill"

call me and I'll take your money"—when you have a weak hand and hope to bluff out the other players.

Now, there isn't anybody over the age of five who doesn't know these tricks, but the whole point of this bluff is to establish a demeanor. By revealing your psychology, you set up an opportunity to bluff more effectively later in the game. For example, you have made a bluff for a small amount of money. The guy calls you; you show him your hand and say, "Oh, I haven't got anything; you win." He logs that away ("Ah! This guy tries to bluff"), and he also remembers *how* you tried to do it. So when the opportunity arises and you make a substantial bet at him, he's going to think, "Well, now; when this guy bluffs, he only bets a little bit, and now he's betting a whole chunk, so therefore he probably isn't bluffing." He folds—but this time you *are* bluffing. You've set him up.

Don't worry about poker faces; watch for "tells." There's a lot of nonsense aired about the "poker face." I suppose the nearest thing I've seen is John Chan, the "Oriental Express," a two-time world champion; he just sits there looking like a lump of stone. But every poker player has mannerisms and physical giveaways, called tells, that reveal what he holds in his hand and so help you to run a bluff against him.

The tells of amateur players are so obvious that you have to be something of an idiot not to notice them. The guy puffs his cigarette like a chimney when he's got a good hand and sets it in the ashtray when he hasn't. He leans forward in his chair or he leans back. Just watch.

With professionals, also, you may detect tells; but the more you play with them, the more you see that they're faking every damn one of them! (One pro told me he figured good players had more fake tells than he'd ever eaten hot dinners.) Pros deliberately make you think you have clues about what's in their hand; but, at the crucial moment, these clues turn out to be misleading.

I have a friend whose entire personality at the poker table is a misrepresentation. He plays the drunk, bluffing a lot and always displaying his cards whenever he wins with nothing. Pretty soon the other players all want to take him on. This is exactly what he wants, because now he reverses and plays a good, tight game while still appearing to be the sot. When they call his bluff, they find that he's got the cards, after all.

Master table talk. In no-limit poker there's a lot of calculated conversation, the idea being to make other players reveal what they hold. Most of the tricks pulled by professionals are vocal intimidation, which is really a form of bluffing. One player will fix another with a goodly old stare and say, "What you got, Fred? Two deuces?" or something like that, and then watch for any hint of a reaction—because the eyes always give away something. Of course, pros are so good at these shenanigans that they shout right back, "Sure, do I need any more?"

My own personality at the poker table is designed to do away with chatter directed at me. I tend to lean into the table a bit aggressively and adopt a quiet glare. It puts people off a bit, so they don't bother me much. Now, the reason I don't want people bothering me is that I have to learn a lot about the other players very quickly, and I don't want any distractions. (In poker, you need to find out as much as you can before you push $50,000 into the pot; it's not recommended otherwise . . .)

Bluff to get some free cards or save money. Sometimes I'll raise just to slow the other player down. If he knows that every time he bets I'm going to raise him, he's not going to bet. He'll check to me, and I can get some cards without paying for them. A particularly good time for this strategy is on the sixth card in stud poker. Then, if you make your hand, you can bet it on the seventh card; if you don't get the cards, you have the chance to check and save the last bet. It's a kind of reverse bluffing; you're just trying to save money on the hand.

Trap the other player. Let's say you've made a good hand after five cards in a game of seven-card stud. Don't bet it until the other player has caught up with you a little bit; let him build some strength so he stays in the game. Then nail him. Of course, he may happen to make a better hand than yours and nail *you*, but that's life. As they say, "Sometimes the lettuces eat the rabbits."

GROW A LAWN TO MAKE YOUR NEIGHBORS GREEN WITH ENVY

Jerry Baker

Jerry Baker has written thirty-seven gardening books, including *Plants are Like People* and *The Impatient Gardener*, which have sold more than seventeen million copies. He is a garden consultant to *The World Book Encyclopedia* and host of the nationwide Saturday morning radio program "On the Garden Line."

If you follow my advice, the greenest grass will be on your side of the fence. The neighbors will probably accuse you of painting it! But forget looking for magic potions at the garden store; a little common sense and some cheap, common materials do the job best.

For the home gardener, the first day of spring is August 15. What you do in the fall will determine the quality and quantity of your lawn, no matter where you live in the United States. Plants do their super growing—which happens below the ground—in the fall more than any other time.

Weeding

When the weather cools down in autumn, that's the time to get out and kill some weeds. Zing them between one and three o'clock on a bright, sunny day, when they are growing their very best.

Before you apply weed killer, give your lawn a bath with a

soapy solution. This washes dirt, dust, and pollution off the leaves so that photosynthesis and osmosis can happen, opens up the pores so that the weed killer can kill the weeds, and softens the soil so that penetration takes place. Use ordinary children's shampoo, which is ammonium lauryl sulfate. (In a garden store, this chemical is labeled "soil softener" and will cost you $18.95 for 8 ounces.) Mix a teaspoon to the quart, a tablespoon to the gallon, or a cup to 20 gallons. Apply it with a hose-end sprayer—that's a screw-on quart jar that says "20 gallons" on it. (You may ask, "How do I get 20 gallons in a quart jar?" You push hard. No—what it means is that when 20 gallons of water have passed through the sprayer, the entire contents of the jar will have been siphoned into the main flow.)

To actually kill the weeds, use another hose-end sprayer; put red nail polish all over it so you can identify it at a glance, and put an orange golf ball inside to act as an agitator to keep things stirred up. Bring the water level up to the 5-gallon mark on the side of the jar, add the amount of liquid or dry weed killer specified for 5 gallons, then put in a teaspoon of children's shampoo (or liquid dish soap, if you don't have children). Start from the left-hand corner of your property and move from left to right. Turn on the sprayer only over the top of weeds; because weed killer slows the production system of grass by 16 to 20 days, you don't want to cover the whole yard. (It's kind of like when you were a kid and your brother got constipated; your mother didn't make *you* take castor oil.) If you have weeds again in the spring, just repeat the procedure.

In places where you're afraid to spray weed killer—for example, around children or pets—you can spot-treat weeds. Take a quart jar of warm water, put in 1 ounce of children's shampoo, 1 ounce of vinegar, and a capful of gin. (I often garden with solutions of gin or beer; people say the crops rotate themselves!) You'll kill everything you shoot with this spray, because you've just made salty, soapy water. The vinegar is salt, the soap makes it cling to the weeds, and the gin is a secondary weed killer.

(You'll notice that plants don't grow very well under juniper trees, and gin is made from juniper berries.) Apply this spot treatment with a Windex-type sprayer, shooting a stream so you hit only the weeds. It works great on sidewalks, driveways, and among other plants.

Feeding

Dry fertilizer is a balanced meal for your lawn, just like having oatmeal every morning. Buy a bag of your favorite brand; it doesn't matter if it's for 2,500 or 5,000 square feet. Mix a 4-pound box of Epsom salts into the bag; in the fall also add a pound of powdered sugar. Epsom salts are the real secret; they're magnesium sulfate, which deepens the color of grass, thickens the petal, and increases the root structure. The powdered sugar is like a Hershey bar; it gets the lawn's engine running. (After all, what do plants manufacture for their own use? Sugar and starch. So supply it in a form the lawn can eat.) To apply the mixture, set your rotary spreader on half the recommended setting; if the fertilizer bag says "6," you set it on "3." Spread the mixture over your lawn before noon. You should apply it both fall and spring.

After you've fertilized, it's time to feed the lawn. You'll need a hose-end sprayer that you've never used weed killer in, with a white golf ball inside as an agitator. Pour in a can of beer—unless your lawn is on a diet; then use Lite beer. Add a cup of children's shampoo; dissolve half a cup of molasses in half a cup of warm water and add that; fill the balance with household ammonia. Spray it on your lawn (right on top of the fertilizer, Epsom salts, and powdered sugar). This mixture rejuvenates old soil that's been lying there, doing nothing, for twenty years; it also stimulates growth. The beer has an enzyme activator that begins organic activity in soil and eats up the thatch—the false earth that's built up by the roots decaying and by grass clippings you've left on top of the lawn. The ammonia is predigested nitrogen, which the lawn can snort right up. The soap cuts surface tension, so the food can penetrate the soil. Feed your lawn every three weeks, and you won't believe the results.

Mowing

Eight sheep to the acre is the best lawn mower in the world; that's what they used to mow the White House lawn when Teddy Roosevelt lived there. Of course, your neighbors may not let you get away with it.

Always mow after seven o'clock on a Thursday evening. That hour is more comfortable for you—and for the turf, because the grass has a chance to recover before the sun comes out, dries out all the tips, and makes your yard look white instead of green. The reason for Thursday is that now Friday, Saturday, and Sunday are open for honey-do jobs—you know, "Honey, do this" and "Honey, do that." Or it gives you a great excuse to go play golf.

A *sharp* blade is the key to mowing. You want to cut your grass, not whack it. A dull mower rips the petals and also pulls at the roots. If it pulls the rhyzomes loose, you get problems such as brown spots. (You may think it's the neighbor's dog, or bugs, when in fact it's the bug pushing the lawn mower.) After every two mowings I sharpen my blade with a #10 rat-tail bastard file, which puts a razor edge on any tool.

> **If the grass is greener in the other fellow's yard, let him worry about cutting it.**
> —*Fred Allen*

These days, it's a fad to leave your grass clippings on the lawn. If you like an ugly lawn, go ahead. Personally, I would love to have the barber leave the hair on top of my head because I don't have any. But on a lawn, grass clippings look unaesthetic. Besides, grass clippings are money in the garden bank: use them on your vegetable patch and between your annuals and perennials; as insulation and weed control, they're very effective.

Always trim very closely along sidewalks and driveways, using an edger or string trimmer. When grass lays too far over these areas, it's a breeding place for insects and disease.

Dealing with insects and disease

The best way to "keep lawn order" and control pests is to prevent them. One method is to give your lawn a springtime bath with old-fashioned Fels Naptha fatty lye soap. Cut a length that's an inch wide and shave it with a potato peeler into a quart of boiling hot water. Add 4 ounces of children's shampoo or liquid dish soap; or, if you want a real kicker, substitute flea and tick shampoo. (The soap is an emulsifier and keeps the Fels Naptha from ending up like a rubber ball that won't dissolve.) Take four fingers of Red Man chewing tobacco—it's been my sponsor since I was nine years old—put it in the toe of a nylon stocking, and marinate that in another quart of boiling water. You'll also need some Listerine or other antiseptic mouthwash. This weird solution packs a wallop. The Fels Naptha solution gives bugs diarrhea; they're so busy going to the bug bathroom, they don't have time to make trouble. It kills diseases, too. Chewing tobacco is a contact and ingestion poison, so the bugs start limping. The mouthwash is a bacteriostat, which inhibits the growth of diseases by screwing up their sex life. Use equal parts of the three ingredients—a teaspoon of each to the quart, a tablespoon to the gallon, a cup to 20 gallons—and apply with a hose-end sprayer. (A cup of each covers 2,500 square feet of lawn.)

Watering

You can't just put your turf on an automatic sprinkler system, set it to turn on every other day, and expect good results. There are too many variables: wind speed, the temperature of the air and the soil, the amount of sunlight that's drawing out moisture. Here's when to water: If you step on your grass and it doesn't pop back up, or if it looks funny and sort of iridescent. Do your watering between 4:30 A.M. and noon, at the latest. And when you water, *water*, at least half an hour on each section; 45 minutes or an hour is better. If you've been using the shampoo, which is a surfactant, you'll get good penetration and deep watering. Remember, shallow watering means shallow rooting—

and shallow roots grow up in thatch, which is the first thing to dry out. Water deeply every time.

One last secret: Always wear your golf shoes when you work on the lawn. They're mechanical penetrators that help foil the biggest killer of your lawn—surface tension. Remember when we were kids and we'd spit in the dust and it wouldn't go anyplace? That's surface tension; no lawn food or weed killer can get through until you penetrate it either chemically (with children's shampoo) or physically (with golf shoes).

If you follow these procedures, your lawn will grow like mad. In fact, you'd better run for the garage, because it will chase you up there and demand to know when you're having another party.

How to Decorate Your Living Room

Val Arnold

The work of Val Arnold, an interior designer based in Los Angeles, has won many awards and has been featured in cover stories in *Architectural Digest*.

Getting rid of things

One of the best ways to improve any room is to clear out as much as you can. A good system is to take out all the furniture and put it in the hallway. Have the room painted, new carpet laid, or whatever needs doing. Then bring back each piece of furniture in order of importance. Look at the stuff in the hall and ask, "What do I need the most?" It will probably be the sofa, then maybe a desk and two comfortable chairs. But at this point people start bringing in end tables and putting all their crap on them, and they stick lamps everywhere. The room starts getting crowded. Don't do this. To make it easy on your eyes, keep the room as simple as possible.

Be sure to leave space to put things—a bowl of flowers or the book you're reading—instead of cramming the room full. Many times I'll put just one thing on a table, but it's an important thing. Rather than spending $1,000 on three or four objects, you can do some diligent shopping and get one interesting head or bronze for the same amount; it won't be museum quality, but it can be very beautiful.

Arranging furniture

One of the master rules of design came from medieval churches, which were generally divided in the shape of a cross. When you look at your living room, divide the room in four. After you put the furniture in, you should be able to examine the four areas separately and have each quarter stand as a design on its own.

A room should have balance, or what designers call an axis. Architecturally, this means that if there's a fireplace on one wall, for instance, the opposite wall should have either a window or a pair of doors to balance it. Following the same rule, you don't want to put all your furniture on one side of the room. But the natural thing in American homes is to group everything around the fireplace—two sofas and a couple of chairs, a coffee table, and maybe a piano nearby. This arrangement totally wastes about two thirds of your space, and the room is so heavily weighted to one side that it looks as if it's going to tip.

I'd recommend that your arrangement not hug the fireplace. A fireplace today is essentially a psychological device that says "hearth and home," and it may as well serve the whole room, not just one side. You can put a big sofa back out of the way, with a pair of chairs to create a large grouping. Then put four good-looking French armchairs and a couple of tables around the fireplace. Four people can sit there, or you can take the two chairs from near the sofa and move them over beside the fireplace to make a larger circle. In eighteenth-century houses, people moved their furniture a great deal. During the winter they'd put screens around the fireplace and sit beside it, bringing chairs over from the side walls. In summertime they'd move everything over by the window and get some fresh air.

TIPS ON WORKING WITH A DECORATOR

Paige Rense

One: Be firm about your wishes. Some decorators have trademark styles, and if you don't want that, before you write a check you must have the internal fortitude to say, "I don't want Treatment No. 22. I want something designed just for me and very personal. If you're not willing to give me that kind of time or make that kind of effort, just tell me in the beginning."

Two: Be objective. If you really don't live the kind of life that involves black marble floors, why kid yourself just because you think you *should* like them? Your decorator can help you be objective by exploring the way you live; for instance, do you really want to spend a lot of money in the dining room if nobody ever uses it?

Paige Rense is editor-in-chief of Architectural Digest.

They also were constantly moving furniture according to what function the room was to serve that day. We can adapt this idea. Some of my clients already have a den, sitting room, and informal room, for example, so they really don't need a full-time living room. I sometimes suggest they use it as an all-purpose room. I make the room beautiful but fairly spare, with a minimum of furniture, and I use good side treatments, which means artwork, mirrors, and nice chairs along the walls. The clients can set up this room in various ways—for dinner tables, a small dance, or whatever the occasion requires.

Hanging pictures

If your pictures are any good at all, put them up. If not, forget it; I'd rather see a blank wall. Don't hang reproductions—Picassos and that sort of thing. Hang real pieces of art.

The most important picture can go above the fireplace. But don't think that you must have something on every wall in the house. One of the most chic places I've ever seen was a New York apartment done by a very well known designer; you walk in and there is one incredible painting, not very large, down at the end of the living room. It's the only piece of art. (The rest of the room achieves its distinction from the lighting, which throws shadows and forms that play upon the walls.)

When hanging pictures, the generally acknowledged rule is that they should be at "eye level"; but some people are 5 feet tall and some are 6 feet, so what do you do? Try compromising, placing the center of the picture 5½ feet from the floor. Still, you may have to make adjustments, using your sense of proportion and design.

Keep Your Cat from Scratching That $5,000 Sofa

Cleveland Amory

• First and most important, don't get your cat declawed. The operation is difficult and cruel, and it leaves the cat totally defenseless if he should get outdoors—which just about every cat does sometime.

• A good trick is to put a plastic cover on the sofa for a while, so he gets used to not using it for a scratching post. At the same time give him enough other things to scratch—maybe a fancy little carpeted "cat tree," or he may prefer just an old piece of wood. That should shift his interest away from your sofa.

• Even if your cat does scratch the sofa, think to yourself, "Which do I like better, my sofa or my cat?" If you have any trouble reasoning that out, you shouldn't have a cat in the first place.

The social critic and author Cleveland Amory is the founder of the Fund for Animals, whose 200,000 members help work to prevent cruelty to animals.

Hang every picture at the same level. Usually, it looks best to keep the tops aligned (although if the room has very high ceilings, you can align the bottoms). The tops will make a regular line around the room.

Hanging a number of pictures together in an attractive grouping takes a knack. You have to sort of wing it. And don't be afraid to make holes in your wall. I'm a hammerer; I figure there's going to be something over the hole, anyway, and it doesn't take much effort to patch and paint. Start with the most important picture in the center; it may be the biggest, the one with the strongest color, or whatever. Everything else should be geared to that. Next, figure out how many verticals and horizontals you have among the rest of the pictures. (Once in a while you'll have a round shape, which can be very interesting.) Decide whether you're going to alternate the verticals and horizontals up and down or from side to side.

When you hang the pictures, keep a consistent amount of space between their edges. And don't worry if something is half an inch off. Your home doesn't have to be perfect; it's much more important that it reflect your personality and have some interesting stuff in it.

Lighting the room

You need three types of lighting. First, some lamps, because you need light at eye level for reading and so forth. Second, some little 75- or 100-watt floodlights or spots in the corners of the room, pointing upward. As their beams shoot up into the corners, the light bounces down into the room. Third, some blasts of "laser light." Choose just a few things in the room to focus on—maybe a painting over the fireplace, a small sculpture on the coffee table, and something else on the other side of the room.

Hitting these objects with sharply focused light will create the excitement your room needs.

Nowadays, people overlight everything. Don't buy dozens of track lights, making the room look like a department store.

Getting a decorator's help at a reasonable rate

Find a good decorator and make a deal. Explain that you don't want him or her to do your house but just to come in and say what *should* be done; you're looking for ideas and creativity. Explain that you're willing to pay by the hour. Most good decorators charge about $150 an hour, with a $500 minimum. It sounds like a lot, but in a full afternoon a decorator can solve plenty of design problems and also save you from making expensive errors.

You can ask the decorator how to rearrange your living room, using the things you're stuck with. (The decorator's assistant can help push and shove the furniture around.) This reshuffling can so completely transform a room that I've had people say, "My God, I didn't think it could look like this!" All you've done is to put everything where it belongs.

How to Fight a Bull

Barnaby Conrad

Barnaby Conrad is the author of eleven books on bullfighting, among them the best-seller *Matador* and *The Encyclopedia of Bullfighting.*

I am fed up with all this mystique, all this moment-of-truth stuff, grace under pressure, oedipal urges, latent castration desires, homosexual aggressions, and so forth. What I have never seen spelled out is the basic, uncomplicated fact that bullfighting is fun. But, you protest, bullfighting is a dangerous and deadly business. How can it be called fun? The fun is in the nonprofessional variety, the amateur caping of young animals in the private arenas of the Spanish ranches where fighting bulls are raised. Any tourist in Spain can visit one of these *tientas*, plunk down a few dollars, and face a bull. (Well, not really a *bull*—more likely a heifer, which can be very tough, nonetheless.) In these amateur arenas there is no killing of animals, merely a caped ballet of bravery and skill. Here are some rules of the art, which will not teach anyone how to become a second Manolete, but could save you a few bruises.

Be sure the calf's horns have been blunted.

The points of the horns should be filed or sawed off; otherwise, even a year-old animal could turn you into a sieve if you make a mistake.

Use a *muleta* (the small cape), not the big cape.

The muleta is a piece of flannel cloth with a 2-foot wooden stick screw-eyed into it for a handle, used during the last third of every fight. It is much easier to manipulate than the heavy and voluminous *capote*, or big cape.

Remember the basic principle: Make the animal charge at the cape—not at your body.

The goal of bullfighting is to guide the beast past your flesh in a graceful and dignified manner. But fighting cattle will always charge at a man unless the man employs a few basic rules for making them go at the cape.

Start with a simple "pass."

Let's learn the basics as they apply to the *pase de la muerte*, or "pass of death." Don't blanch at the name; this is the easiest pass of all to do.

Adopt the correct stance. When charged by an animal, a man's first instinct is to clutch the *muleta* to himself in the subconscious hope that, since the animal seems to be attracted to it, maybe if he hides it the vicious little beast will go away and leave him alone. This is a disastrous move, as the animal will follow the cloth into the man's body. The man's next instinct is to bend his knees, hold the lure away from his body, and, at the charge, jump back out of danger. This may be safe, but it is incorrect and unaesthetic: People watch bullfighting to see a man behave exactly opposite to the way *they* would behave if down in the arena, to see him defy his natural instinct for self-preservation. Therefore, the proper posture for most maneuvers is standing straight, back arched, chin down on chest, feet planted firmly on the sand.

Spread the muleta *with your "sword."* Actually, a wooden imitation of a sword is used by *toreros* until the moment of the kill. Insert the point in the folds of the *muleta* and spread the cloth. What you have now is a target twice as big, twice as attractive to the heifer, and hence twice as safe for you.

Step toward the line of the calf's intended charge. Walk not toward the heifer, but parallel to it, with your *muleta* spread wide. Keep your back to the wall, because the animal will tend to swerve away from the wall—and you. It knows that a wall is solid; it doesn't know what you are yet.

When you are about 15 feet away, you stop, shake the *muleta*, and call: "Ah-hah, *vaca!*" (Shouting "Hey, cow!" in English, German, or Swahili will attract her attention just as well.) The heifer, suddenly aware of your presence, will drop her head and charge at you. At this moment you should be standing profiled to the animal, feet together, with the *muleta* in the path of the intended charge.

Do nothing. That is why the "pass of death" is so easy. You just stand there as the animal bears down on you. Don't move! She will head straight for the cloth, because she is intrigued by its size and quivering movement. Once the heifer is launched in its charge, make no abrupt motions, no jitterings with your feet, that might attract her away from the cloth and into your body. Stand as though dead—the reason for the name of this pass. (The only exception is if the animal should appear to be heading for your body; then give the cloth a sharp shake, but don't move your feet.)

With a great *swooooosh*, the heifer will charge into the cloth. That sound is tantamount to a bullet's whine—when you hear it, you know the danger missed you. The bulk of the heifer will hurtle under the cloth, the horns will skim by your legs, and the animal's momentum will take her several feet beyond you before she realizes that she has been duped and skids to a stop.

The audience will yell "*olé*" and you will feel a tremendous rush of elation, not because of the crowd but from the amazing fact that for a moment you controlled this wild creature. You avoided mayhem. But do not just stand there now with self-applause deafening you, or you will be in trouble.

Get ready for the next charge. The moment the heifer passes, take two or three steps back toward where she came from. This way, when she cuts her charge short and wheels quickly for the next attack, you will have a little distance between the two of you, a few seconds to prepare without being crowded and on the defensive.

Provoke a charge, if necessary. If she is slow to recharge, and is looking at you, not the cloth, take one step forward—that is, not toward her but toward the center of the ring, across the line of the heifer's intended path—and shake the cloth. This will cause her to charge, and you repeat the pass.

Retire gracefully. Do the pass several more times. Then it might be wise to withdraw from the animal and retire to the safety of the *burladero*, the section of fence near the side of the ring that serves as a protective barrier. When you get there you will discover that you have not taken a real breath during all this. Your hands are atremble and your knees are a little weak. But it wasn't as bad as you expected—it was a thrill, it was fun! *Olé!* Look out, Manolete!

GIVE A
CARTOON CHARACTER
A FUNNY EXPRESSION

Russell Myers and "Broom-Hilda"

A long time ago I wanted to learn how to draw facial expressions. What I did was to stand in front of a mirror and make faces at myself, portraying different emotions. Then I'd try to draw my cartoon character with the same facial expressions.

Here's how Broom-Hilda and I do this little exercise:

Russell Myers draws the syndicated comic strip "Broom-Hilda," which appears in more than two hundred newspapers and has been a feature of the comics page since 1970. "Actually," says the cartoonist, "it was brought over on the *Mayflower*, but it took five hundred years for public taste to deteriorate to the point where someone would print it."

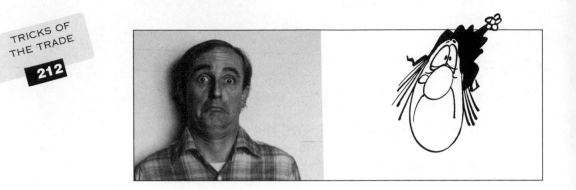

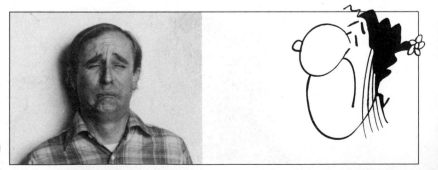

Eventually your characters take on lives of their own, as you can see:

"Annual Salary Negotiations"

WHITTLE A CHAIN FROM A SINGLE PIECE OF WOOD

Jim Porter

According to "Ripley's Believe It or Not!" Jim Porter's whittled chain is the longest one in the world. He lives in Galena, Kansas.

Whittling is relaxing. If you've got a pocket knife in your hand, you're thinking of something other than your own little hard luck. I get out there underneath a shade tree, and I turn that radio on a good country and western tune, and I just set there and whittle, that's what I do. My chain is working its way toward 1,000 feet long. There are five links in 1 foot of chain, and it takes me about 30 minutes to whittle one link—so you can see I've spent some time at it. A good way for you to try whittling is with a three-link chain:

Mark the wood.

You'll need a piece of basswood that's 1½ inches square and 6 inches long. Use a pencil to draw these guidelines on all six sides.

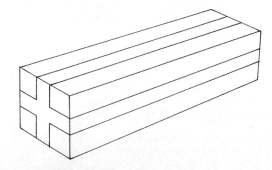

Cut away the extra wood.

Make sure your pocket knife is sharp. Now cut away the dark areas. Be sure to make little cuts, or you'll have your piece split or broken.

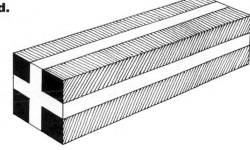

What you'll have left is a block 6 inches long and shaped like a cross at the end.

Draw and whittle the links.

On one plane of the cross, draw the two links that butt together; each link is 3 inches long. Then give the block a quarter turn, and on the other plane of the cross mark off 1½ inches from each end; the center 3 inches will be the third link, which you also draw.

Cut away the dark areas outside the links, and you'll end up with the outlines of your three links.

Next, whittle away the wood on the inside of the links. Carefully cut a little bit on all sides. Pretty soon, the links will be free. There's your chain!

There's only one secret to whittling: Just be patient and take your time. Whittling's not something to get in a hurry with.

DETAIL YOUR CAR
SO IT LOOKS LIKE NEW

Mike Slama

The owner of the Polished Image detail shop in Portland, Oregon, Mike Slama also meticulously restores antique gas pumps.

I'm a car buff and went into the business of automobile "detailing" ten years ago. If you want to restore your car to the way it looked when you drove it off the showroom floor, either for your own enjoyment or so you can sell it for a higher price, I've got a lot of trade secrets.

The interior

For general cleaning you'll need a toothbrush, a long-bristle paintbrush, a terrycloth towel, a car-wash mitt (made from sheepskin or a good imitation and sold at auto supply stores), a good all-purpose cleaner like Formula 409, and some vinyl dressing.

The paintbrush is handy for whisking dust out of tight places, such as around the levers on the heater. Use the toothbrush and some Formula 409 to clean in cracks and corners—the instrument panel, gearshift, and so forth. You can use Q-Tips to get into the holes of vents and radio speakers, especially if you want to put the car in show condition.

With a rag and some 409, wipe down the dashboard and door panels. (Don't let a cleaner dry on anything, though, since it can leave a stain; wipe it off.) If there are gummy spots, try mineral spirits or lacquer thinner; but be sure to test it first on a small, hidden spot, because it can remove the dyes in vinyl.

Now take a car-wash mitt—a nice clean one that's fluffed up and dry—and mist it with a light coating of vinyl dressing; a good brand is Turtle Wax's Clear Guard. Apply it to your dashboard and door panels, then wipe it off with a towel, lightly buffing out any streaks. The longer you leave the dressing on, the shinier the result. If you want a dull or satin finish, take off the dressing right away; if it's still too shiny, dampen a towel with warm water and use it to bring the finish down to a dull gloss.

Wood (or imitation wood) on the dash or instrument panel can be cleaned with Pledge. On older cars with painted dashboards use a paste wax, just as on the exterior paint.

Chrome trim can get a film on it, particularly if somebody has smoked a lot in the car. Using #0000 steel wool (a very fine grade available at paint stores), carefully wipe all the interior chrome. When you've removed the film, apply a light coat of wax; the metal will look like new again.

The gauges usually have plastic windows, which you should wipe with a soft towel, lightly dampened with water; use no cleaner. If the plastic is scratched, polish out the scratches with Meguiar's plastic polish, sold at auto supply stores; it also clears up fogginess in the plastic. (It does a good job on convertible-top windows, too.)

Windex works fine on glass. (Don't use 409-type cleaners, which can streak.) Spray two windows at a time; as you're working on the first one, the cleaner can be sitting on the next one, cutting the film. One little trick is to use two towels—the first to clean, the second to actually polish the windows, using light, quick strokes. Hockencrash towels—similar to terrycloth but without the little loops of thread pulled in them—work great because they don't leave behind any lint. (You can find them at any linen or bar supply house.)

The secret of cleaning in tight spots—for example, where the glass meets the dash, especially with today's aerodynamically slanted windshields—is to fold the towel over a rubber kitchen spatula. Because it's thin and firm, yet flexible, a spatula can get into the deep corners of the windows.

Next, we'll do the carpets and upholstery. Does your car have any odors, perhaps from heavy smoking? Usually a good cleaning will get rid of them. But if there's an unpleasant or mildewy smell, treat it by spraying Lysol or another disinfectant on the fabric the night before you clean the car. Let it sit overnight, and the odor should disappear. In my experience, sprays claiming to give an old car that "new car smell" don't work.

Now vacuum the interior thoroughly. Most of the dirt in the carpets and upholstery is loose dirt that can be sucked out. But your home vacuum cleaner probably isn't strong enough to do a good job, so take your car to one of those quarter car washes and use its vacuum.

Next, shampoo the carpets and seats. Usually the dirt is right on the surface, and I have a special technique for removing it. Wet a car-wash mitt in a bucket of warm water, wring it until it's just damp (not sopping), and spray some 409 on it. Shampoo the fabric vigorously; the suds will lift the dirt away. After you shampoo an area, run a dry terrycloth towel over the surface to pick up the foam and any loose dirt. It's important to remove *all* the cleaner, because soap leaves a light residue that actually attracts dirt. Dip a rag into the warm water, wring it out, and wipe everything down. By the way, I don't recommend those foaming carpet cleaners; they make a car look good but are hard to rinse away, so your carpet becomes a dirt magnet.

Here's a trick for anyone who has a home shop with an air compressor. If a spot just won't come out of your carpet (or seat), spray the cleaner directly on the spot, let it sit there for a few minutes, and then lay the hose down flat on the carpet so you can spray across the surface. Move the air nozzle back and forth, and it will literally blow the dirt out of the carpet. Be sure to hold a rag on the other side, so that sand and grit don't fly into your face or all over the car.

Sometimes there are more serious stains, but you can't quite tell what they are. Did someone spill grape juice? Ink? Cut a finger? You can remove many stains with lacquer thinner or mineral spirits; but be sure to test it first on a small area, somewhere out of sight. Look at your rag to see if it's pulling out dirt—or pulling out dye and ruining the fabric. Proceed very cautiously, and do a small area at a time.

On leather seats, don't use anything but saddle soap. Follow with a leather dressing, such as Lexol or Hide Food.

After you shampoo, roll down the windows and let the car dry out. (If you leave the windows up, you'll get a mildewy odor.)

The exterior

Most people wash a car with a garden hose and a bucket of soapy water, but that can't match the results I get with a pressure washer. You'll want to use one of those high-pressure wands at quarter car washes. Get the car wet all over. Spray a cleaner like Formula 409 on the tires, underpanels, wheel wells, under the front bumper, and anywhere else that's heavily soiled. Keep the car wet, to prevent the cleaner from drying onto the paint and possibly damaging the finish. The cleaner will loosen up heavy dirt; to knock the dirt off, rinse the car with a powerful spray.

To wash the entire car, fill a bucket with cool water and add a soap that's made especially for the purpose; don't use a dishwashing liquid, whose high pH strips the wax off cars. You'll also need a car-wash mitt. Start by washing the top surfaces, where there's less dirt; you want to avoid rubbing grit into the paint. If you see an area starting to dry off, stop and rinse the car again, so that soap doesn't dry onto the finish. Work your way around the sides of the car. And fill your bucket with fresh water occasionally; you don't want to rub dirty water on a car you're trying to get clean.

When the car looks generally clean, it's time for some detail work. Especially on lighter-colored cars, a film seems to form around the edges of the emblems on the hood and trunk. Spray each emblem with 409, gently scrub around it with a tooth-brush, and flush the area with water. Next, open the doors and clean all the edges with 409; spray the hinges, too, and wipe them off. I also open the little door of the gas-cap compartment and rinse out any dirt there.

If there is road tar, tree sap, bugs, or bird droppings on the paint, about 90 percent of the time I use kerosene as a solvent. (Be sure to test it on a hidden area of the paint first.) Wipe off the kerosene thoroughly. Later, you'll have to wax the spots where you used kerosene, because it strips the old wax.

Scrub the tires with a hand-held brush and Formula 409. On whitewall tires use Westley's Bleche-Wite, sold at auto parts stores, where you might also get a brush with fine brass bristles, the best kind for cleaning whitewall or raised-letter tires. To clean magnesium or wire wheels, apply a mag-wheel cleaner like Eagle I, which is basically muriatic acid diluted down to a safe level. Use a baby-bottle brush to plunge through the slots in the wheel or through the wire spokes. (Special brushes for this pur-pose are also sold through advertisements in the car magazines.) To rinse the wheels, hold the nozzle a few inches away and spray thoroughly from every side; too often people just wave the wand a few times and think they're done.

If your paint is dull or oxidized, you'll want to polish your car. This livens up the paint, brings back its shine, cuts any dirt or oxidation that's embedded in it, and prepares the paint for wax. (A lot of people don't understand this. They think you can have a horrid-looking car that's all scratchy and dull, put on a coat of wax, and fix everything; it doesn't work that way. Wax is just a protection, a finish step.)

You can't predict how an off-the-shelf polish from an auto parts store will work on your car, so I recommend using Zymöl polish, which is available by mail (Maru-West Enterprises, 3825 River Road North, Salem, Oregon 97303). A fantastic product, Zymöl is a real trade secret, known only to detail shops and true car buffs. If you don't want to wait for mail order, most auto body or auto paint houses sell a range of professional polishes; they'll recommend the proper grade. Apply any polish with a soft towel and follow the directions.

If your paint appears to be in good condition and feels smooth to the touch, you can get by without polish and just wax the car. You'll get back what you put into waxing, so avoid the creamy-looking waxes that are "easy to apply," like Raindance. They have cleaners in them, and if your car is slightly faded or oxidized, you're going to get streaks in the paint. I use a good carnauba paste wax. Meguiar's makes a couple of types sold in auto parts stores; but again, Zymöl makes the best product I've found. It has a heavy carnauba content, plus natural oils that work especially well on black or red paint.

Apply the wax with a soft cloth. Work on a small area, and don't let the wax sit for more than five minutes. Wax metal parts, too. Buff lightly with a cloth diaper, rubbing in small circles. I wouldn't recommend using a buffer attachment on an electric drill unless you're really skilled at it. But an orbital buffer is almost foolproof if you're careful and your buffer pad is clean, dry, and fluffy.

Now your car is shiny clean, inside and out. Why not take a spin around the block?

Oh—one more thing. You can't wash and wax a car without listening to the radio. It's the American Way! The younger guys in my shop like hard rock, cranked up; I'd rather listen to jazz. And there's nothing like a sunny day and some Beach Boys music.

TEACH YOUR HOUSE CAT TO RETRIEVE

Cristie Miele

Cristie Miele is a trainer at Animal Actors of Hollywood. Her credits include *Pee Wee's Big Adventure* **and television's** *Full House.* **She has trained reindeer in Norway and cheetahs in Africa for Disney studios.**

Your friends will be dumbfounded when they see your cat retrieve a stick. To train him, you use positive reinforcement—which basically means you give him food when he does things right.

First, you'll need to teach your cat to jump onto a stool about a foot high. Put the stool and the cat on a table; that's so you don't have to bend over during the training session. Now hold out a goodie and encourage him to come onto the stool. Meanwhile, you say "seat," because you want him to associate that word with jumping onto the stool. Work with him about four times a day in five-minute sessions. Within a few days, he'll be jumping onto the seat gladly, because he knows he'll get all sorts of treats when he arrives.

Now put away the seat. At this point you'll use a "retrieve stick," a wooden dumbbell that you can buy at a dog show or order from a pet store. Get the smallest size, meant for a tiny dog like a Yorkshire terrier. Lay the retrieve stick in front of the cat, and when he sniffs it, you exclaim "good!" and give him a treat. Animal trainers call this sequence "bridging," because you're helping the cat to build a mental bridge that connects his action to a sound (in this case, a word) followed by a food reward. When

> **Cats are smarter than dogs. You can't get eight cats to pull a sled through snow.**
> —*Jeff Valdez*

the cat hears the word "good," he knows immediately that he's done something right and will get a treat.

Having received a goodie for sniffing the stick, it's ten to one that he's going to sniff it again. When he does, give him another treat. It will take days for you to get him consistently interested in that stick. (The first time or two he sniffed it, it was probably by chance, and it takes a while to click in the cat's head.)

When he's gotten pretty good at it, you change the routine. Now when he sniffs the stick you don't reward him. He starts getting frustrated and thinks, "Gosh, initially I sniffed this thing and she gave me food. Now, nothing." So he might try and mouth the stick. (You can even try to put it in his mouth, although that usually doesn't work.) What can help things along is smearing a little bacon grease on the stick, to get him interested in biting it. Each time he puts his mouth over it, you praise and reward him. Go through this routine at least four times a day for a full week.

Once the cat knows to bite onto the stick, you bring back the seat. He'll want to get on it since he knows he'll be rewarded, and you'll have to restrain him for a moment. At this point, he's not really holding the stick in his mouth yet, so you place it in there just as you let him leap onto the stool. The moment he lands you say "good," he drops the stick, and you pay him his reward. Eventually, he figures out that he's supposed to bring this stick with him when he jumps onto the seat.

Next, each time you put the stick in his mouth, you say, "Pick it up." Soon he'll associate these words with having the stick in his mouth. You also begin to move the cat away from the stool—maybe a foot to start. Gradually it will click in his mind: "Oh! I only get my reward when this thing is in my mouth and I land on the stool." He'll take the stick with him when he leaps.

So far you've been placing the stick in the cat's mouth. Now

> ## Cat Facts
>
> • In 1950 a group of climbers in Switzerland was followed to the top of the 14,691-foot Matterhorn by a four-month-old kitten.
>
> • A Missouri woman left all her worldly belongings, valued at $250,000 in 1978, to her pet alley cat.
>
> • A cat named Towser, who worked as a mouser in a Scottish distillery, killed almost 30,000 rodents during her career.
>
> *(All cited in The Guinness Book of World Records)*

you lay the stick in front of him and say, "Pick it up." Because he's learned he gets a reward, he'll pick up the stick and jump onto the stool.

Finally, you can throw the stick a short distance and say, "Pick it up." He'll get it and bring it to the stool. Your cat is now a retriever!

For film work, it's good to have a cat bring the stick (or whatever it is) to a specific spot. If you want him to bring it to your hand, just modify the training a little, using a pie tin instead of a stool. As before, you get him interested in the stick by giving him food each time he sniffs it. Eventually (with the help of some bacon grease) he'll bite on the stick, and you'll reward him.

> **Cats are intended to teach us that not everything in nature has a function.**
> —*Garrison Keillor*

All this takes place over the pie pan. After he bites the stick, he drops it into the pan and eats his treat. Pretty soon the cat makes the necessary associations (the noise of the stick hitting the pan acts as reinforcement), and he realizes that he's got to drop the thing in the pan to get a reward. Now you move him a foot or two away. He wants to get to the pan and collect his reward, so you restrain him a moment, putting the stick in his mouth and saying "Pick it up" as he moves toward the pan. He soon figures out that he must hold the stick in his mouth until he gets to the pan.

Once you gain a little distance, you can start throwing the stick; tell him to "pick it up," and he'll bring it to the pan. Then try putting your hand *over* the pan and have him drop the stick in your hand. Soon he won't need the reinforcement of the pan anymore. You just toss the stick, say "Pick it up," and he'll bring it right to you.

With four or five short training sessions a day, the average cat will take about four weeks to learn to retrieve a stick. (Some cats *never* learn, so don't be discouraged if yours won't.) You'll need patience—but at the end you'll have the most amazing cat on your block!

Spit Shine Your Shoes like a U.S. Marine

Sergeant Eric Berger and Staff Sergeant Steven Williams

A Marine for nine years, Sergeant Berger is a senior drill instructor. Staff Sergeant Williams, who has served for twelve years, is a chief drill instructor. Both are stationed at the Marine Corps Recruit Depot in San Diego, California.

Sergeant Berger:

We train ninety privates every three months, and we have to teach these kids how to shine their boots. If you asked five drill instructors, you'd probably get five different pet methods. I say that my way is better than Staff Sergeant Williams's way!

When the boot comes from the factory, it has an outer black coating on it to protect the leather. I firmly believe that in order to get the leather to accept the polish, you have to remove that outer coating. So when the privates get their boots, they need to take them out to the wash rack and take a scrub brush to them. I tell them to use shaving cream; there's some kind of chemical in it that strips off the coating. You actually get the boot very wet, and there may be a couple of tan areas where you've removed the color. Then the boots should dry for twenty-four hours.

Now you need to apply about four or five coats of Kiwi black dye; the stuff is alcohol based and dries really fast.

For shining, in my opinion spit has never worked very good;

your saliva has acids that I think actually break up shoe polish. You need to take a T-shirt and wash it with soap and warm water, so there's no dirt or dust in it that can get into the polish. Wrap the T-shirt tight around two fingers. To get the ultimate spit shine, use a *very* small amount of polish; regular Kiwi black. If you wipe the T-shirt in a fast circular motion in the polish, that picks up the oil in it. Polish the boot in a 1-inch circle and work that small amount of polish in; the leather will suck up the oil.

It's a long process. A real good spit shine—we're talking garrison-inspection quality—takes about four days, working an hour and a half or two hours a day. So I have to build a positive mind-set into these privates' minds. The way I do it is, I talk very highly about these boots. I tell them that a Marine is on his feet about 90 percent of every day, and his boots are his lifeline in the field. I point out that these boots are the Cadillac of the industry when it comes to shoewear, and that they'll last forever if a Marine takes care of them properly. That's how I get the privates to put some quality time into their work.

> **I like work; it fascinates me. I can sit and look at it for hours.**
> —*Jerome K. Jerome*

After a year or so of keeping the boots in topnotch condition, you need to repeat the process. You tear off all that old shoe polish, because dust gets into it. (That's why I say use just a little polish each time, so it doesn't build up too thick.) Break down the boot and do it all over again; that's what keeps the boots in inspection condition.

Staff Sergeant Williams:

Okay, my way's a lot different. I don't scrub down boots. They come from the factory with a preservative-type coating, right? I don't take that coating off. I take a can of Kiwi black polish. I take my bare fingers and dip them in the wax and just rub it all over the boot. I rub in about ten coats—and I use a *lot* of polish for big, thick coats. I like to get a good base coat, to where it fills up all them pores in the leather. The whole idea with leather is it's porous, as you know, right? It breathes, it's got holes in it. When we spit shine shoes, we actually ruin the boot, because we fill in all these holes. But you've got to do that if you're going to get that nice gloss shine. Putting on these ten coats is a continual process; you don't even need to let the boot sit and dry.

Then what I do is, I take a big goddang table candle, and I light it, and I melt that Kiwi black polish right into the leather. I hold the boot over the candle and go all around the boot. The wax melts right into the boot itself, so it closes up all the pores. (Which is the same thing that happens to Sergeant Berger's boots after another six months of shining!) At this point, the boots have a dull, Hershey bar look.

Then I take a diaper—not a T-shirt, because a T-shirt is coarse—and wash it a few times, get it nice and soft, and dry it in a dryer. (That's the only thing I use that diaper for—unless my wife finds it!) I put it tightly around my fingers, and I dip it in water. The reason for the water is because any cloth material when it's dry is going to be coarse; the water softens the fibers, okay? I use small amounts of polish, like Sergeant Berger described. And it takes me a good 30 minutes to get a high spit shine all around the entire boot. I'm using a fast circular motion. And that'll bring out a shine so shiny you can shave in it!

There's lots of different ways to spit shine boots—but mine's probably the best.

PROMOTE YOUR COMMUNITY EVENT

Sonny Bono

Sonny Bono wrote "Baby, Don't Go" for Cher and created their image, launching a career that included hit records and a prime-time television show. Later, he became a restaurateur in Los Angeles and then in Palm Springs, where he was elected mayor.

Whether you are working on a charity fund-raiser or on a campaign for a new city park, you must organize and publicize your cause so that everyone gets behind it and it becomes a success. Here are the secrets I've learned, from my careers in show business, restaurants, and politics, that apply to promoting any event:

Get the attention of the press.

The press just loves people who create news—especially through controversy or audacity. Take Sonny and Cher in the sixties. Back then everyone was wearing suits with skinny legs and thin ties, and then—wham!— we came along with long hair and bell-bottom pants. It was a controversial look, so we got a lot of publicity.

Be able to deliver what your publicity promises.

If Sonny and Cher had had nothing to offer but a new look, we may have simply been classified as rebels. But we were able to perform—we had the songs—and that established us, beyond our appearance. You have to have the product to back up your

PR. Look at Muhammad Ali; he was audacious, but he always delivered.

Treat your project as a production.

To promote your community project, you must apply production values and create the sense of a big event.

Develop a "hook." In show business, the special thing that makes a performer different is called a hook. This is the sizzle that sells the steak. The hook is up to your imagination. Say you're going to stage a special event: What will make it unique and exciting? In Palm Springs, there was a vintage auto race that was always held at the airport, a drab location that didn't have the necessary glamour. But when I was elected mayor, I ran the beautiful old formula Ferraris right through the streets. The race became like Monte Carlo's, with a European feeling. That gave it an appealing "hook"—and attendance shot up from 4,000 to 30,000 people.

Enlist celebrities in your cause. It adds excitement if a famous person participates in your event. For example, if I want next year's vintage auto race to be even more successful, maybe I can get Tom Cruise to race in it. I'm always looking for another hook.

Choreograph your production. Let's say your town needs a new park and you want to make it happen. It may not be effective to just say, "Hey! We need a park!" First, you can stage a concert outdoors somewhere, which people will enjoy. Next, you start holding events outside every week, so more citizens come. Pretty soon they're saying, "Wouldn't it be nice if we had a whole park for things like this?"

The idea is to choreograph your production in small steps instead of one giant step; this leads to success. To put it another way, the secret is to draw one line at a time until the lines form a complete picture that people can see and respond to.

Help other people visualize your idea.

A promoter is really a salesman. Because you're selling a package no one can see yet, however, you have to create a clear picture of it for other people. To do this, you must have a specific vision in your mind; it's almost like a movie that's already played in your head. If you're vague and can't see every detail, then you won't be able to sell it properly. But if you're very clear, the idea can have as much reality for other people as it already does for you.

As an example, I always wanted to be a singer, but I don't really have much of a voice. A lot of people who listened to me said, "Forget it!" But I visualized my goal very clearly and didn't let anyone put up stops in my way. In the end, other people saw me as a singer, too.

How to Tell if
That's a Bear Track
Outside Your Tent
231

HOW TO TELL IF
THAT'S A BEAR TRACK
OUTSIDE YOUR TENT

William Gordon

William Gordon, of
SES Associates in
Cambridge,
Massachusetts, found-
ed the Trackmaster
nature center system.

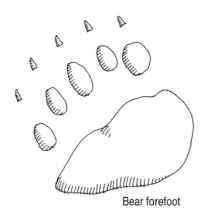

Bear forefoot

Bear hind foot

Yep. That's a bear track, all right. But what does it mean? Each set of animal tracks presents you with clues. You can be a wildlife detective—reading the woods, sharpening your analytical skills—and solve the mystery. The scenes illustrated here represent familiar animals in new encounters.

Clue: Consider the size of the slashes on the tree.

Story: The bear approached the tree and clawed it. Bears claw trees to mark their territory. Their long, strong claws get cleaned in the process.

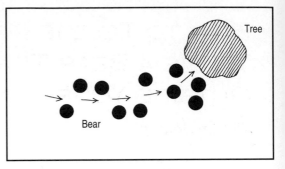

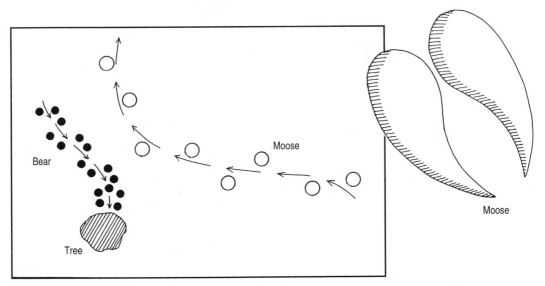

Mystery: Where did the bear go and why?

Clue: Observe the steady pace of the moose.

Story: The ambling moose was a sufficient threat to the bear to send him up a tree. A moose, with his enormous horns and huge size, is extremely undependable—timid one day and fiercely aggressive the next. A moose has been known to drive its front hooves right through the body of an automobile. Therefore, this bear was not being overly cautious in going up the tree even before the moose came into view.

How to Tell if
That's a Bear Track
Outside Your Tent

233

Story: There was no confrontation here. The fox tracks are on top of the bear tracks, which proves that the fox came *after* the bear.

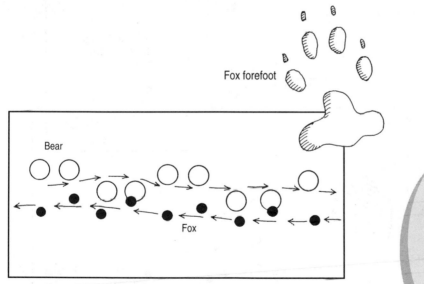

Fox forefoot

Bear

Fox

> **I'd rather wake up in the middle of nowhere than in any city on earth.**
> —*Steve McQueen*

Here are some encounters with other animals:

Mystery: What became of the rabbit?
Clue: Figure out where the bobcat came from.
Story: The bobcat dropped on the rabbit from a branch, killed it, and carried it off to a hiding place to eat it in private. The rabbit didn't know what hit him.

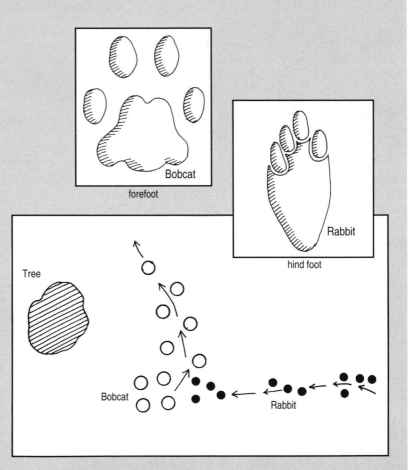

Bobcat
forefoot

Rabbit
hind foot

Tree

Bobcat

Rabbit

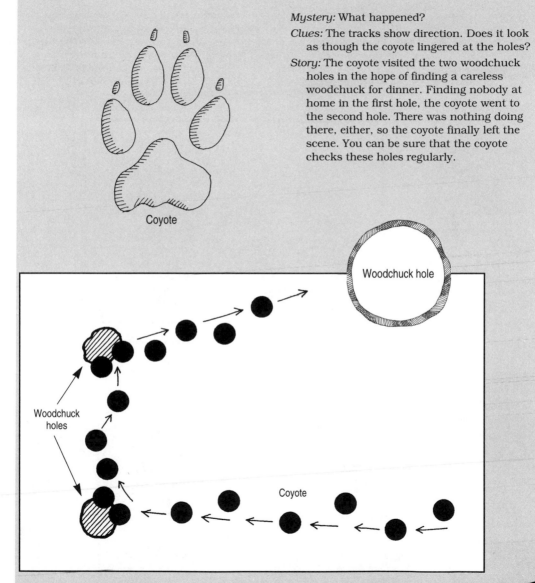

Mystery: What happened?

Clues: The tracks show direction. Does it look as though the coyote lingered at the holes?

Story: The coyote visited the two woodchuck holes in the hope of finding a careless woodchuck for dinner. Finding nobody at home in the first hole, the coyote went to the second hole. There was nothing doing there, either, so the coyote finally left the scene. You can be sure that the coyote checks these holes regularly.

Coyote

Woodchuck hole

Woodchuck holes

Coyote

Story: The weasel chased the rabbit right into his hole. The fact that there was an escape hole did the rabbit no good. When he made it inside the first hole, he must have paused for breath on the assumption that he could wait there or take off through the second exit when the coast was clear. He forgot that a weasel can get into any hole that a rabbit can use. Thus, we see the weasel tracks emerging from the second hole. We can assume that he is picking his teeth after a delicious dinner.

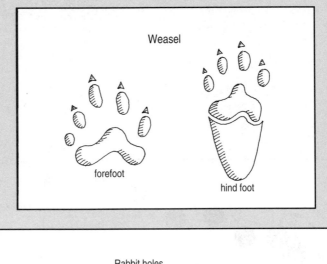

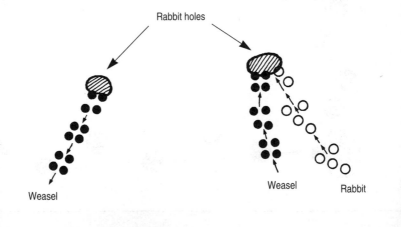

HOW TO COLLECT THAT $500 YOUR BROTHER-IN-LAW OWES YOU

A. Michael Coleman

The author of *Collection Management: The Art of Getting Paid,* Mike Coleman has collected millions of dollars owed by professional check bouncers, con men, white-collar credit criminals, and even the lieutenant of a Mafia crime family.

Remember the movie *10*? After it came out, everyone was saying, "How would you rate this or that on a scale from 1 to 10?" I turned this idea into a collection strategy. The script goes like this:

> "Brother-in-law, do you recall the Bo Derek movie *10*? Well, on a scale from 1 to 10—10 being that you're going to come to terms with your obligation and resolve this, and 1 that you're going to leave me stuck out in the rain—where are we?"

Notice that I don't use the words "pay" and "not pay." I substitute "obligation" and "leave me stuck," both to create guilt and to sidestep words that connote money. However, we still pass "Go." This technique also injects the element of humor. People like to laugh, and when you can extract a chuckle, especially in serious debt collection, you increase your chances of getting paid.

Most important, this technique instantly gauges where you are with respect to getting paid. About 99 percent of debtors will respond somewhere between 5 and 8. If your brother-in-law answers in that range, it means he is acknowledging the debt but is not willing to bring the ball over the goal line. So the next part of your script is:

"Fine. How do we get to 10?"

"Well," he says, "I'm a little short right now."

In response to that, *never* ask, "What can you afford to pay?"—because the debtor will, naturally, pick the lowest amount. On that $500 debt, your brother-in-law will say something like, "All I can afford is $10 a month." So never let him dictate the terms; you put yourself in a position of weakness in the negotiations. Instead, ask him:

> **The richer
> your friends,
> the more they
> will cost you.**
> —*Elisabeth
> Marbury*

"Well, how short are you of the $500?"

He'll say something like, "I'm $400 short."

That's fine. Now you're going to get $100 right away rather than $10! Collect the hundred, and set up a payment schedule for the balance.

IF YOU HAVEN'T LENT THE MONEY YET . . .

Remember my motto: "A friend in need is a pest indeed." Hard experience has taught me a lesson: Don't extend credit to relatives or friends. Strange as it sounds, the most difficult debt you'll ever collect is from someone close to you. When it comes time to pay the piper, they will intuitively put you last on the list, because they're relying on your friendship and goodwill.

If you must lend money to someone you know well, get it in writing. Be sure the loan is secured, or at least get a Confession of Judgment. A promissory note isn't enough, because it is only a *promise* to pay. But if he signs a *secured* instrument, you know he can't stick you. A

borrower should collateralize the loan to guarantee satisfaction and to show good faith—putting up a car, house, whatever.

"Wait!" you protest. "I'm not about to make my friend (relative, co-worker) sign over his car for a $100 loan." In that case, secure a Confession of Judgment, a standard legal form available at commercial stationery stores. If the debt goes sour, the signed and notarized Confession of Judgment becomes an automatic legal judgment in your favor, without going through litigation. Now you are in a position of strength and security. (Confessions of Judgment are legal in only about forty-two states, so check your state's law.)

WHAT TO DO WHEN "THE CHECK'S IN THE MAIL"

This strategy works when there's a larger amount of money involved and not necessarily a personal relationship. You telephone and ask for payment, and Mr. Pastdue says, "Let me write you a check and put it in the mail." Here is your script:

"Mr. Pastdue, I appreciate what you're telling me. I know your intentions are honorable. However, to make sure I can clear this up, what I need to do is satisfy my lawyer, who is filing legal papers [or "my accountant, who will enter the debt into a national credit-reporting data base"]. At my expense, I will arrange to pick up the check Federal Express, and that way we can credit your account and avoid any legal or credit ramifications. By the way, would you prefer that I have the check picked up this morning, or would you prefer this afternoon?"

Notice that you start with an empathy-building statement; you don't make it appear that you doubt the debtor's integrity and are actually saying, "I think you're a liar and aren't going to mail the check, so I want it sent Federal Express." It's not done that way; it's accomplished by establishing a sense of urgency, leading him to believe there are (a) potential legal consequences or (b) dire credit consequences.

> **There is no money in poetry, but then there is no poetry in money, either.**
> —*Robert Graves*

TAKE BETTER
SPORTS PHOTOGRAPHS

Brian Lanker

The photography of
Brian Lanker appears
regularly in *Sports
Illustrated* and won
him a Pulitzer Prize.

Anticipate the important moment.

The vital element in sports photography is
anticipation. If you wait until you actually *see* the important
action—when you think, "Oh, that's wonderful. Shoot now"—
you've missed it. It takes too much time to get your eye-hand
coordination in gear. At a boxing match, for instance, if you see
the glove smashing into the other boxer's face and then take the
photograph, you'll find when you look at your film that the two
boxers are now standing about 4 feet apart, looking quite silly.
It's when the boxer lowers his shoulder and you *think* he's going
to deliver a punch that you should be taking the picture.

Capture the peak of the action.

If your subject is a youngster doing the high jump, don't photograph him as he's leaving the ground but as he's rolling over
the bar. In all sports there is a peak moment, which you can
freeze.

Isolate your subject as the center of attention.

To emphasize your subject, make the background less clut-
tered. If a Little Leaguer is batting at home plate, move around
until you can see him without the snack bar and the Coke sign

in the background. Or let's say you're focusing past the coach's head to shoot the action—the coach may end up as a big, blurry object in the foreground. Move to the side and try to clean up the photo.

Learn to "follow focus."

Imagine that a soccer team is running toward you down the field. Here comes a player with the ball, about to kick a goal. But you have trouble keeping him in focus as he approaches. A simple exercise can take care of this difficulty. Go out to a running path and practice turning the focus ring on your camera as the joggers come closer or move away. You're working for a smooth

PROPER EQUIPMENT FOR SPORTS PHOTOGRAPHY

To stop the action, you want to shoot at a speed of 1/250 of a second or faster. That means having a 35mm camera with variable shutter speeds up to 1/500 of a second.

Your lens must not only allow you to record the action but also get you out of the middle of it; that means a telephoto. A lot of people make a big mistake by buying an inexpensive 300mm telephoto lens with an f-stop of 4.5 or 5.6, thinking it will give them great closeups. The problem is, given the light level of so many sporting events—especially anything at night or indoors—you often end up shooting at slow speeds, such as 1/30 or 1/60 of a second, to get a proper exposure. At that speed you can't hold the camera steady enough to avoid moving it, and because the participants are moving quickly, they're a blur. What you may want is a telephoto of only 105mm or 135mm with an f-stop of 2.8 or 2.5. Then you'll have the flexibility to photograph sporting events both indoors and outdoors.

With the new high-speed color films you can use a faster shutter speed, which will help you get a sharper image. Of course, everything's a sacrifice: You'll also get more grain in the picture, but that's better than uncontrolled blurring.

People think, "If I turn on this motor drive for a couple of seconds during the peak of the action and make a burst of shots, I'm bound to get the right photograph." But that doesn't happen; inevitably, the best moment happens between the frames. Also, you use up far too much film. I recommend using a motor drive (or an automatic winder) for a different purpose—to free you from having to take the camera away from your face or jar it to advance the film. A motor drive allows you to shoot a frame and still stay fixed on the action; you can concentrate on the image itself.

Buy a new piece of equipment *only* when you feel that your gear isn't allowing you to take a kind of photograph you want. Don't go equipment happy and look like a walking camera shop.

flow of focus, without any jerking. Don't bother to shoot any film; your practice will be rewarded the next time you take pictures.

Pick your spot.

I always like to stand wherever the other photographers aren't. Ask yourself, "Where can I be out of the way so I don't disturb the game but still have a nice angle on the person I'm trying to photograph?" Sometimes it's in the thick of things; other times it's off to the edge. You have to judge each situation.

Vary your shots.

If you want full coverage of a sports event, you should work different angles and look at the event in a number of different ways. Perhaps back off with a wider-angle lens to get a sense of where the event took place. After you've set the scene journalistically, then come in with tighter photographs. And be sure not to sit in just one spot in the grandstand, shooting with a long lens, or all your pictures will have the same look. Moving around to get variety will add interest to your slide show or photo album.

Look for the telling moments.

Try to be aware and open-minded at all times. For instance, sometimes the best picture takes place when the action is over. Maybe the great play at home plate has ended. The dust is still in the air, although nobody's sliding anymore, but the catcher is looking down at the ball on the ground, and meanwhile, someone is jumping in the air and running off.

Other times, just a face can tell the whole story. Maybe it's the elation of the pitcher coming off the mound after winning the game. You can capture the essence of an entire sport in a single, tight portrait.

HOW A PETITE WOMAN CAN APPEAR TO BE STRONGER THAN SEVERAL MEN

Merry Vaughan

Because she is petite, Merry Vaughan enjoys appearing to be stronger than she really is. She has been a zookeeper and magazine writer, but she learned these stunts at parties.

Vaudeville audiences were mystified by an act called "The Girl You Cannot Lift." A slip of a girl would come onstage and ask for a volunteer committee from the audience—all of them men who considered themselves pretty muscular specimens. With only the power of her mind, she said, she would make herself stronger than they were; then she would become so heavy that none of them could lift her. To the consternation of the husky volunteers (and the amusement of the audience), she did just that.

The secrets of this traditional act have rarely been discussed outside show business. The stunts can be performed anywhere, from a living room to a stage; I do them at parties.

At your fingertips

Announce that you will create such powerful magnetism between your fingertips that no one will be able to separate them. Hold your elbows bent and out to the side; your fists are against your chest, with the forefingers extended; press the tips together firmly. Ask two strong men to stand beside you, one at each elbow. They are to grasp your forearms and attempt to pull your hands apart. (When working with just one person, have him stand in front of you and grasp both your forearms.) Caution the volunteers to exert a continuous, steady pressure, with no quick jerks, in order "not to interrupt your concentration."

As you'll discover, they won't be able to separate your fingertips. You have a mechanical advantage: In this position, moving your fingertips would almost require pulling your upper arms out of their sockets. Although the secret is physical, there's also a mysterious mental component: If you truly *feel* that an irresistible magnetism is welding your fingertips together, the stunt seems to work much better.

THE LIGHT AND HEAVY GLASS

This experiment (actually an old magician's trick) demonstrates your strange power to make a drinking glass so heavy that no one can lift it. You need a hardcover book, a glass, and two handkerchiefs or bandannas. Hold the book flat in your right hand, with your fingers underneath and thumb on top. Place the glass on the book and spread a handkerchief over the top. Ask someone to lift the glass—which, of course, he or she can do easily.

Now claim that by putting the second handkerchief inside the glass, you will make the glass too heavy to lift. Tuck the handkerchief into the glass, then spread the other hanky over the top, hiding your right hand and fingers. Under this cover, shift your forefinger from the bottom of the book to the top and grip the glass firmly between your forefinger and thumb. Challenge anyone to lift the glass. No one will be able to. Before whisking away the handkerchief, be sure to move your forefinger back to its original position below the book. Tell everyone that your mental powers caused the glass to become so very heavy.

The witch's broom

In this experiment, a powerful man is unable to push you off balance, due to your "mental powers." Hold a broom horizontally about a foot in front of your chest. Your hands are held wider than your shoulders, and your arms are bent at about a 90-degree angle. A burly volunteer grips the broomstick; his hands go outside yours. With all his might he is to press against the broom—smoothly, with no jerking—and try to push you over. As long as you keep the broom in front of your chest (lift up on the stick if necessary), he won't be able to budge you. His energy will be displaced into thin air.

The girl you cannot lift

For a finale, you apparently make yourself so heavy that a powerful man can't lift you off the floor.

First, demonstrate that he can lift you with relative ease until you exert your mental forces. Stand sideways to the viewers and face the volunteer, who places his hands at your waist. Ask him to hoist you off the ground; just ride along and let him lift you, as in an acrobatic stunt. Then he is to put you down again.

Look him in the eye and claim that you will cause yourself to grow heavy . . . very heavy. Say you'll also "drain his strength"; place your right forefinger against the side of his neck and your left hand on top of his right wrist (which is at your waist). Apply pressure to both spots at once. Your burly volunteer won't be able to lift you a fraction of an inch.

HOW TO DEAL WITH YOUR LAWYER

William French Smith

The late William French Smith was the attorney general of the United States from 1980 to 1985. He was a senior partner in one of America's largest law firms, a labor negotiator, and Ronald Reagan's personal attorney. He recruited Sandra Day O'Connor for nomination to the U.S. Supreme Court.

Be businesslike.

The only thing a lawyer has to sell is his time, and whatever fills it takes away from other things he could be doing. Therefore, nonproductive time may be chargeable. Limit pleasantries, and get down to business.

Prepare your records.

It's like going to a tax accountant: If you just dump a bundle of papers on his desk, he's got to go through them all and charge you for his time. Anything you can do that the lawyer (or a paralegal) would otherwise have to do will save you money. You can write a summary of the facts in the case. You can provide the names, addresses, and telephone numbers of the people involved. If you're going to be negotiating a contract, you can organize all the relevant information. In some states you can even serve subpoenas!

Don't try to play lawyer.

You shouldn't try to do things that are in the attorney's area of expertise and not yours, things for which he's charging you. You've employed somebody to do a job for you: Let him or her do it.

> Lawyers,
> I suppose,
> were children
> once.
> —*Charles Lamb*

Let the attorney prepare you for the courtroom.

Your lawyer will carefully instruct you, not only in the do's and don'ts of testimony, but also on your appearance, demeanor, and general approach. There are certain standard rules; for example, on cross-examination, "Answer the question, and don't volunteer." The rest depends on the ambiance and context of the particular case, and the lawyer will advise you.

If you think a lawyer has done a bad job, you have recourse.

There are different degrees of competence and culpability. These can range from bad judgment—whether or not to settle the case, for example—all the way through negligence to gross negligence or downright malpractice, which is a failure to do those things that a lawyer is supposed to do and is paid to do.

You can't sue in the event a lawyer's decision just turned out to be poor judgment. But you can sue for malpractice. At what point you can call it malpractice depends on the facts in the case; it's a hard line to draw. What you do is go to another attorney and determine if what happened in your case is actionable.

I'm not an ambulance chaser. I'm usually there before the ambulance.
—Melvin Belli

4

NEW TRICKS FOR OLD DOGS

HOW TO PUNCTUATE

Russell Baker

A winner of the Pulitzer Prize, Russell Baker developed his rules on punctuation as part of a project for the International Paper Company.

When you write, you make a sound in the reader's head. It can be a dull mumble—that's why so much government prose makes you sleepy—or it can be a joyful noise, a sly whisper, a throb of passion.

Listen to a voice trembling in a haunted room: "And the silken, sad, uncertain rustling of each purple curtain thrilled me—filled me with fantastic terrors never felt before."

That's Edgar Allan Poe, a master. Few of us can make paper speak as vividly as Poe could, but even beginners will write better once they start listening to the sound their writing makes.

One of the most important tools for making paper speak in your own voice is punctuation.

When speaking aloud, you punctuate constantly—with body language. Your listener hears commas, dashes, question marks, exclamation points, quotation marks as you shout, whisper, pause, wave your arms, roll your eyes, wrinkle your brow.

In writing, punctuation plays the role of body language. It helps readers hear you the way you want to be heard.

"Gee, Dad, have I got to learn all them rules?"

Don't let the rules scare you. For they aren't hard and fast. Think of them as guidelines.

Am I saying, "Go ahead and punctuate as you please?"

Absolutely not. Use your own common sense, remembering that you can't expect readers to work to decipher what you're trying to say.

There are two basic systems of punctuation:

1. The loose or open system, which tries to capture the way body language punctuates talk.

2. The tight, closed, structural system, which hews closely to the sentence's grammatical structure.

Most writers use a little of both. In any case, we use much less punctuation than they used 200 or even 50 years ago. (Glance into Edward Gibbon's *Decline and Fall of the Roman Empire*, first published in 1776, for an example of the tight, structural system at its most elegant.)

No matter which system you prefer, be warned: Punctuation marks cannot save a sentence that is badly put together. If you have to struggle over commas, semicolons and dashes, you've probably built a sentence that's never going to fly, no matter how you tinker with it. Throw it away and build a new one to a simpler design. The better your sentence, the easier it is to punctuate.

Choosing the right tool

There are thirty main punctuation marks, but you'll need fewer than a dozen for most writing.

I can't show you in this small space how they all work, so I'll stick to the ten most important—and even then can only hit highlights. For more details, check your dictionary or a good grammar.

Comma [,] This is the most widely used mark of all. It's also the toughest and most controversial. I've seen aging editors almost come to blows over the comma. If you can handle it without sweating, the others will be easy. Here's my policy:

1. Use a comma after a long introductory phrase or clause: *After stealing the crown jewels from the Tower of London, I went home for tea.*

2. If the introductory material is short, forget the comma: *After the theft I went home for tea.*

3. But use it if the sentence would be confusing without it, like this: *The day before I'd robbed the Bank of England.*

4. Use a comma to separate elements in a series: *I robbed the Denver Mint, the Bank of England, the Tower of London and my piggy bank.*

Notice there is no comma before *and* in the series. This is common style nowadays, but some publishers use a comma there, too.

5. Use a comma to separate independent clauses that are joined by a conjunction like *and, but, for, or, nor, because* or *so*: *I shall return the crown jewels, for they are too heavy to wear.*

6. Use a comma to set off a mildly parenthetical word grouping that isn't essential to the sentence: *Girls, who have always interested me, usually differ from boys.*

Do not use commas if the word grouping *is* essential to the sentence's meaning: *Girls who interest me know how to tango.*

7. Use a comma in direct address: *Your majesty, please hand over the crown.*

8. And between proper names and titles: *Montague Sneed, director of Scotland Yard, was assigned to the case.*

9. And to separate elements of geographical address: *Director Sneed comes from Chicago, Illinois, and now lives in London, England.*

Generally speaking, use a comma where you'd pause briefly in speech. For a long pause or completion of thought, use a period.

If you confuse the comma with the period, you'll get a run-on sentence: *The Bank of England is located in London, I rushed right over to rob it.*

> **Is sloppiness in speech caused by ignorance or apathy? I don't know and I don't care.**
>
> —William Safire

Semicolon [;] A more sophisticated mark than the comma, the semicolon separates two main clauses, but it keeps those two thoughts more tightly linked than a period can: *I steal crown jewels; she steals hearts.*

Dashes [—] and Parentheses [( )] Warning! Use sparingly. The dash SHOUTS. Parentheses whisper. Shout too often, people stop listening; whisper too much, people become suspicious of you. The dash creates a dramatic pause to prepare for an expression needing strong emphasis: *I'll marry you—if you'll rob Topkapi with me.*

Parentheses help you pause quietly to drop in some chatty information not vital to your story: *Despite Betty's daring spirit ("I love robbing your piggy bank," she often said), she was a terrible dancer.*

Quotation Marks [" "] These tell the reader you're reciting the exact words someone said or wrote: *Betty said, "I can't tango."* Or: *"I can't tango," Betty said.*

Notice that the comma comes before the quotation marks in the first example but comes inside them in the second. Not logical? Never mind. Do it that way anyhow.

Colon [:] A colon is a tip-off to get ready for what's next: a list, a long quotation or an explanation. This article is riddled with colons. Too many, maybe, but the message is: "Stay on your toes; it's coming at you."

Apostrophe ['] The big headache is with possessive nouns. If the noun is singular, add *'s*: *I hate Betty's tango.*

If the noun is plural, simply add an apostrophe after the *s*: *Those are the girls' coats.*

The same applies for singular nouns ending in *s*, like Dickens: *This is Dickens's best book.*

And in plural: *This is the Dickenses' cottage.*

The possessive pronouns *hers* and *its* have no apostrophe.

If you write *it's*, you are saying *it is.*

Keep cool You know about ending a sentence with a period (.) or a question mark (?). Do it. Sure, you can also end it with an exclamation point (!), but must you? Usually it just makes you sound breathless and silly. Make your writing generate its own excitement. Filling the paper with !!!! won't make up for what your writing has failed to do.

Too many exclamation points make me think the writer is talking about the panic in his own head.

Don't sound panicky. End with a period. I am serious. A period. Understand?

Well . . . sometimes a question mark is okay.

ICE SKATE BACKWARDS

Tai Babilonia

I've been skating backwards since I was a little girl, and it's become completely natural. But beginners find it a challenge. (No wonder—you can't see where you're going!) Let's start with a few general tips; then a simple method and a more advanced one.

How to stand

Go out on the ice with your skates on (of course!). Bend your knees slightly, and hold your back straight and upright. Hold your arms out to the side at shoulder level. (Your outstretched arms work like a tightrope walker's pole to keep you balanced.)

Doing "fishes"

This is the simplest method and a good way to start. You stand a little pigeon-toed and push both feet outward. This propels you, so you glide backwards. Your feet will separate. Then they come back together as you point your heels inward; your heels just touch. Now push outward again with both feet. As you repeat this, your skates make a pattern on the ice that looks like a fish, or a series of fishes. (That's where this technique got its name.) You really don't have to think about it. It's just heel, toe, heel, toe—a rhythm of out and in. Because you're switching the angle of your feet, you push yourself along.

Tai Babilonia and her skating partner, Randy Gardner, earned the highest score ever recorded in pairs skating at the U.S. National Figure Skating Championships, won the U.S. senior pairs title five times, received the first Olympic Spirit Award, and won the world championship in Vienna, Austria.

Back crossovers

This really looks like skating backwards the way the pros do it. Let's try "right over left" crossovers:

You're standing backwards. Push off with your right foot, so you're gliding backwards on your left foot, and lift your right foot. Cross it over the left foot, and place it on the ice again. At this point, both feet are on the ice and your feet are crossed as you glide backwards. Then "unhook" your left foot, lifting it from the ice, and bring it back under the right leg. As it touches the ice, your feet are in starting position again. Push backwards again with your right foot, so you glide on your left, and repeat the crossover. You're skating backwards!

You can do this to either side—what skaters call right or left crossovers—depending on which direction you want to skate. Crossovers are difficult. It's all in the timing and in holding yourself with lightly bent knees, back upright, and arms out at shoulder height. Once you get going, though, there's no stopping you!

The Little Matter of Falling Down

• It sounds funny, but everyone should know how to fall. It's one of the first things I learned when I started skating twenty-five years ago. When you realize you're going to fall, put your arms out behind you to catch yourself, so you don't slam down. This will break your fall, so you'll slide instead of hitting the ice—bam!

• Another key is not to stiffen up, because you're more likely to get hurt when your body is tight than when it's loose. Just go with the fall and don't fight it.

RAISE YOUR SCORE ON I.Q. AND OTHER STANDARDIZED TESTS

Dr. Abbie F. Salny

A twenty-five-year member of Mensa, the high-I.Q. society, college psychology professor Abbie Salny is a specialist on standardized tests. Her *Mensa Genius Quiz Books* (written with Marvin Grosswirth) have sold 300,000 copies.

Find out the type of test.

Never, ever walk into a test without knowing what kind of test it is. True-false, multiple-choice, essay, or completion—the kind of test determines how you'll prepare for it. For true-false tests, you only have to recognize the truth or falsity of a statement; for completion (fill-in-the-blank) tests, you've got to do more memory work. In other words, the first type of test requires recognition; the second, recall. For an essay test you want to have your ideas organized, so that you can get them down in the appropriate form as rapidly as possible.

Find out how the test will be scored and adjust your technique accordingly.

Most of the big test companies are willing to discuss their scoring methods; just write or telephone for information. Their way of scoring helps you decide whether or not to make guesses. If there is no penalty for guessing, go ahead, because you won't get a point off for every wrong answer. On the other hand, some tests dock you two points for every miss, so don't answer a question unless you're absolutely certain of the right answer.

It's not hard to figure out the appropriate strategy. If you think you know the correct answer on a true-false test that subtracts one point for every miss, go ahead and guess; you've got a 50–50 chance. But if it's a multiple-choice test with four possible answers, the odds are 3 to 1 against you; unless you can discard two choices immediately, skip the question.

Organize your time.

Find out how much time you have, then analyze your approach. For instance, let's say the test has 100 items and you have an hour. If you can't solve number 11, leave it and go on. The reason is obvious: If you get only 10 questions right because you're stuck on number 11, you are far worse off than if you skip the 15 you can't do and answer 85 right.

The best approach is to go through the whole test, doing all the questions you *can* do as fast as you can. Then go back and answer the ones that are moderately easy and take a little longer. Leave the hardest to the very end, and if you get really stuck on one question, just move on to the next one.

Before starting an essay test, place your watch on the desk to time yourself. If you have four essay questions and two hours to do them, you cannot allow yourself more than half an hour per essay—or you'll zonk the questions at the end. I had an aunt who took the insurance brokers' licensing test, and although she got 100% on the first two sections, she flunked the test because 70% was a passing grade and she never got to the last two questions. Be sure you stick to your schedule, or you're likely to run out of time.

Practice the kind of test you'll be taking.

Most of us haven't taken timed tests in years, so we need to practice. Test companies will give you samples of their old exams, and there are books available to help you practice for many tests—SATs, GREs, and so forth.

After taking the practice tests, go back and analyze your answers to see which type of question gives you the most trouble. Perhaps you're confused by analogies, the questions that require you to analyze and complete a comparison, such as "*Hot: Cold* as *White:* ____." Go to a bookstore or library, get a book on analogy tests, and work on them until you understand what they're about. If you have trouble with vocabulary, a subject that most tests play on heavily, then do some vocabulary building with one of the many specialized books available.

An I.Q. test measures your intellectual ability in a number of categories, particularly in vocabulary, reasoning, mathematics, recall, and analogies. To boost your score on an I.Q. test, get practice books on these subjects.

Clearly, this approach doesn't apply to subject tests where you actually have to know a body of material. Nobody can help you pass an Advanced Chemistry Graduate Record Exam unless you know advanced chemistry.

Adopt the right mental attitude.

Lots of tension is destructive, but a mild degree of anxiety seems to sharpen you up for a test, the way a bit of stage fright can boost an actor's performance onstage. Another desirable attitude is confidence, which you achieve by going over practice tests until you see that you have them knocked. A bit anxious but reasonably confident—that's the ideal state of mind for taking a test.

Want to Join Mensa, the High-I.Q. Society?

• Mensa accepts members who score in the top 2 percent on any standard I.Q. test or equivalent. There are 150 local groups, which get together for meetings and an annual gathering. "Members join for the fun of associating with people with whom they can have intelligent conversations," says Dr. Salny. "You should see fifteen hundred bright people all effervescing. It's quite a sight."

• For information on membership and testing, write or telephone:

American Mensa
2626 East Fourteenth Street
Brooklyn, New York 11235
(718) 934-3700

PLAY ROCK 'N' ROLL PIANO LIKE JERRY LEE LEWIS AND FATS DOMINO

Jeffrey Gutcheon

The rock and country pianist Jeffrey Gutcheon has played with Ringo Starr and Maria Muldaur, was a writer of the Broadway show *Ain't Misbehavin'*, and is the piano player on Gladys Knight's recording of "Imagination" and on Willie Nelson's album *Shotgun Willie*. His instructional books, *Improvising Rock Piano* and *Teach Yourself Rock Piano*, are compendiums of rock piano styles.

To play rock 'n' roll you kind of sit down on your haunches, launch yourself from your heels, and pounce on the piano for all you're worth. You've got to hit every note from your feet up; the fingers are only the last part of the message. In fact, the key to playing like Jerry Lee Lewis or Fats Domino is to make believe that you have only half as many fingers as you actually do and to get the job done with less. Dexterity is not the point. Instead, the hammer and the steam drill come into play.

Rock piano, while it derives from the same blues roots that jazz does, is a rhythm style. The most satisfying way to play it is with a heavy and deliberate hand in the bass and midrange part of the piano—as if you're the underpinning of a rock 'n' roll band. The piano is seldom a lead instrument in a rock band, because it doesn't project the way electric guitars and horns do. So pianists like Jerry Lee Lewis and Fats Domino play mainly rhythm accompaniment, with occasional solos or riffs.

Fats Domino's style

Fats Domino's style is purely physical. So it helps to get into his frame of mind—or, rather, frame of body. Take the posture: Fats Domino really leans into the piano and puts his weight into it. He's a two-handed rhythm player, and his style is basically rhythmical.

"One Starry Night" (see excerpt) sounds a lot like "Blueberry Hill." It's written in 12/8 rhythm, which simply means that each quarter note gets three beats; these are called triplets. The right hand pounds out the triplets, and to make them sound right, each one of the triplets should be played heavy and even tempered, with no special accents. Just keep those beats rolling out there with equal force. Meanwhile, the left hand plays a simple New Orleans–style bass; its roots can be traced all the way back to Jelly Roll Morton's time.

"One Starry Night" contains the familiar "Blueberry Hill" introduction, a chorus, and a conclusion.

> I don't know anything about music. In my line you don't have to.
> —*Elvis Presley*

Jerry Lee Lewis's style

Jerry Lee Lewis is not only the front man of an act, he's the lead instrument. So he plays more solos and lots of flourishes in between his vocalizing. One of his trademarks is the glissando. This flashy swooping up and down the keyboard is basically theatrical, to cut through the other instruments in the band and to attract a lot of attention.

To do a Jerry Lee Lewis glissando, you have to pitch yourself into it with abandon. Get used to the fact that it's probably going to hurt you a little bit, since you'll use your fingernails. But you can make it easier on yourself. As you go up the keyboard, try to back up your fingers with your thumb; as you're coming down, back up your thumb with your fingers. That way you'll be using not a single digit, but more of your hand. If you can imagine the thumb, forefinger, and middle finger unit as something close to a piece of wood, you'll be on the right track.

Another important thing about Jerry Lee Lewis's style is the

One Starry Night

Medium (Heavy Handed and Even Tempered)

Introduction

16th note tremolo

J. Gutcheon

Jerry Lee's Boogie

pretty damn fast

(as fast as you can play)

J. Gutcheon

simile

solo begins

steadiness of his boogie-woogie bass. To achieve the correct rhythm, be sure to accent every note evenly with your left hand. As for the right hand, Jerry Lee Lewis gets a lot of mileage out of a very few notes. He doesn't play an awful lot, but what he plays is neatly articulated and fits well. So it's not as if you have to be technically flashy to evoke his sound. But brevity—if not necessarily wit—is really important in his right-hand figures. A couple of little licks and flashes, played in the right way, will get the point across.

"Jerry Lee's Boogie" (see excerpt) has an introduction that illustrates the way he would play behind a vocal; then a little figure leads into a near transcription of the solo from "Whole Lotta Shakin'."

Rock 'n' roll is the hamburger that ate the world.
—*Peter York*

TAKE BETTER
TRAVEL PHOTOGRAPHS

Wilbur E. Garrett

**Wilbur Garrett was
editor of *National
Geographic Magazine*
for more than a
decade.**

Photographing people

Take your time. Don't run up to someone, go "click, click," and
run away. There's nothing to be embarrassed about; most people
aren't offended if you take their picture. If you've got a really nice
person who's cooperating—some nice *babushka* at a Russian
marketplace selling sausages—take a few shots so that she'll get
used to you. Then, when a customer comes and the woman gets
animated and forgets you're there, you can take better ones.

Catch people acting naturally. If a farmhand pitching hay is looking straight at you instead of at the hay wagon, you know he's
conscious of the camera. That's not what you want. When this
happens, explain, "I'd appreciate it if you wouldn't look at me."
Or just lower the camera until he goes back to what he was
doing. You don't want your subject staring at the camera unless
you're shooting a portrait.

Use good manners. The camera has become so ubiquitous that
there's hardly a quaint subject on earth who hasn't been
harassed by someone taking photos. Instead of trying to sneak a
shot, it's often better to walk up and say, "Would you mind if I
take a photograph?" Most people don't mind, but they usually

appreciate being asked. You can pick up the appropriate phrases in any language—French, Hindi, or whatever.

If you're in a crowd or a big marketplace where there's a lot going on, you don't really have to ask permission. But sometimes there are other reasons people stop you from taking a picture. Once I was chewed out by a Russian woman in Siberia for taking a picture of lovely old wooden houses. She considered them outdated, reflecting poverty and backwardness. "Why don't you take something modern?" she said. I pointed to a 1930s streetcar going past: "Like that?" "Yes," she said. The streetcar would have made Russia look far more backward than the houses, but I learned something about people's sensitivities.

Most people don't want to be photographed when they're sweaty and dirty, because they know that in a way you're picking them at their worst moment. Just put yourself in the subject's position and imagine how you'd like to be treated.

Don't offer people money to pose. If somebody came up, took my picture, and then offered me a quarter, I'd get mad. I think most people have pride. Here's a better idea: If you take some shots of a person and get to know him, write down his address and offer to send a picture. It may start a nice correspondence.

Photographing landscapes

Beware of the empty landscape shot. If you point a snapshot camera with a wide-angle lens at a mountain ten miles away, it will record as a little pimple. Later you'll say, "It was so pretty, I don't understand what happened." You should usually fill the frame, either by moving closer or by adding something in the foreground.

Frame the subject. To fill the empty space with something besides sky, frame the mountain with a tree branch or something else compositionally pleasant. There's also a good trick for framing scenery or a city view without even leaving your hotel room. Maybe you have the Kremlin outside your window, and you also want your shot to include something in the room, perhaps a person. Wait until the light outdoors is about the same as the light inside the room, and you'll get a balanced exposure. It's easiest at dusk, but you can always move a lamp closer to the subject to help balance the light. You have to look; it's just a matter of the eye.

PHOTOGRAPHY BASICS

Don't buy a camera that's over your head. Many good cameras are available with all kinds of jazzy features. But for snapshots, you just need a little one with automatic focus, a built-in flash, and one lens. (Some add a built-in zoom lens, which gives you more flexibility.) These "point-and-shoot" cameras work equally well for photos of people and for your average mountain view. I carry one in my briefcase all the time.

Prevent blurry pictures. *Brace your camera.* About 99 percent of fuzzy photos are caused not by bad lenses but by camera movement. Hold your camera steady. Be extra careful in late afternoon or in a place that's dimly lit, where your shutter speed is slow. At an exposure of less than 1/100 of a second, the best professionals try to use a tripod. It doesn't have to be the three-legged kind: You can brace the camera against a tree, on a chair back, or flat against a building. Or just brace *yourself*—against a light pole, for example. The camera will be less likely to move.

Squeeze the shutter button. Don't hit the button like you're trying to drive a spike. Push it gently, so the camera won't shake.

Avoid the most common composition blunders. *Fill the frame.* Amateurs almost never fill the frame, and they usually stand too far away. Even if it's only a group shot of three relatives, chances are they'll walk back 15 feet, just to be safe. The people end up tiny. Remember, the viewfinder is to be trusted. Fill it—because what you see is what you get.

Notice the background. Most people never see what's *behind* their subject—until they get the pictures back and find that Uncle Charlie has a tree growing out of his head. So don't just compose the foreground; be sure the subject blends with the background.

Be alert in backlit situations. Your camera's built-in light meter will be confused when a subject is backlit—let's say, a person standing in front of a bright window or a sunny background. The meter may read the sunlight, the lens will close way down, and the person's face will come out too dark. To prevent this, make sure that the subject is at the center of the frame, because the center is where your light meter usually takes a reading. Now the camera lens will open up for a proper exposure.

Another tip: Even though it's bright daylight, turn on your automatic flash to fill in the shadows on people's faces. A person can come out a little overexposed if you use a flash too close, though; usually 4 to 8 feet from the subject is about right.

All rules are made to be broken. If you must, do it with style and you may get the rule changed. That's creativity.

START A <u>TWO</u>-MATCH FIRE IN YOUR FIREPLACE

Pete Luter

A resident of the piney woods of Roanoke Rapids, North Carolina, Pete Luter has served as president of the National Chimney Sweeps Guild.

How did I get into the chimney sweep business? Well, I guess everyone has a little pyromania inside . . .

I wear traditional black clothes every day, but I've opted for a baseball cap instead of the usual top hat. Top hats are difficult to work in; when you bend over to look up the chimney, you knock it off your head.

In the little North Carolina town where I've lived for fifty years, people keep asking me how to light a fire so that smoke doesn't fill the living room. They've heard the myth of the "one-match fire"—but the secret of a great fire is to use *two* matches. Before we light it, let me explain a few things.

First, you must be sure that your fireplace and chimney are in good shape. The chimney may be old, unlined, or laden with heavy creosote buildup. If you are unsure of the condition of your chimney, it would be wise to employ the services of a certified chimney sweep before attempting to use it. You don't want a rip-roaring chimney fire on your hands!

As a chimney sweep, I'm always being asked what kind of wood to burn. And I answer, "The best firewood is free firewood." Fruit woods, like peach, apple, persimmon, and cherry, produce a nice aroma as well as pretty flames that have colors in them.

Pine and any of the other "soft" woods work just fine, although you will make more trips to the woodpile; a piece of pine weighs half as much as the same size piece of oak, which basically means that it will burn half as long. The only wood to avoid is "salt-treated" commercial lumber, which produces a cyanide gas that can be harmful if you burn large quantities of wood over a long period of time. Also, don't burn saltwater driftwood in metal fireplaces, because it corrodes them.

The average fireplace is about 36 inches wide, so firewood about 24 inches long is well-suited. Good firewood should be well seasoned; technically, that means it has about a 20 percent moisture content. Green wood, oddly enough, is usually a white color. Well-seasoned wood is starting to turn a darker brown. You'll also notice that it is starting to split on the ends as it dries.

If your fireplace has a grate, it will be easier to get the fire going, but wood fires do not *require* a grate; they will burn in a bed of ash. By the way, when you clean your fireplace don't remove all the ashes. Leave some in the area right under and alongside the grate. Ash acts as an insulator, throwing heat back into the fire, and it helps the fire take off quicker.

To build a fire, the first thing you do is crumple up some sheets of newspaper. It's actually best to put the newspaper *under* the grate. And set the newspaper slightly toward the front, because the natural draft of the chimney will bend the flame toward the back of the fireplace. (You can also use those "magic log" fire starters, cut into little sections.)

Now you need an ample supply of kindling wood. Probably the best is kiln-dried fir or pine, which you can find as scraps around building sites. And don't be stingy with it; using lots of kindling helps your fire get going much quicker. When you lay the kindling in the grate, "cross-hatch" it—place some one way, some the other. That way the kindling stays in position, gets enough air so that the fire can spread easily, and supports the heavier wood that you now place on top. (I've seen people just lean kindling against crumpled newspaper and lay firewood on top, but when the paper burns away, the support is gone, the whole thing collapses, and the fire dies.)

I said I'd tell you how to light a two-match fire. You're about to use the first match. Take one double spread of newspaper from the center of the paper and twist it up; do this tightly enough so that you can hold it kind of like a torch, but loose enough so that it will burn. Open the damper. The chimney is probably full of cold air, especially if it is on the north side of the house or on the windy side, or the weather is cold. Cold air is heavy, so if you light your fire at the same time you open the damper, you get this big whoosh of cold air falling down the chimney—which pushes smoke right out into the house. To prevent this, light one end of your "torch" and hold it right up in the damper. The paper will burn very quickly, which heats up the flue and gets the hot air rising.

If this bit of "priming the chimney" goes well (you may have to repeat it if you still feel cold air coming down), you're ready to light the fire with the second match. Once the kindling has caught and you're pretty well satisfied in your mind that the fire is going to take, then you can slowly add more firewood. Now sit down and put your feet up!

Gamble on the Seven Best Bets in a Casino

Henry Tamburin

On his first visit to Las Vegas, Henry Tamburin lost all his money within two hours, then vowed to learn to gamble properly. A chemist with a Ph.D., he used computer technology to analyze the best casino bets. Among his books is *Henry Tamburin on Casino Gambling.*

If you decide to gamble in a casino, you must choose among more than fifty different bets. Some bets offer much better odds than others. So limit yourself to the seven bets that give you the best chances of winning. Then, with a little luck—the right cards or a fortunate throw of the dice—you have a shot at coming out ahead.

> **You can't expect to hit the jackpot if you don't put a few nickels in the machine.**
> —*Flip Wilson*

There's a big difference between a good bet and a bad bet. Take the craps table: If you put your chips on "Any 7," the odds against you are about 17 percent; that means the casino will win 17 percent of your money over the long run—quite an edge for the house. But if you play properly at blackjack, the odds are just .5 percent against you. Comparing 17 to .5 percent reveals that the first bet will lose thirty-four times more money over the long run than the second one. That's why you should stick to the seven best bets. Only the first requires learning a playing strategy. For the others you just put down your money and hope that Lady Luck is on your side.

1. Blackjack—played with perfect basic strategy

By far the best bet is at the blackjack table. But you must learn how to play each hand properly—that is, know when to hit, stand, double down, and split pairs (see chart, "Basic Strategy for Blackjack"). If you play with perfect basic strategy, you can almost neutralize the casino's advantage, which falls to about .5 percent. Most blackjack players lose simply because they don't play this basic strategy.

Coupling good basic strategy with card counting can actually give you an advantage over the casino—in Las Vegas, about 1 percent *in your favor.* "Card counting" is keeping track of the cards that have been played, so you know the ratio of high-value cards (10, J, Q, K, Ace) to small-value cards (2,3,4,5,6) that are still left in the dealing shoe. This ratio is important, because if there are more high-value cards left, your advantage goes up— and that's when you want to bet more. Card counting systems, which help you calculate a simple index to this ratio, are explained in reference books on casino gambling and blackjack.

Casinos are well aware of card counting, of course, and if they detect a player doing it, they will shuffle the cards often, change dealers, or, in extreme cases, actually ask the player to leave. So you must disguise your card counting. The main point is not to continuously wager $5 on every hand, then suddenly jump up to a $100 bet when you have the advantage; instead, vary your wagers in smaller increments. Also, don't appear to focus too closely on the cards as they're played; certainly don't tell anyone you're counting cards; and try not to win too much or play too long at any one table. These actions would attract the attention of the casino management.

2. Craps—the Don't Pass/Don't Come line, with odds

This is a two-part bet. On the "come out" roll (the first roll by a new shooter) you bet on the Don't Pass line. (Or if a point has already been established, you would wager on the Don't Come.) The shooter throws the dice and, let's say, rolls an eight. You'll win your Don't Pass bet if the shooter throws a seven before throwing another eight. Now you have the opportunity to make a secondary bet, called the "odds bet." All casinos allow single

BASIC STRATEGY FOR BLACKJACK

4, 6, 8 decks

Your hand	Playing strategy vs. dealer's up card
5 to 8	Always hit
9	Double on 3 to 6; otherwise hit
10	Double on 2 to 9; hit on 10, A
11	Double on 2 to 10; hit on A
12	Stand on 4 to 6; otherwise hit
13	Stand on 2 to 6; otherwise hit
14	Stand on 2 to 6; otherwise hit
15	Stand on 2 to 6; otherwise hit
16	Stand on 2 to 6; otherwise hit
17	Always stand
18	Always stand
A, 2	Double on 5, 6; otherwise hit
A, 3	Double on 5, 6; otherwise hit
A, 4	Double on 4 to 6; otherwise hit
A, 5	Double on 4 to 6; otherwise hit
A, 6	Double on 3 to 6; otherwise hit
A, 7	Double on 3 to 6; stand on 2, 7 or 8; hit on 9, 10 or A
A, 8 to A, 10	Always stand
A, A	Always split
2, 2	Split on 2 to 7; otherwise hit
3, 3	Split on 2 to 7; otherwise hit
4, 4	Split on 5, 6; otherwise hit
5, 5	Never split; treat as 10 above
6, 6	Split on 2 to 6; otherwise hit
7, 7	Split on 2 to 7; otherwise hit
8, 8	Always split
9, 9	Split on 2 to 6, 8 or 9; stand on 7, 10 or A
10, 10	Always stand

The previous strategy is valid if players are allowed to double down after pair splitting. If doubling down is *not* allowed after pair splitting, use the following pair splitting rules.

2, 2	Split on 4 to 7; otherwise hit
3, 3	Split on 4 to 7; otherwise hit
4, 4	Never split; always hit
6, 6	Split on 3 to 6; otherwise hit

Single deck

Your hand	Playing strategy vs. dealer's up card
8	Double on 5 or 6; otherwise hit
9	Double on 2 to 6; otherwise hit
10	Double on 2 to 9; otherwise hit
11	Always double
12	Stand on 4 to 6; otherwise hit
13 to 16	Stand on 2 to 6; otherwise hit
17 to 21	Always stand
A, 2 to A, 5	Double on 4 to 6; otherwise hit
A, 6	Double on 2 to 6; otherwise hit
A, 7	Double on 3 to 6; stand on 2, 7, 8 or A; hit on 9 or 10
A, 8	Double on 6; otherwise stand
A, 9	Always stand
A, A	Always split
2, 2	Split on 3 to 7; otherwise hit
3, 3	Split on 4 to 7; otherwise hit
4, 4	Same as 8 above
5, 5	Same as 10 above
6, 6	Split on 2 to 6; otherwise hit
7, 7	Split on 2 to 7; stand on 10; otherwise hit
8, 8	Always split
9, 9	Split on 2 to 9 except 7; stand on 7, 10 or A
10, 10	Always stand

The previous chart assumes the casino doesn't allow doubling down after pair splitting. If the casino *allows* doubling down after pair splitting, then use the following pair splitting rules.

Your hand	Playing strategy vs. dealer's up card
2, 2	Split on 2 to 7; otherwise hit
3, 3	Split on 2 to 7; otherwise hit
4, 4	Split on 4, 5 or 6; otherwise hit
6, 6	Split on 2 to 7; otherwise hit
7, 7	Split on 2 to 8; stand on 10; otherwise hit

odds, which means the size of your odds wager must be such that, if it wins, the payoff should equal the size of the original Don't Pass bet. Many casinos allow double or triple odds, and a few even allow ten times odds. Place your odds bet next to the original Don't Pass bet on the layout. You will be "laying" odds; that is, betting more to win less. The reason for this is because once a point is established, the Don't Pass bettor actually has the advantage over the casino.

The odds bet is extremely important, because it's the only bet in the entire casino where the house's advantage is zero. The casino pays you off exactly what the mathematical probability dictates. If you win, the original bet is paid at 1 to 1; the secondary odds bet gets paid at the actual odds that the shooter will not make his point.

Overall, your original bet plus the odds bet trim the casino's advantage to just .5 to .8 percent.

3. Craps—the Pass/Come line, with odds

This bet is exactly like #2, except that your original bet is on the Pass Line (or Come), and you are betting that the shooter will make his point before throwing a seven. You make the secondary odds bet (single, double, triple, or more) once the point is established. Place your chips on the table behind the original Pass Line bet. You will be "taking" odds, because once a point is established, the casino has the advantage over the Pass Line bettor. The house's edge is a fraction higher than for bet #2.

> **The house doesn't beat a player. It merely gives him the chance to beat himself.**
> —Nick "the Greek" Dandalos

4. Baccarat—the Bank Hand

At the baccarat table there are three possible bets—on the Bank Hand, on the Player Hand, and on a Tie. If you look at the percentages, a bet on the Bank Hand puts the odds at about 1.17 percent against you, which is relatively small.

5. Baccarat—the Player Hand

The house edge on the Player Hand is just 1.36 percent.

6. Craps—the Don't Pass/Don't Come line

This bet is like #2, but without the secondary odds bet. The house's advantage is less than 1.4 percent.

7. Craps—the Pass/Come line

This bet is like #3, but without the odds bet. The house edge is about 1.4 percent.

How to Win at Video Poker

• One of your best bets is video poker—but only when you play certain machines and use perfect strategy in playing your hands. If you do this, the casino's edge can drop to less than 1 percent.

• **Pick a machine that pays:**

• *Jacks or better.* Some machines return your bet on a pair of 10s or better—an even better bet.

• *9 coins for a full house and 6 coins for a flush.* These are known as "9–6 machines." Most video poker machines pay 8–6 or 8–5; better to find a 9–6 machine. (On a "progressive machine," where the jackpot continually increases until it's paid out, 8–5 is standard and acceptable.)

• *A 4,000-coin jackpot on a royal flush.* Some machines pay less; just pass them by. (On a progressive 25-cent machine, play only when the jackpot rises past $2,200.)

• **Play your hands perfectly.**

• Video poker is a game of skill. You must know when to stand, when to discard, or when to go for a straight or royal flush. Computer studies have determined the optimal playing strategies, and these are taught in standard texts on video poker or casino gambling. To maximize your chances of winning, you must learn these strategies.

Wash Windows Without Streaking

Don Aslett

I do windows—and if you take five minutes to learn these professional secrets, you'll find that doing windows is fun. Really!

But first, here's what not to do:

Forget the old wives' tales about using vinegar and newspaper. Vinegar is not a cleaner; it squeaks, and that's why everyone thinks it cleans. (It makes a great rinsing agent, but it won't cut grease, exhaust fumes, and so forth.)

> Based in Pocatello, Idaho, Don Aslett has been in the cleaning business for more than thirty years, and his company employs two thousand cleaners in sixteen states. His books, such as *Is There Life After Housework?* and *Clutter's Last Stand*, have sold well over a million copies.

Also, forget glass-gunking aerosols. Many foaming glass cleaners and waxes leave a residue that actually builds up on windows. The buildup is what you see in the streaks. Windows cleaned with sticky products attract dust and get dirty faster.

Here's the right way.

Use "the right stuff."

Go to a janitorial supply store and buy a professional brass squeegee with a 12- or 14-inch blade. (The Steccone brand is best.) Make sure the rubber blade sticks out on the ends. Keep the blade in good shape, and replace it if it gets nicked or damaged. Save your window squeegee just for windows; don't use it on the floor.

> **Cleaning your house while your kids are still growing is like shoveling the walk before it stops snowing.**
> —*Phyllis Diller*

By the way, don't go to the supermarket and get one of those all-in-one, sponge-on-one-side, blade-on-the-other monstrosities—they are meant for your car. They just don't work well, even in a professional's hands.

Cleaning solution.

Half a dozen drops of dish soap in a bucket of water—that's what we professionals use. You can call it secret formula X1900-32 if you like; but Dawn or Joy is superb. Don't be tempted to add more soap or you'll get streaks; a few drops is plenty for a gallon of water. It's all the cleaner you need—one bucket will do the whole house.

Step by step to sparkling windows.

1. Lightly wet the window using a clean sponge, soft-bristle brush, or wand applicator dipped in cleaning solution. You don't need to flood the window. Just clean it, don't baptize it. If the window is really dirty or has several years' worth of buildup from miracle-gunk window cleaners, go over it again.

2. Before you start to squeegee, wipe the rubber blade with a *damp* cloth or chamois. The damp cloth lubricates the squeegee so it will glide. A dry blade will skip (and make that *gee-bee, gee-bee, gee-bee* sound).

3. Tilt the squeegee at an angle, pressing one end lightly against the top edge of the *glass* (not the window frame or house shingles). Pull the squeegee across the top horizontally. This will leave a 1-inch dry stripe across the top of the window. (Remember all those drips that came running down from the top of your clean window when you tried squeegeeing before? By making this move across the top, you've removed potential drips.)

4. Place the rubber blade in the dry stripe and pull down. Repeat this across the window, lapping over into the dry part with each stroke. Wipe the blade after each stroke.

A window can be cleaned from top to bottom or side to side using this technique. Just be sure to cut a dry stripe across the lead edge of the glass to eliminate potential dripping.

5. Wipe the windowsill with your damp cloth.

What about drips, marks, and lines?

Use your bare hand! The cleaning solution will have removed the oils from your skin, making your finger the best touch-up tool. You can hit the small spots without leaving a mark. As for the tiny strip of moisture along the edge, perhaps ½ inch, leave it! It will evaporate and go unnoticed. Avoid the temptation to wipe it with a finger or cloth or you'll end up with a half-inch strip.

Hard water buildup.

"Sprinklered" windows call for more drastic action. Using the pad side of a scrubbing sponge, apply a mild phosphoric acid solution. (I use Showers 'n' Stuff; similar products are available at a janitorial supply store.) Follow the directions on the label. Let the chemical work for a minute or two and agitate it with your pad. Rinse and repeat until the mineral buildup is gone.

Your windows are still white and opaque? They may be etched and damaged; no cleaner I know can repair this. Replace the glass, or draw the drapes.

> I am a
> marvelous
> housekeeper.
> Every time
> I leave a man,
> I keep
> his house.
> —Zsa Zsa
> Gabor

Getting to high windows.

Where windows are out of reach, use an extension handle, which is much easier than dragging out the ladder, and it keeps your feet on the ground. Mine is 4 feet long and extends to 8 feet. You can attach a cleaning head or a squeegee, and you can maneuver it with surprising accuracy. Instead of wiping the blade after each stroke, just hit the pole with the palm of your hand to release the water from the blade.

A few tiny smudges or drips won't hurt anything, so don't try to be a perfectionist; it isn't worth the stress or time. Clean glass always looks good!

THE "ROPE-A-DOPE" AND OTHER SECRETS OF BOXING

Muhammad Ali

Muhammad Ali ("I Am the Greatest!") was the first boxer ever to win the world heavyweight title three times. He earned more than $50 million in the ring and became perhaps the most widely recognized person on earth.

For young fighters, here are my secrets of the sweet science of boxing.

Do the rope-a-dope.

That's how I handled George Foreman during the "Rumble in the Jungle" in Zaire. I'd attack, then hold my hands and gloves in front of my face, with my elbows and forearms tucked against my chest and stomach. If you do that for five or ten seconds, just to cover up, the punches won't hit your face or body. I named this technique for Foreman—the "rope-a-dope." All that punching wore him down. In the eighth round I knocked him out.

There are more pleasant things to do than beat up people.
—*Muhammad Ali*

Tire out the other fighter.

Wearing the other guy down is a science: Put your head within range so he has to try to hit you, then lean back and away. It saps the other fighter to throw blows that land in thin air.

Be a moving target.

Dancing on my toes—that's how I protected myself from getting punched. Move to the left and right; bob up and down; move from front to back. Being fast on your feet is the best defense. It's hard to hit a moving target.

Learn to "float like a butterfly, sting like a bee."

You want to hit the other guy without being hit yourself. The secret is to move in when you attack and then *move out*. I had a natural way of doing this. Say I threw a jab; I knew my opponent would return a punch, so I pulled back. His glove might reach right to my nose, but because I moved an inch back, he'd miss.

Study your opponent.

Rope-a-dope was a good strategy for George Foreman, whereas in New Orleans with Leon Spinks, who doesn't tire so easily, it was better to do pretty straight boxing; I was just jabbing and scoring points. But if I'm fighting a guy like Joe Frazier, who's shorter than I am, powerful, and can outpunch me, then I'd plan to keep my distance—an arm's length and a half away—so he can't touch me.

Win on points.

If you find a guy who's too hard to knock out, who has a good record and has never been out—like me!—you have to beat him on points. At the end of each round he goes back to his corner, and his trainer tells him, "You lost that one." He says, "I cornered him and I chased him, but I can't hit him! I try to throw a punch, he's gone." A man who's fast on his feet and can really move will always outpoint the other fighter.

Tie up the other fighter.

One way to keep your opponent from getting a swing at you is to hold on to him: Put your hands behind his elbows and pull him to you. That's just for a few seconds until the referee breaks you up.

Keep your eyes open wide.

You want to be able to see *everything*, so you can sidestep or dodge any punch.

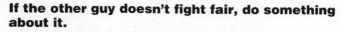
If the other guy doesn't fight fair, do something about it.

There are tactics that are hard for the referee to spot, such as when your opponent drags the laces of his gloves across your ears or head-butts you. If that happens, stop boxing and tell the referee.

Don't deliberately hurt your opponent.

If a guy has a cut over his eye, it's a natural strategy for the other boxer to work on it and try to close up the eye so the fight gets stopped and that boxer wins. But it's so barbaric, even to talk about. I never could deliberately hurt anybody; my Muslim religion got in the way.

I always lightened up when I saw them going down.

> **My toughest fight was with my first wife.**
> —*Muhammad Ali*

HOW TO TALK AT WARP SPEED

Fran Capo

Although most people cannot speak intelligibly at a speed of more than 300 words per minute, Fran Capo earned a place in *The Guinness Book of World Records* by rapping out the 91st Psalm at an incredible 603.32 words per minute. A comic by trade, her act includes a bit called "Evelyn Wood Reads Her Kids a Bedtime Story."

Being able to speak at a mind-boggling rate can come in handy—for instance, when I get into an argument with my husband, I talk so fast he doesn't even realize he's been in a fight. If you want to challenge my *Guinness Book* record for speed-talking, I'm happy to share my training methods.

Practice talking with a cork in your mouth.

It may sound silly, but it develops good enunciation. When you talk fast, you still want people to understand every single word. For training, take a wine cork and place it vertically between your front teeth; your teeth should be about an inch apart. Then say paragraphs. It won't sound very good, but when you take the cork out of your mouth and actually do some fast talking, you'll articulate everything much clearer. I got the idea from a Greek tale about a guy who wanted to learn to speak clearly, so he practiced with marbles in his mouth. Marbles sounded dangerous, so I came up with the wine cork.

Work on tongue twisters.

Auctioneers use this technique for practice. Start slowly, then gradually pick up speed. When you first try a tongue twister, you moosh it up and trip over the words. But the more you practice, the better your mouth will be able to form sounds that are normally hard to say in succession. Try "A big brown bug bit a big brown bear" and "I slid a sheet, a sheet I slid, and on the slidded sheet I sit." One of the hardest tongue twisters is just two words: "toy boat"—repeat it fast!

Practice anytime you can.

I live in New York, and if I'm riding on a train, I'll read all the advertising placards above the seats. I read each one quickly, take my eyes away, read it again, take my eyes away, and so on. The idea is to become good at picking things up quickly. When doing this, I don't speak loudly but just mumble— it's a great way to keep muggers away!

The sixth sick sheik's sixth sheep's sick.
—said to be the hardest tongue twister in the English language

For the *Guinness Book* speed-talking competition, you pick a passage from either Shakespeare or the Bible and repeat it as fast as you can for 60 seconds. Driving in my car, I'm always practicing the 91st Psalm. To build up your speed, time yourself, starting in 15-second increments, and work up to the full minute.

Don't use artificial means.

You may imagine that drinking will relax you or that coffee will make you talk even faster, but I don't agree.

Breathe properly.

Breathing takes more time than anything else, so when I do my spiel for the Guinness competition, I take only two breaths during the whole minute. You can mark the text to indicate where you're going to breathe. And before you start speaking any passage, be sure to take three deep breaths.

DRESSING FOR
SUCCESS AND STYLE:
SIX TIPS FOR MEN

Bill Blass

Bill Blass has won the Coty fashion award three times, including the first Coty award for menswear. Women who wear his designs include Candice Bergen, Barbara Walters, Mrs. Vincent Astor, and Barbara Bush.

1. In business, dress the part as if you already have the position you want. This makes you appear to be the right candidate for advancement. Be alert to your corporation's signals for the appropriate dress code.

2. Try on your business and evening clothes, taking a good, honest look at yourself in a three-way mirror. Keep these general rules in mind:

A suit looks good on a short man, but avoid a jacket and contrasting slacks; these cut you in half and make you look shorter. Heavy men should wear dark colors, which are more slimming, and should avoid big, bold patterns. If you're very thin, don't wear suits with vertical stripes, because they elongate your figure; you can wear double-breasted suits and contrasting slacks and jackets to advantage.

3. If you have gray hair, suits of charcoal gray or navy blue set it off nicely. (I don't advocate black for men's clothing except for tuxedos.)

4. At night, men's clothes should be a backdrop for women. If it's not a black-tie occasion, wear a dark suit and a dark tie.

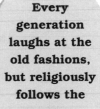

Every generation laughs at the old fashions, but religiously follows the new.

—Henry David Thoreau

5. The less a cleaner cleans your clothes, the longer they'll last. Freshen and care for your clothes yourself as much as possible.

6. Don't be sentimental about your clothes. Give away anything you haven't worn in the past year.

> I base my fashion taste on what doesn't itch.
> —Gilda Radner

A Style Secret for Men

• When you're in doubt, a white shirt and a white linen pocket handkerchief are your best friends. They always look crisp, clean, and classic; they show off good clothes to advantage. Avoid matching neckties and pocket squares.

> I should warn you that underneath these clothes I'm wearing boxer shorts and I know how to use them.
> —Robert Orben

DO A COBWEB PAINTING

Mabel Wood

A resident of Horseheads, New York, Mabel Wood first painted on a cobweb when she was seventy-three years old. "I haven't painted any big pictures on canvas since that day," she says.

Painting on cobwebs is an art that's been lost and revived five times since it originated 250 years ago in a remote valley in the Tyrolian Alps. According to "Ripley's Believe It or Not!," who researched it in 1980, I'm the only person in the world painting on cobwebs. I'm eighty-eight years old now, so I'm teaching my daughter; we thought we'd better keep it going.

The webs are okay to gather only about three weeks during the year, along in May. (That's in my territory, which is southern New York; it may be different in your part of the world.) Then they're more likely to be clear; after that, they get dusty and dirty. One reason the art's been lost so many times is probably because webs are so scarce to get. You forget that it's time to gather them, and first thing you know, the year's gone by and you don't have any more webs. You can't go get your "canvases" at any art store!

In the old days they used webs spun by the funnelweb spider and the large brown grass spider, but they're extremely fragile, and these spiders don't live in the United States anyway. Luckily, the old masters found that the webs of the tent caterpillar work just about perfectly. You can find the webs out in fields or by the roadside; they grow over the branches of trees and bushes. The webs are a little thicker than a spider web and almost as clear as a piece of glass. They're small but very pretty. Sometimes they're ball shaped and sometimes flat, according to how the worms chose to build them. The caterpillars start with a little tiny web and lay their eggs in it; the little ones live in the web, eating leaves, and the caterpillars keep laying more eggs and building the nest bigger and bigger.

Before going out to gather the webs, you'll need to cut some frames from heavy paper or light cardboard. The hole in the center should only be 1½ by 2 inches to 3 by 4 inches. In order to pick up the webs—now, this is something I've never told before—you put a border of glue around the hole on your frame. Then you move the frame up behind the web to capture it. Next, you cut the web loose from the tree or bush. Let it dry, and take it home.

Then there's a cleaning job to do. The web will be speckled with dirt and worm residue where the little baby worms have lived. You need to take round-pointed tweezers and pick all that material off the web. I use my own eyes, not a magnifying glass. It takes me about five hours to clean a web. And do be careful—if you get a hole in the thing, you have to start all over with a new one. When your web is clear, then you're ready to paint.

The webs are dense enough so you can paint in real detail. I use the smallest, softest brushes I can find (a #0 or the smallest one they sell at the art store). You have to elevate the frame—either tilt it up against something or set the edges on something—because the paint makes the web stick to anything underneath. Don't just lay the frame on the table.

I use acrylic paints because they dry quickly; I don't like waiting for oil paints. You can choose any subject. I've painted everything from birds to toadstools, covered bridges, railroad stations, barns, and all sorts of scenery. My paintings are very detailed, and I don't hurry.

When you're finished, you'll want to frame your cobweb painting. Cut two mats and use two pieces of glass—one in the back, one in the front. Then you can see the painting from either side, because the web itself is nearly transparent.

Maybe cobweb painting won't be a lost art, after all.

A primitive artist is an amateur whose work sells.
—*Grandma Moses*

Two New Ways Students Cheat on Tests

Howard Baker, Jr.

Howard Baker, Jr., is
the author of *And the
Cheat Goes On*, an
exposé of cheating
methods used in
schools.

Electronics

In the old days a student wrote a "cheat
sheet" in teensy printing on a scrap of paper
and pasted it somewhere accessible, like the face of his wristwatch. Today there are Seiko digital watches that a cheater can
plug into the back of his IBM-PC at home and load up with vast
amounts of information. Even inexpensive memo watches will
hold quite a few screens full of words and numbers. The cheater
merely has to "check the time" on his wristwatch.

Another electronic cheating method: Students are allowed to
use calculators in class nowadays, and some of them have tiny
typewriter keyboards, so a cheater can write information into the
calculator's memory. A student in physics class says to a friend,
"Hey, can I borrow your calculator?" and the other student
hands him a machine with the test answers freshly typed into
it—all right under the teacher's nose.

Fashion Statement

We all know the old ploy in which students write answers on
their shirt cuffs and roll up their sleeves to conceal the evidence.
But a new camouflage trick is being used in schools where it's a
fad to doodle geometric patterns all over Levi's. Hidden among

the doodles you may find a weird word like "AADDACABB." These letters are the answers to a multiple-choice test, which a friend has supplied to the cheater after taking the test earlier; the cheater simply scribbles the answers among the scrawled patterns already on the blue jeans.

A thing worth having is a thing worth cheating for.
—*W. C. Fields*

HOW TO SKIP STONES

W. T. Rabe

A photojournalist and PR man, W. T. Rabe directs the annual Fourth of July tournament sponsored by the Stone Skipping and Gerplunking Club of Mackinac Island, Michigan, which is also the sport's official advisory body and reviewer of claims for *The Guinness Book of World Records.*

Certain scientists allege that it takes no skill to skip stones. Some nerve! The top man in stone skipping, Arthur "Babe" Ring, set the world record with a run of 29 skips—14 plinks and 15 pittypats. His ability is the stuff of legend.

How can you, too, develop such awesome prowess? Use a stone that fits comfortably between your thumb and index finger. Don't choose a round stone (it won't skip well) or a flat stone that's too big (the wind will pick it up and make it unsteady) or too small (it will be hard to control and impossible to count the skips). In official tournaments, all stones must be genuine; barbecue "lava rocks" aren't allowed, nor fake stones manufactured commercially for skipping. Some people dip their stones in water first or pour beer over them, although you're not allowed to grease them.

Here are a few skipping tips: (1) wade right out in the water (the drip-dry trouser revolutionized our sport) and assume a solid spread-legged stance; (2) wind up horizontally; (3) release the stone close to the water; (4) skip it *between* the troughs of incoming waves, not across them; and (5) follow through.

I'm often asked how tournament officials count the number of skips. The standard answer: "With great difficulty." As in all professional sports (except football and horse racing), videotape is not employed to resolve scoring. The tournament's high commissioner and panel of judges use their eyes only—yet they almost always concur on the number of skips a stone has taken.

Good plinking! Just don't plonk out or throw an agnew (see "A Brief Glossary of Stone Skipping").

A Brief Glossary of Stone Skipping

• To discuss this venerable sport—supposedly invented by an English king who skipped gold sovereigns across the River Thames—you'll need to study its special vocabulary.

Agnew A wildly skipped stone that clonks someone in the crowd

Blinchki Russian term for stone skipping, literally "little pancake" (e.g., the circle a stone makes on the water)

Chukker Equivalent to an inning in which each contestant throws one stone; there are six chukkers in a tournament

Drakes and ducks British term for stone skipping

Little David Trophy A 75-pound rock that is the Stanley Cup of amateur stone skipping

New Orleans dispensation Lacking stone on the Mississippi delta, New Orleans skippers may use oyster shells

Pittypat Short skip at the end of a "run"

Plink Long skip at the beginning of a "run"

Plonk If your stone sinks without any skips at all, you are said to "plonk out"

Run What one stone does; a throw

Skronker A thrown stone that never touches anything

Smut Danish term for a skip

U.S.S. An Unidentified Skipping Stone that enters the official skipping lane

Vet's out Michigan tournament veterinarian may reject off-island stones if he believes they will contaminate the Straits of Mackinac

TEACH YOUR DOG TO BE AN ACTOR

Bob Weatherwax and Lassie

Bob Weatherwax learned his craft from his father, Rudd Weatherwax, who trained the original Lassie half a century ago. He continues the tradition, training many television and movie dogs, including the star of *The New Lassie*. He has also released a videotape on dog training and tricks.

Motion picture dogs don't just do tricks; they *act*. If your dog wants to have a Hollywood career, there are two things you must teach him to do. One is to perform on command, which is a matter of training and repetition. The other is to capture the mood of a scene, which depends on the trainer's voice inflection.

Lassie has about a hundred different behaviors that he will do on cue. ("He" is correct; Lassie is a male collie.) The trick is to string three or four segments together for a dramatic purpose, to convey action and emotion.

Scene 1: Lassie swims out of a river, crawls exhausted onto the bank, and struggles toward you.

My father's dog, Pal, performed this trick at MGM Studios as a "double dog" in *Lassie Come Home*, the first Lassie movie. He did it so well that he replaced the star and became Lassie. There have been seven generations of Lassie now, all descended from Pal.

This sequence has several parts, most of them standard tricks. First is teaching your dog to come, to sit, and to lie down.

You'll also need to teach him to crawl. Do this by having him continue to lie down while you encourage him to come forward.

Lassie was able to appear "exhausted" by lying on his side. And since the dog knew how to dig, my father taught him to make digging movements while still remaining on his side. This way it appeared that Lassie was struggling to pull himself along the ground, too weak to stand up. (However, I wouldn't recommend teaching your pet to dig, because he might practice on your flower beds!) My father also figured that if a dog coming out of a river was really tired, he wouldn't shake off the water; so in this scene Lassie wasn't allowed to shake.

A lot of people think that you work a dog silently in a movie, using hand cues. But almost everything involves voice commands, which aren't audible in the edited version of the picture. Through your tone of voice you induce a dog to convey the emotional mood of a shot—and that's the real key to working a picture dog. In this scene you want Lassie to come out of the water looking very subdued rather than racing toward you excitedly. So you say, "Easy, easy," using a quiet inflection. You have him come forward slowly and stop, come forward and stop, as if he's too tired to go on. Then he lies down and rolls over on his side; he makes the digging motion, which looks like he's struggling but can't get to his feet. Finally, he lies very still. All this creates a perfect impression that he's too exhausted to move.

Scene 2: Lassie looks sad.

You can transfer your mood to a dog through voice inflections. Dogs are very closely bonded to human beings, and your tone of voice has a big effect on them.

Let's say you want to shoot a really sad scene. Maybe there's something wrong in the household; the little boy is being punished. As Lassie comes into the boy's room, I'd have him walk very slowly, with his head down, then lie on the floor and put his head down. It's all done through my voice: "Lassie, come in. Ah! Ah! Ah!" I actually use a correctional tone of voice. I might even say, "Stop it! Easy! Lie down!" Because of the displeasure in my tone and the "down" mode of my voice, Lassie will start to show a change of expression, which evokes the sad mood.

Scene 3: Lassie has a message.

If it's the opposite sort of scene, and I want Lassie to come in very excitedly, then *I* get very excited: "Come on! Attaboy! Come on! All right!" After he comes into the room, I may have him speak, as if he's trying to tell the boy: "Follow me! There's something outside!" Then I cue Lassie, "Go on!" After the dog starts to leave, I turn him back around and have him speak again, as if he's beckoning for the boy to follow.

This is a little different from what people usually teach their pet dogs. But it's all based on standard tricks like "lie down" and on using the appropriate voice inflection. These secrets make it look like acting!

I loathe people who keep dogs. They are cowards who haven't got the guts to bite people themselves.
—*August Strindberg*

How Jigsaw Puzzle Designers Challenge Puzzle Fans

John Robrock

John Robrock has designed the dies to cut every puzzle in Hallmark's Springbok line, a chore requiring at least forty hours for a 500-piece puzzle. "People imagine I can put puzzles together well," he says, "but I even trick myself."

The pieces of a jigsaw puzzle give you two clues to help put them together: shape and color. My job as the puzzle designer at Hallmark is to use these same two elements to make a puzzle challenging and fun.

As far as shapes go, the first thing most people do is look for the four corner pieces, which stand out like sore thumbs. After finding them, they start working the straight lines to complete the border of the picture. To fool people, I sometimes split each corner in half by cutting a line at a 45-degree angle right through it. That makes eight corner pieces instead of four.

Sometimes I'll copy the shape of one of those split corner pieces almost exactly but in the *middle* of the puzzle. (It can't be exactly the same shape, because then it could fit into the corner.) This ploy confuses people who think they've found a corner piece.

The puzzle's overall shape can also make things interesting. At Hallmark we've done octagonal puzzles, which have a lot more "corners." We've also done round puzzles. One looked like a pizza. Another had maybe forty-five different birds painted on it, and they were arranged so that whatever edge was up, the birds on top were right-side up. That meant there was no top or bottom to the puzzle. This was confusing, because you couldn't tell whether any given piece was right-side up or upside down.

I've done puzzles in the shapes of states, and the irregular outlines make these puzzles a challenge. Using maps also brings back an element of education, the reason that jigsaw puzzles were invented in England in the 1700s: maps were cut up to help schoolchildren learn the different countries and oceans.

A puzzle designer also works with colors. Our art department tries to choose subjects whose pictorial elements will make the puzzle harder and more entertaining. For example, we did a puzzle called "The Battle of Gettysburg." There are hundreds of soldiers who all look pretty much alike, and that's one trick of good puzzle design—to have lots of similar elements in the picture. Another design principle: Using uniform color makes individual pieces more difficult to find. After all, if a scene has some bright red patches, it's easy to find the pieces of that color. But if there's a big sky that's pretty much all the same color, as in "The Battle of Gettysburg," it's much harder.

The ultimate in color confusion was a round puzzle we made called "Little Red Riding Hood's Hood." It was entirely red. Putting it together depended solely on your ability to recognize shapes. (Some puzzle addicts actually flip puzzles face down and work them on the blank side to create a similar challenge.)

Working jigsaw puzzles is a friendly, nonthreatening pastime, the kind of thing you can do alone with a cup of coffee or among friends and family. Of course, there are some people who are especially good at it, who can fit ten or twelve pieces while you're still scratching your head. Curious about this, Hallmark hired a university psychologist to analyze the kind of person who works puzzles quickly, and we learned something surprising. The jigsaw puzzle expert shares an ability with a race car driver, who can roar into a curve at 150 miles an hour, with other cars all around him, yet knows exactly where everyone will end up and how his car fits into the "puzzle." He somehow recognizes patterns on an instinctive level—just like a person who speedily puts together jigsaw puzzles.

RENOVATE A HOUSE ATTRACTIVELY AND INEXPENSIVELY FOR RESALE

Brooke Whitney Pattengill

A designer and artist in Los Angeles, Brooke Whitney Pattengill has been renovating houses for more than twenty years; her work has been featured in numerous magazines and newspapers.

Having started in the 1960s, I consider myself sort of a pioneer among women in the house renovation field. I got into it by accident when I was newly divorced and my mother had died, leaving me some money. A friend said, "Why don't you buy a little house?" I was living in a charming apartment building that once belonged to Errol Flynn, but the landlord was mean. He wouldn't let me garden or even put up a pretty Moroccan door knocker I'd bought. The situation was ridiculous, so I forged out with my door knocker—but no house. After some painful struggles at the bank, I got a loan and bought a house of my own.

Since then I've redone quite a few houses for myself and others. I look for a house that has architectural character; then I can enhance what's already there. I keep within the style; if it's a Spanish house, I wouldn't add aluminum sliding windows. I work with paint and color, landscaping, and other visual elements that are relatively inexpensive—what you might call "more flash than cash"—but which make a big difference. I don't remodel, because moving walls or adding on is too expensive. I stick to a simple formula, doing things that I know will work well.

Interior

New paint makes the whole house look fresh and rejuvenated. And color is really magic. I often paint my ceilings sky blue. It's not obviously noticeable, but gives a nice feeling to the room and lifts it up. It's also very calming, which helps to make the house a peaceful shelter in these crazy times. On walls I usually use shades of white (cream, off-whites) or champagne. This neutral background lets you completely change a room's appearance without having to alter the room itself. You can bring in new artwork, for example, or new slipcovers that lend a summer or a winter look.

One way to give any room a more finished or architectural look is to add crown and baseboard moldings. Moldings tie rooms together and beautify the nondescript areas where the ceilings and floors meet the walls.

Good doors also make a big difference. I bought fifteen pine doors for the house where I live now. Wood adds warmth, and solid doors (rather than hollow core) give a house a substantial feeling. I always replace the hardware. Usually I use Baldwin brass hardware, but I also find old doorknobs at estate sales and in funny old hardware stores.

As a collector, I'm a nut on storage and shelves, since I never have enough room. My favorite solution comes from Cliff May, the architect who did so many ranch houses in Southern California. He always built floor-to-ceiling shelves. They're not only handy, but in an otherwise ordinary space they can make one wall interesting and give focus to the room. The shelves can be built around a fireplace, French doors, or a window; I even have shelves surrounding my front door. Art objects, plants, and books go on them. This open storage space lets me enjoy my collection of blue and white china, and whenever I need something, I just take it from the shelf.

I also love to put shelves above doors and up high near the ceiling. In my kitchen, these shelves hold baskets and other decorative things, making the room look like a little country store.

One of my houses had an awkward bit of wall space, where I built a floor-to-ceiling storage rack for china. Only four inches deep, it created the old-fashioned look of an Irish dish rack. Almost every house has spaces that don't seem to be good for much, but that can be used to display and store things.

Beams add real character to a room—but not those fake hollow beams. I try to find used wood, maybe from an old building or barn. The beams bolt right into the ceiling rafters, and although they don't bear any load, they look strong and seem to have been there all along. (In all my renovations, I try to make things look original, not added on.)

If a house has wall-to-wall carpeting over hardwood floors, I take up the carpet and pad. I'd much rather expose the wooden floors and use area rugs. A good trick is to have a craftsman groove the planks; you can groove every board or every fourth one, whatever you like, depending on the scale you want. You can also put in pegs. Then refinish the floors. This treatment will give the house a whole new look.

I love fireplaces, especially in bedrooms, so I've bought handsome wooden mantels at house sales or from people who are moving. One of my houses had no fireplace at all, but I mounted a mantel on a wall and made it look sort of like a fireplace. It added visual interest and at least evoked the mood. If a fireplace is unattractive—ugly brick, let's say—I paint it so that it blends into the color of the room and doesn't stand out.

Stencils can add flair. Once I decorated a den in a country theme (horse tack and a collection of ceramic roosters and chickens), and over every door I had an artist paint a rooster with a little spray of wheat. It was a relatively inexpensive way to create a country mood.

In bathrooms I try to keep the existing tile if it's in good shape. If it's not a pleasing color, you can often overcome that problem by using a wallpaper border in the room. Let's say there's a bathroom with maroon tile, which you don't love. Next to the ceiling you install a wallpaper border that has maroon in it, along with two or three other colors that you like better. (I learned in design school that if a room has a color you don't care for, you can make it kind of go away by using it again somewhere; it's strange but it works.) Add towels and bath accessories in the prettier colors of the wallpaper border. (You can also spray-paint baskets in these colors.) You'll find that the maroon will recede, while the more pleasing colors dominate the room.

Exterior

Good landscaping does wonders for any house. I always try to retain the trees and plants that are already there. (In fact, I look for houses in older neighborhoods, where the trees have had a chance to mature.) If you plant geraniums and other flowers in pots, you can move them around wherever you want them, which is especially nice when you have a party—or an open house, when prospective buyers come through.

Split rail fences create a warm feeling around the house. I like to put climbing roses on them, usually pink Queen Elizabeths.

A great brick mason taught me the trick of making a concrete walkway warmer and more charming by covering it with used brick pavers, which are about half an inch thick. Concrete driveways can be improved by adding brick inserts—panels, strips, or whatever. I also like to put up arbors of cross-rafters above a patio, to add shade and charm to the garden.

There's only one problem whenever I fix up a house this way: It looks so pretty that I don't want to move.

MOMENTS OF MAGIC

David Copperfield

The Linking Paper Clips

Effect: Two paper clips are clipped on a folded dollar bill. The ends of the bill are pulled and the paper clips *jump* from the bill. Upon inspection, the paper clips are found to be linked!

Method:

1. Fold a dollar bill in thirds (illus. 1).

2. Take a couple of paper clips from your pocket and place one around the first and second folds. Place the other clip around the second and third folds (illus. 2).

1

2

3. If you pull the upper corners away from you in a quick motion, the paper clips will link and drop to the table (illus. 3).

3

A fancy version:

1. As you are folding the bill, place a rubber band around the dollar and position it in one of the folds (illus. 4).

2. This time, when you pull the ends of the bill, not only will the paper clips become linked, they will also end up attached to the rubber band (illus. 5).

4

5

The Mystic Papers

Effect: The magician sits at a table and asks members of the audience to call out the names of famous people. He writes down each name on a separate piece of paper, then folds the slip and throws it into a bowl. Next he invites a member of the audience to remove one of the folded papers and hold it up against his brow. The magician burns the balance of the papers in the bowl, gazing mystically at the ashes as if looking for a message. He then announces very slowly the name written on the folded slip. When it is opened, his prediction is verified.

Method:

1. Have members of the audience call out famous names while you appear to be writing each name on pieces of paper. The secret is that you write the *first* name called on *each* slip of paper. Fold each piece into quarters as you go, and toss them into the bowl.

2. Have a spectator pick one of the folded papers and hold it against his forehead.

3. Burn the rest of the papers to destroy the evidence. (If this isn't safe or practical, just rip them up and hold the scraps tightly in your hand.)

4. Appear to be contemplating the ashes (or scraps) and the slip held by the spectator. Very slowly, announce the predicted name—which, of course, turns out to be the same as the one chosen by the spectator.

Performing hint: You can repeat or vary the trick by asking the audience for the names of cities, animals, or colors.

HOW TO MAKE A MAGIC TRICK
LOOK LIKE A MIRACLE

Dai Vernon

Be natural. Be sure that any movement you make to accomplish a secret "sleight" is a natural movement. It should look exactly the same whether you really transfer a coin or ball from hand to hand or only pretend to do so.

As an example, here is a way to make a coin vanish. First, determine how it looks if you don't do any sleight-of-hand. You might display the coin on your right fingers, then dump it onto your left palm in an unhurried way, close your left hand, and reach for a wand (you can use a pen) with your right hand. To cause the coin to vanish, you make *exactly* the same movements—but this time simply move your right thumb onto the coin as that hand turns palm down, retaining the coin against the fingers. Close your left hand into a fist, which conceals the fact that no coin is there, and turn all your attention to the wand, reaching for it with your right hand. During this movement curl the right second, third, and little fingers gently around the hidden coin; then pick up the wand with thumb and forefinger. Use the wand to tap the left hand, pause for a magical moment, and open the left hand to reveal the vanish. (A fine point: You have provided a logical reason for transferring the coin from hand to hand—to pick up the wand—so no suspicion is aroused by an unnecessary, *unnatural* action.) Done properly, this simple trick will elicit gasps.

Another meaning of "be natural" is to be yourself. A magician often has difficulty fooling his wife or friends because they are so familiar with his natural movements. When he does something that appears foreign, it registers immediately as a clue that trickery is taking place. Even strangers sense that something is happening, because a movement out of keeping with the general makeup sounds a discordant note. If you have a low-key manner, therefore, don't suddenly take on a theatrical personality when you do a magic trick; nor should you make false or exaggerated movements as you do a sleight. These things will ring hollow and create the suspicion that all is not as it seems. You will fool people more completely when your movements and speech are exactly the same when you are performing magic as when you are doing anything else in your daily life.

Use your head. To get the most from a magical effect, don't simply buy a trick at the magic shop and do it. You must apply thought. For example, every shop sells the Rattle Bars—three little tubes, of which only one rattles. The game is to keep your eye on that one, as in the old shell game. In fact, none of the tubes makes a noise. A fourth tube with a rattle inside is concealed in the magician's hand, so he can apparently cause any of the tubes to make the rattling sound. The trick is old and overused, and many people know the secret. But a one-armed magician named McDonald—who, because of his handicap, had to think carefully about every trick he did—devised a clever dodge to make the Rattle Bars a fooler once more. McDonald concealed the little fake, the tube with the rattle in it, inside a lit cigarette. He could show his hand openly, yet when he picked up an empty tube, he created the illusion of its being the one that rattled—because he held his cigarette in the same hand. This deception is a fine example of using your head.

Don't run when nobody's chasing you. This was a favorite saying of a great magician named Al Baker. It means don't try to prove something when it's not necessary. For instance, don't have the audience examine an everyday item like a playing card or say to them, "Here I have a perfectly ordinary coin." This only plants the idea in the audience's mind that the card or coin could be gimmicked, and it prompts them to watch your every move. If you do use a faked prop, just handle it naturally, as if it were innocent.

Practice diligently. Some people look upon practice as a dull pastime, but there is a terrific incentive to progress once the first glimmers of achievement are apparent. So practice not only until you can do the "secret move" or operate the apparatus you bought at the magic shop, but until the trick looks entirely natural in your hands.

Instead of trying to perform many tricks—and probably doing none of them very well—select two or three effects and work only on those. A few tricks done well can gain the performer a reputation for being a first-class magician.

Although not well known to the public, Dai Vernon is considered by many sleight-of-hand artists to be the greatest magician who ever lived. He helped advance conjuring from the threads and mirrors of the Victorian era into the modern age. Now in his nineties, he still spends his evenings at the Magic Castle, the Hollywood conjurors club, and he has taught such famous performers as Doug Henning.

How to Improvise Humor

Jonathan Winters

For forty years Jonathan Winters has built a career on his ability to adopt the facial expressions, voices, and accents of other people and then to get inside their heads and improvise—whether it's a sweet grandma (Maude Frickert), a Mafia hit man, or a chicken farmer (Elwood P. Suggins).

I'm not one to tell jokes. It's more fun to improvise, just to think up things on the spot and do them. In my everyday life I improvise all the time. For instance, passing the Empire State Building in a taxicab, I once pretended to be an out-of-town rube. I asked the driver, "Say, where's the monkey on the building?"

"What monkey?"

"King Kong," I said. "Come to think of it, I read where he'd moved to Florida."

The driver stared at me. "Naw, naw, mister. Dat was just a *movie*. They were kiddin', ya know? Whatsa matter wit' you?"

"Sorry," I told him. "I had no way of knowing. Thank you so much for briefing me on this."

At that point, you're on a roll. And it's no different in front of an audience. It's fun to have people say, "God, he's off the wall now! He's really doing his thing." People sense that you're out on a tightrope, taking a chance, and they applaud when you make it to the other side. That's improvising. Here are some tips if you want to try it.

Talk to yourself.

This presents a problem for some people. ("Look over there, he's talking to himself! That poor man.") But it's the best way to let your imagination go. Just driving in the car by myself, I can talk to an imaginary person on my right. Let's say I'm a highway patrolman:

> "Ed! Don't eat all them doughnuts. You know we're going to a shoot-out! Why don't you save some for afterward?"
>
> "Hmmph! Why don't you mind your own business? I hate you anyway. I never wanted to be partners with you."
>
> "Hey, look at your gun—it's got jelly all over it! That's from that doughnut. Get out of the car!"

Because I was an only child and was often told to play in my room, I learned that if there's nothing in that room but you, you've got to fill it up with some friends. You've really got to call on improvisation. I think it's a great way to train yourself.

Be an observer.

No matter what you want to be, no matter what courses you take in college, you must learn to observe. It means looking around and taking lots of pictures with those wonderful lenses, your eyes. When I travel in other countries, I observe people and listen to them even if I don't speak their language. I do it *everywhere*, hoping to get some material and just store it in my head.

Take risks.

When I was a little boy in Dayton, Ohio, I may have put on a red sock and a blue sock, maybe a necktie that was far too long, and some kind of fright wig. I would wear this in front of my father, and he would say in a serious tone: "You're not going downtown like that. You'll merely draw attention to yourself." But to improvise, you have to get over your fear of going downtown and acting funny. You have to be willing to gamble—which is a big word.

You can practice even at a party. Someone asks, "What do *you* do?" You may put on a British upper-crust accent: "Well, I have never known *work*, as it were. I always wanted to find something constructive to do, but my family has just—it's tragic—has just dumped *millions* on me."

I've carried stuffed animals into major department stores, where I stood by the perfume counter and talked to the rabbit: "Woodrow! Look, you've already gone to the bathroom how many, *many* times? Those little pellets are most unattractive. I'll have to freshen you up—pardon me, ma'am, can I use some of this perfume?"

You've got to be a little bit of the devil. I've always said, "God is in my mind, and the devil is in my pants," so it kind of evens things out.

Develop your own sense of humor.

It should go without saying, but hang on to your own approach. You must trust yourself. When I was on Johnny Carson's show, Johnny understood my style and would say something like, "Well, I understand you were born on a farm." Then I'd make something up—how we had thirty cows until some hungry neighbors sneaked in one night and—butchered is such a terrible word—"relocated" the cattle. And so we had to put up cardboard cows and lean them up against things in the pasture. We had a little mooing machine—"Mmmmooo, mmmoooo"—which took the edge off the farmers' never seeing anything but weeds at our place.

On that show I could just go off freely in any direction. And that's the joy of improvising. I think it's surprising what you can get away with, as long as you don't start taking your clothes off.

HOW TO ATTAIN
ENLIGHTENMENT

There is no cure for birth and death, save to enjoy the interval.
George Santayana

Row, row, row your boat
Gently down the stream.
Merrily, merrily, merrily, merrily,
Life is but a dream.
Children's song

Life is a tragedy full of joy.
Bernard Malamud

Everyone is in the best seat.
John Cage

It is only with the heart that one can see rightly; what is
essential is invisible to the eye.
Antoine de Saint-Exupéry,
The Little Prince

Such is the vocation of man: to deliver himself from blindness.
Max Ernst

If you think you're free, there's no escape possible.
Baba Ram Dass

The final delusion is the belief that one has lost all delusions.
Maurice Chapelain

We have met the enemy and they are us.
Walt Kelly,
"Pogo"

One has two duties—to be worried and not to be worried.
E. M. Forster

There is only one sin: fretting.
Neal Cassady

In the end, everything is a gag.
Charlie Chaplin

Life without jokes is like a road without inns.
Henri Pourrat

I'm just a duck man . . . strictly a duck man.
Carl Barks,
creator of Uncle Scrooge comics

Show me a sane man and I will cure him for you.
Carl Jung

A man needs a little madness or else he never dares to cut the rope and be free.
Nikos Kazantzakis,
Zorba the Greek

The advantage of the emotions is that they lead us astray.
Oscar Wilde

If I had to live my life again, I'd make the same mistakes, only sooner.
Tallulah Bankhead

It has been my experience that folks who have no vices have very few virtues.
Abraham Lincoln

O Lord, help me to be pure, but not yet.
  St. Augustine

When choosing between two evils, I always like to take the one I've never tried before.
  Mae West,
  Klondike Annie

Try everything once, except incest and folk-dancing.
  Sir Thomas Beecham

I believe in sex and death—two experiences that come once in a lifetime.
  Woody Allen

Everybody should believe in something. I believe I'll have another drink.
  Anonymous

Have fun; if not, you'll bore us.
  Marcel Duchamp

Speak in French when you can't think of the English for a thing—turn out your toes as you walk—and remember who you are!
  Lewis Carroll,
  Through the Looking Glass

Stay high and keep moving and give all of yourself away.
  Neal Cassady

Make sure you're right, then go ahead.
  Davy Crockett
  (television character)

Few things are harder to put up with than a good example.
  Mark Twain

Living with a saint is more grueling than being one.
  Robert Neville

If you can get through the twilight, you'll live through the night.
  Dorothy Parker

I've developed a new philosophy . . . I only dread one day at a time.
  Charlie Brown

It's not that I'm afraid to die. I just don't want to be there when it happens.
  Woody Allen

I don't fear death because I don't fear anything I don't under-stand. When I start to think about it, I order a massage and it goes away.
  Hedy Lamarr,
  Ecstasy and Me

The mistake you make is trying to figure it out.
  Tennessee Williams,
  Camino Real

We are here and it is now. Further than that all human knowledge is moonshine.
  H. L. Mencken

Apart from the known and the unknown, what else is there?
  Harold Pinter

The reverse side also has a reverse side.
  Japanese saying

The intelligent man finds almost everything ridiculous, the sensi-ble man hardly anything.
  Goethe

Fill what's empty. Empty what's full. Scratch where it itches.
  Alice Roosevelt Longworth

Life only demands from you the strength you possess. Only one feat is possible—not to have run away.
  Dag Hammarskjold

If I seem free, it's because I'm always running.
   Jimi Hendrix

Live fast, die young, and have a good-looking corpse.
   John Derek,
   Nicholas Ray's *Knock on Any Door*

We're all in this alone.
   Lily Tomlin

Separate we come and separate we go
And this, be it known, is all that we know.
   Conrad Aiken

Friend . . . GOOD.
   Frankenstein's Monster

What I say is that, if a fellow really likes potatoes, he must be a
pretty decent sort of fellow.
   A. A. Milne

Guns aren't lawful
Nooses give
Gas smells awful
You might as well live.
   Dorothy Parker

Happiness is a way station between too little and too much.
   Channing Pollock

Happiness is not best achieved by those who seek it directly.
   Bertrand Russell

I can detach myself from the world. If there is a better world to
detach oneself from than the one functioning at the moment, I
have yet to hear of it.
   P. G. Wodehouse,
   at age ninety

The true value of a human being is determined primarily by the measure and sense in which he has attained liberation from the self.
Albert Einstein

When the mind soars in pursuit of the things conceived in space, it pursues emptiness. But when the man dives deep within himself, he experiences the fullness of existence.
Meher Baba

You do not need to leave your room. Remain sitting at your table and listen. Do not even listen, simply wait. Do not even wait, be quite still and solitary. The world will freely offer itself to you to be unmasked, it has no choice, it will roll in ecstasy at your feet.
Franz Kafka

The advantage of the incomprehensible is that it never loses its freshness.
Paul Varley

The most beautiful thing we can experience is the mysterious.
Albert Einstein

Show me a man or woman who cannot stand mysteries and I will show you a fool. A clever fool—perhaps—but a fool just the same.
Raymond Chandler

The wise man is astonished by anything.
André Gide

Everything is miraculous. It is miraculous that one does not melt in one's bath.
Pablo Picasso

Complacency in the presence of miracles is like opening the door to your own tomb.
Rod Steiger

The only way to discover the limits of the possible is to go beyond them, to the impossible.
   Arthur C. Clarke

If you do not raise your eyes, you will think you are the highest point.
   Antonio Porchia

We are all in the gutter, but some of us are looking at the stars.
   Oscar Wilde

You've nothing to give the world that anyone else can't give, except yourself.
   Quentin Crisp

The fabled musk deer searches the world over for the source of the scent which comes from itself.
   Ramakrishna

Through the years, a man peoples a space with images of provinces, kingdoms, mountains, bays, ships, islands, fishes, rooms, tools, stars, horses and people. Shortly before his death he discovers that the patient labyrinth of lines traces the image of his own face.
   Jorge Luis Borges

You don't look in the mirror to see life; you gotta look out of the window.
   Drew "Bundini" Brown

Stained glass, engraved glass, frosted glass; give me plain glass.
   John Fowles

That the world is, is the mystical.
   Ludwig Wittgenstein

The gods sell all things at a fair price. There is no entrance fee to the starlit hall of night.
   Axel Munthe

Whether invoked or not, God will be present.
Carl Jung
(inscription over his front door)

It's all soul.
Junior Wells

I love God, and when you get to know Him, you find He's a Livin' Doll.
Jane Russell

Before God we are all equally wise—and equally foolish.
Albert Einstein

The wise man doesn't give the right answers; he poses the right questions.
Claude Lévi-Strauss

It is better to know some of the questions than all of the answers.
James Thurber

An answer is always a form of death.
John Fowles,
The Magus

Discard all theologies and belief . . . the whole principle that someone else knows and you do not know, that the one who knows is going to teach you.
J. Krishnamurti

Only the hand that erases can write the true thing.
Meister Eckhart

Among the great things which are to be found among us, the Being of Nothingness is the greatest.
Leonardo da Vinci

INDEX

Names

INDEX

Subjects